DESCARTES

Books in the RENAISSANCE LIVES series explore and illustrate the life histories and achievements of significant artists, rulers, intellectuals and scientists in the early modern world. They delve into literature, philosophy, the history of art, science and natural history and cover narratives of exploration, statecraft and technology.

Series Editor: François Quiviger

DESCARTES

The Renewal of Philosophy

STEVEN NADLER

REAKTION BOOKS

Published by Reaktion Books Ltd
Unit 32, Waterside
44–48 Wharf Road
London N1 7UX, UK
www.reaktionbooks.co.uk

First published 2023

Printed and bound in India by Replika Press Pvt. Ltd

A catalogue record for this book is available from the British Library

ISBN 978 1 78914 683 7

COVER: Frans Hals, *René Descartes*, 1649, oil on panel.
Statens Museum for Kunst (SMK), Copenhagen.

CONTENTS

RENATUS. DESCARTES, NOBIL. GALL. PERRONI DOM. SUMMUS MATHEM. ET PHILOS.

Introduction

hen exactly does philosophy become 'modern'? There is no clean beginning or end to the medieval period, nor is there some year that represents the commencement of the Renaissance. Why, then, should there be a specific point that marks the start of modernity in philosophy or a single thinker who can be undisputedly identified as the *first* modern philosopher? René Descartes is often called 'the father of modern philosophy', and understandably so. Many of the metaphysical and epistemological questions that have come to dominate philosophy since the early twentieth century are expressed, quite beautifully and some for the first time, in his works. But plausible claims to the title could also be made on behalf of such luminaries as Galileo, Thomas Hobbes, Francis Bacon or Michel de Montaigne, all of whom made significant, but very different, contributions to what we now regard as modern philosophical thinking.

Less well known are the so-called *novatores*, a loosely defined, international coterie of figures in the sixteenth and seventeenth centuries. These 'innovators', united by little more than their rejection of the traditional Aristotelian natural philosophy that dominated late medieval and early modern academic and scientific culture, pursued various different paths to a new way of looking at the world. The list, usually drawn up by their contemporary opponents, often named Bernardino Telesio, Francesco Patrizi,

Unknown artist, *René Descartes*, 17th century, engraving.

Giordano Bruno and Tommaso Campanella in Italy, Jean Bodin in France, David van Goorle (Gorlaeus) in the Netherlands and William Gilbert in England, among many others – including, sometimes, Descartes himself.[1]

However, we might want to save the founder's honour for some figure later than Descartes, one whose thought seems less entangled with medieval Scholasticism and less informed by theological assumptions and ostensible religious motivations – say, Bento (Baruch) de Spinoza, who scandalized his contemporaries with his radical claims about God, nature and the human being; John Locke, with his uncompromising empiricist theory of knowledge; or, even later, the sceptical atheist David Hume.

Of course, labels such as 'medieval' and 'modern' are highly relative scholarly impositions. (Whereas modern philosophy is generally agreed to arise in the seventeenth century, the beginning of 'modern' literature and 'modern' art is typically situated in the early twentieth century.) While these terms may be convenient for organizing the historiography of philosophy, they do not represent precise and absolute distinctions. What, after all, does it mean for a philosophy to be 'modern'? From a trivial historical perspective, Aristotle is more modern than the pre-Socratic thinkers Thales (who said that 'all is water') and Heraclitus ('all is fire'), Descartes is more modern than Aristotle, and Hume is more modern than Descartes. But chronological posteriority is neither necessary nor sufficient for intellectual modernity. Being a philosopher in the nineteenth or twentieth century does not by itself guarantee that one is more 'modern' in one's thinking than Hume or Kant in the eighteenth century. In any given historical period there will be philosophical continuity with past traditions, transitional figures and even some backsliding. The seventeenth century had its share of 'medievals', and some of Descartes' contemporaries were just as wedded to the categories of old-fashioned Aristotelianism as was Thomas Aquinas in the thirteenth century. At times, Descartes himself can seem more like the last of the medieval philosophers than the first of the moderns. Moreover, the early modern period, like any other, also had ecumenical types committed to marrying the old and the new – thinkers such as Pierre Gassendi, a latter-day follower of Epicurus, or the German polymath Gottfried Wilhelm Leibniz, who, late in the century, sought to reconcile the new science with the resuscitation of some elements of Aristotelian metaphysics. Does this desire to accommodate the past make them less 'modern'?

Still, debates about the meaning of 'modernity' aside, there can be no denying that in the seventeenth century something special happened in philosophy, broadly construed to include natural philosophy, or what we now call 'science'. Roughly between 1600 and 1700, there emerged new ways of thinking about the world and about the human being's place in nature, in society and in the cosmos. This did not happen all of a sudden, and the way was certainly paved (and often blocked) by earlier thinkers. It was also conditioned by developments in the historical, political and religious domains. Continuities abound, and the so-called age of reason – a somewhat outdated moniker invented to contrast it with what had been labelled the 'age of faith' – was not immune to the internal dialectical developments and the external influences that generally govern the history of philosophy. Nonetheless, there was a remarkable and decisive change – or, better, given the number of philosophical traditions flourishing in the early modern era, a series of changes – that took place in the seventeenth century. Moreover, the change was in effect a permanent one. A fairly direct line of descent can be drawn between these innovations and how philosophy and science are done today; the ancestry of contemporary physics, for example, clearly lies in seventeenth-century natural philosophy. By contrast, it is more difficult to find such affinity between contemporary thought and medieval Scholastic theories and methods. It really does not seem unwarranted, in referring to this early modern period, still to use that other old-fashioned term 'scientific revolution' – where 'science' is taken to include the study of human nature as well.

Methodologically, the 'new philosophy' (for this is how contemporaries often referred to it), despite important differences among its various strains, involves a general tendency to rely on reason rather than authority to determine what is and what is not philosophically and scientifically legitimate. In other words, the limits of truth are a matter of discovery, not decree. Whether the alleged authority was supposed to be located in sacred texts, ecclesiastic or academic dogma, the opinions of the civil sovereign, or even earlier philosophical traditions (such as Plato and Aristotle), all must now give way to the independent epistemic testimony of the human rational faculties. The new philosophy also involves a commitment to perspicuous and predictively reliable causal explanations of phenomena – explanations which, in turn, are made possible by the evidence of experience, the use of experiment and, perhaps most radically of all, the application of mathematics, or at least quantitative models, to nature's processes.

Substantively, the new philosophy's proponents in the seventeenth century are also committed to thinking of most of nature – and, in the case of some thinkers, *all* of nature, including the human mind – as operating on the same basic principles as artificial machines. The modern philosophers, unlike their medieval predecessors and less progressive contemporaries, regarded terrestrial and celestial phenomena as constituted by one and the same kind of matter and governed by the same set of laws. They believed that all of the visible and invisible events in the world, no matter how wonderful – the changes we see and the hidden causes we postulate – are nothing but the motion and rest of pieces of matter and alterations in their properties brought about by contact. At the end of the century, Isaac Newton will call this fundamental assumption into question when he allows for mathematically expressed forces in nature that do not operate 'mechanically'. But before Newton, a significant part of what made modern philosophy 'modern' – what made it *new* – was a devotion to the idea that everything in nature could be explained by the collision, conglomeration and division of parts of matter of varying size, shape and hardness.

In the search for the origins of modern philosophy, then, there does seem to be something special about the seventeenth century. And if there is, lurking somewhere in that century, a work that constitutes the *Ulysses* or *Les demoiselles d'Avignon* of philosophy's modernity – a treatise both so original and iconoclastic in its conception and so extensive in its influence that it effects a kind of renewal, even a paradigm shift, within philosophy; a treatise that not only self-consciously represents a break with the principles and categories of past thinking but succeeds in setting the agenda, in substance and in style, for philosophizing for subsequent generations – there is no better place to look than the oeuvre of Descartes.

A Frenchman who spent most of his adult life in self-imposed exile in the Dutch Republic to pursue his investigations in peace and quiet, Descartes was indeed a bold innovator. Despite the fact that, for rhetorical and defensive reasons, he occasionally disclaimed that label and insisted that his work was not especially novel, and with all due respect to scholarly efforts to make his philosophy seem less of a departure from the reigning Aristotelian paradigm, Cartesian philosophy was indeed a new starting point for understanding the world. Descartes did not see himself as continuing the development of any particular tradition, and he explicitly rejected the philosophy of medieval and early modern Scholasticism (though he was not above using its vocabulary and even its conceptual apparatus). As he says, 'I want people to recognize the difference that exists between the philosophy I practice and that which is taught in the Schools.'[2] Rather than working within some well-established, even codified, system, Descartes sought new methodological, epistemological and metaphysical bases for the discovery of truth in the sciences.

Among Descartes' extant philosophical, physical, medical and mathematical writings, there are several works that stand out in their time for their avant-garde character. These include two treatises that most readers today associate with his name – the *Meditations on First Philosophy* and the *Discourse on Method*. There is also the less familiar but, in the period, more important *Principles of Philosophy*, the grand *summa* of his philosophical system that Descartes published in 1644 and that he hoped would supplant the neo-Aristotelian textbooks used in the schools and colleges. Equally important is an early work that, to readers today, will be the least familiar of all of Descartes' writings: *The World*. This investigation into 'all the phenomena of nature' was totally unknown to his immediate contemporaries, with the exception of his most intimate friends, because it was never published in his lifetime.

Descartes began the research that informs his writings somewhat haphazardly, several years after discovering his philosophical vocation but while still in the process of figuring out how to go about realizing it. It all started with a number of particular problems of optics, and the result was supposed to be nothing more than a compendium of topics in what he called 'physics'. But over the course of several years, as one question led to another and his investigations expanded to cover a greater variety of scientific subjects, the boundaries of the project swelled immensely. The goal eventually became, in essence, an explanation of everything, grounded in secure epistemological and metaphysical foundations. As the scheme grew, however, so did the apparent risks. What might have been a small and harmless treatment of the physics of light ended up being a series of grand, certainly controversial and (he suspected) probably heretical treatises that discussed God, the soul, knowledge, the origins and structure of the cosmos and the nature of human life.

ONE

Man of Touraine

major theme of the philosophy of the seventeenth-century French thinker René Descartes is the radical separation of mind and body. These are, in his view, two distinct and independent substances; they have absolutely nothing in common in their respective natures and properties, and the existence of one does not require the existence of the other. While the doctrine is not new with Descartes – it goes back to antiquity – he defended it in a particularly clear and systematic way, and it was crucial for his grand scientific project. It thus seems appropriate, and yet not a little ironic, that while Descartes' intellectual legacy – the contribution of his mind – is well established, his life story is bookended by disputes about his body.

Descartes spent his final days in Stockholm. He had been summoned to the Swedish capital by Queen Christina to serve as her philosophy tutor. It was with great reluctance that he left his comfortable abode in the Dutch Republic, where he had been residing for most of his adult life, 'to go live in a land of bears, among the rocks and ice'.[1] Within just a couple of months, rising early in the morning to give the queen her lessons, Descartes caught pneumonia and died, on 11 February 1650.

The philosopher's remains were eventually sent back to France, sixteen years after his death, and interred in Paris in the church of Saint-Geneviève-du-Mont. When the church was threatened by mobs in 1792, in the wake of the French Revolution, his casket was supposed to have been dug up and, along with other church property, taken away for safekeeping. While various works of art and other items from the church did indeed make it to a sanctuary, it seems that Descartes' bones did not. Their exhumation and transport were but another victim of the turmoil of that time. Thus, despite the great reburial ceremony of 1819, there is no telling who now lies in the tomb marked *Memoriae renati Descartes* in the church of Saint-Germain-des-Près. Almost certainly it is not Descartes. The whereabouts of his remains are unknown. Moreover, something rather important was missing from the casket that had arrived from Sweden: the skull. Descartes' head was said to have been left behind in 1666, and only later sent to France. It is now, we are told, sitting in a cabinet in Paris's Musée de l'homme.[2]

Questions, albeit less morbid ones, also surround the beginning of the journey of Descartes' body. The family home of Joachim Descartes (1563–1640) and his wife Jeanne Brochard (d. 1597) was in the village of Châtellerault, in the province of Poitou. However, Joachim, a counsellor for the king in the *parlement* of Brittany, often resided in Rennes for months at a time. Descartes' niece Catherine, the daughter of his older brother Pierre, thus claims that her uncle was 'conceived among the Bretons'.[3] It is highly unlikely, though, that Jeanne accompanied her husband on his extended business trips. The philosopher must have been conceived at home, in Châtellerault. With Joachim then away for a while, Jeanne and her two older children, Pierre (1591–1660) and Jeanne (1593–1641), relocated to the town of La Haye, in the neighbouring province of Touraine. There, at the home of her widowed mother, Jeanne Sain, Jeanne would spend the final months of her pregnancy. The third child of the Descartes family to survive infancy, to be named René at his baptism, was born on 31 March 1596. (La Haye itself would later be rechristened 'La Haye–Descartes', in 1802; in 1967 it became simply 'Descartes'.)

Provincial rivalries being what they are, Poitou was not so willing to give up the title to being the birthplace of France's most famous philosopher. Thus there emerged in the early nineteenth century a story about how, on her way to her mother's home in La Haye, Jeanne's carriage went off the road, whereupon she went into labour in a ditch near a farm named La Sybillière. After taking a day to recover from her ordeal, she continued on to La Haye, where the child was baptized. Old myths die hard, and to this day locals near Châtellerault still refer to Descartes as 'a man of Poitou'.[4]

There is no good reason to believe this convenient tale, other than devotion to Poitevin honour. It is true that Isaac Beeckman, whom Descartes would befriend in 1618 while journeying through the Dutch Republic, refers in his journal several times to Descartes as 'from Poitou' or as 'Poitevin'.[5] But Descartes was, we can be sure, born in Touraine. After all, he tells his friend Henri Brasset, secretary to the French ambassador in The Hague, that he is 'a man . . . born in the gardens of Touraine'. He also probably spent a good deal of his childhood in those gardens, at the home of his grandmother. This is because his mother (along with her baby) died in childbirth the following year. Curiously, Descartes would later offer one of his correspondents a different account of his mother's death: 'I was born of a mother who died, a few days after my birth, from a disease of the lungs, caused by distress.'[6] If he did in fact believe that he was partly responsible for the loss of his mother – was this what he was told by a relative? – it would have been a heavy burden to bear.

With his mother buried and his father so often in Brittany, care for the young boy devolved to the many family members in the vicinity: his grandmother in La Haye, and other grand-parents, great-uncles and -aunts, and godparents in and around

Châtellerault. Descartes' first four years were probably split between the two towns. But when his father remarried in 1600 – his new wife was Anne Morin de Chavagnes, from Nantes – and moved to Rennes for good, rather than accompany him so far from the family lands, Descartes and his siblings moved in with their maternal grandmother in La Haye.[7]

Later in life, Descartes would refer to himself as the 'Sieur du Perron', after a small farm in Poitou that he inherited from his father and which he later sold to finance his intellectual vocation. This is a bit of pretension, since the extended family did not belong to the old landed nobility, the *noblesse d'épée*. Rather, they were members of the *noblesse de robe*. Their roles and nominal titles were purchased, not landed. In this period it was possible to enter the second estate through 'venal' office, as a public bureaucrat or administrator. Local royal counsellors, jurists and tax officials were among the lucrative positions that could be bought. They did not come cheap – in some cases upwards of 100,000 *livres* – but they brought in a good income, and could be passed down to the sons in the next generation. (Not incidentally, such positions also exempted one from paying the steep royal taxes.)

Descartes' father Joachim had a comfortable position in Brittany as the crown's legal attaché. Those relatives in Poitou and Touraine who looked after the young Descartes when his father was in Rennes also occupied high professional positions, as lawyers and surgeons or physicians. While Joachim had opted for a legal career, his father Pierre Descartes, his grandfather Jean Ferrand and his uncle Jean Ferrand II were all medical doctors. In the political, legal and financial domains, a great-uncle on Descartes' father's side, Michel Ferrand, was the lieutenant general of Châtellerault, while a great-uncle on his mother's side, Pierre Sain, was the town's tax official. One uncle on his mother's side was royal counsellor in Poitiers, and another served as a deputy to the États Généraux. Descartes' brother Pierre, meanwhile, would follow in his father's professional footsteps and also become a royal counsellor in the Brittany parlement.[8]

It probably seemed to the young Descartes, and to his family, that he, too, was destined for a lucrative legal career of some kind. In the end, though, it was not to be.

THOUGH HE WAS BAPTIZED as a Catholic, Henri de Navarre was raised by his mother in the Protestant faith. After successfully defending his claim to the French throne against other contenders, however, he formally converted to Catholicism before being crowned Henri IV in 1594. If this mollifed his many opponents, their concerns about Henri's true loyalty were revived just a few years later when, in 1598, he granted official, if limited, toleration to Protestants with the proclamation of the Edict of Nantes.

Over the years, both before and after his coronation, Henri managed to survive several assassination attempts. But fate finally caught up with him in 1610, when a fanatical Catholic assassin, maddened by concessions to Huguenots, jumped into the king's carriage in Paris and stabbed him to death. Most of Henri's body was laid to rest in the Basilica of Saint-Denis, near Paris – all except his heart, which made the three-day journey by carriage to the town of La Flèche, in the Loire Valley, where the king had grown up.

In 1604 the Jesuits established in La Flèche a royal *collège* or preparatory school. Henri had expelled the order in 1594, after one of their members tried to kill him, but allowed them to return in 1603, and even invited them to open a new educational institution in one of his chateaus in the area. This school had a special place in the king's heart, and so would have the honour of being its final home.

The Collège royal de la Compagnie de Jésus (La Flèche) offered a traditional Jesuit curriculum, as set by the order's *Ratio*

studiorum of 1599. The focus was on classical languages and the
liberal arts, broadly construed to include the 'humanities' disciplines as well as fields now classified as 'sciences'. The classes in
the nine-year course of study were all conducted in Latin. They
were intended to properly cultivate students – intellectually,
socially and religiously – in order to prepare them for professional
careers and, if such was their vocation, higher studies in the university faculties of theology, law or medicine. (Students seeking
to become ordained Jesuit priests could also remain at La Flèche
for an additional three to four years of theology.)

The programme began with a six-year sequence of Latin and
Greek grammar, rhetoric and literature, so that 'the youths
entrusted to the Society's care may acquire not only learning but
also habits of conduct worthy of a Christian'.[9] The texts were
drawn from both classical antiquity (Homer, Hesiod, Pindar,

Étienne Martellange, *Veüe du Collège Royal de la Flèche*, 1612, pen and brown ink,
blue wash.

Demosthenes, Thucydides, Plato, Aristotle – including the *Poetics* – Cicero, Caesar, Horace, Ovid, Livy, Virgil, Quintilian) and early Church writings (the *Ratio* lists saints Gregory of Nazianzus, Basil and John Chrysostom). After completing this elementary stage, students moved on to the three-year 'philosophy' curriculum, which involved logic, physics (supplemented by mathematics, mainly Euclid), metaphysics and moral philosophy, all based almost exclusively on texts from Aristotle: selections from the *Prior Analytics, On Interpretation, Topics, Physics, On the Soul, On Generation and Corruption, Metaphysics* – 'passing over the questions on God . . . which depend on truths derived from revelation' – and, the syllabus notes, 'all ten books of Aristotle's *Ethics*'. They also read commentaries on these works by medieval and early modern Aristotelians, such as Thomas Aquinas and the sixteenth-century Jesuits Francisco de Toledo and Pedro da Fonseca.

Classes at La Flèche were primarily lectures by professors, whose job was to 'interpret well the text of Aristotle and be painstaking in this', although afterwards the students were expected to gather in small groups of about ten and spend half an hour reviewing on their own the lecture just given.[10] This lecture/discussion format was supplemented once a month by a disputation, in which students would 'pose objections' on a given topic, to which other students were to respond, followed by an hour-long argument or debate overseen by a professor or theologian. In both structure and content, it was a classic and conservative Scholastic education, subject to minor modifications here and there, and consistent with the Counter-Reformation principles of the Council of Trent in the sixteenth century. According to the *Ratio*'s 'rules for the professor of philosophy', the teachers should have 'a heart set on advancing the honor and glory of God . . . and above all lead [students] to a knowledge of their Creator'.[11]

Among the students being duly edified and who would have been present at the elaborate ceremony on the occasion of the

arrival of the king's heart at La Flèche in June 1610 was Descartes'
older brother Pierre, who had enrolled in the school soon after
its opening and was now in the upper level. By his side, and still
in the elementary classes, was the fourteen-year-old Descartes,
who had left the comfort of his grandmother's home in La Haye
three years earlier and matriculated at the *collège* as well, as a
boarding student.[12]

Whatever may have been Descartes' experience during his
time at La Flèche, in later years he did not look back fondly on
the education he received from the Jesuits (which was not all that
different from the education he would have acquired at most
French *collèges* in the first half of the seventeenth century). Writing
in the mid-1630s, he admits that 'I was at one of the most famous
schools in Europe, where I thought there must be learned men if
they existed anywhere on earth.' He also recognizes the value of
having been taught the languages essential to participating in learned
discourse in the Republic of Letters and the familiarity with great
literary works he gained as a younger man. 'I knew that the languages learned there are necessary for understanding the works
of the ancients; that the charm of fables awakens the mind, while
the memorable deeds told in histories might uplift it and help to
shape one's judgement if they are read with discretion; that reading
good books is like having a conversation with the most distinguished men of past ages.' This positive assessment should not
be taken at face value, however; there is an undercurrent of irony
here. Referring to the study of rhetoric, poetry, morals and other
topics as taught by the Jesuits, he notes that 'it is good to have
examined all these subjects, even those full of superstition and
falsehood, in order to know their true value and guard against
being deceived by them.'[13]

Descartes found even the philosophy lessons at La Flèche
less than illuminating. Despite later telling a correspondent that
'nowhere on earth is philosophy better taught than at La Flèche,'

he was clearly dissatisfied with the intellectual tools with which he had been provided by his teachers.[14] All they really did, he notes, was give him 'the means of speaking plausibly about any subject and of winning the admiration of the less learned'.[15] The texts and topics he studied and the methods of inquiry he learned were, to his mind, rather sterile.

> When I was younger, my philosophical studies had included some logic, and my mathematical studies some geometrical analysis and algebra. These three arts or sciences, it seemed, ought to contribute something to my plan [of seeking true knowledge]. But on further examination I observed with regard to logic that syllogisms and most of its other techniques are of less use for learning things than for explaining to others the things one already knows or even, as in the art of Lully, for speaking without judgement about matters of which one is ignorant. And although logic does contain many excellent and true precepts, these are mixed up with so many others which are harmful or superfluous that it is almost as difficult to distinguish them as it is to carve a Diana or a Minerva from an unknown block of marble.[16]

Philosophy as taught by the Jesuits was not so much a discipline of discovering truth as of demonstrating it to others – and even, through rhetoric, of persuading others of things that were in fact false. 'In my college days,' he would write, 'I discovered that nothing can be imagined which is too strange or incredible to have been said by some philosopher.'[17]

It is, of course, not unusual for students to complain that what they are learning in school is useless and out of date. In this case, such complaints were not without some justification. After all, in the age of Copernicus, Galileo and Kepler, they were studying physics and astronomy from 2,000-year-old treatises, supplemented by medieval commentaries on these. Aristotle was still 'The Philosopher', and the teachers at La Flèche, who might add their own clarifications to the assigned texts, were required to show him due deference. It was explicitly stipulated in the *Ratio* that the lecturer 'shall not depart from Aristotle in matters of importance, unless he find some doctrine contrary to the common teaching of the schools or, more serious still, contrary to the true faith'. He was to be 'very careful in what he reads or quotes in class from commentators on Aristotle who are objectionable from the standpoint of faith'. Above all, the instructor is to avoid as much as possible quoting anything from Averroës, a medieval Arabic commentator on Aristotle whose thought was regarded by the Church as irreconcilable with Christian dogma, 'but if he quotes something of value from his writings he should do so without praising him'. However, the lecturer 'should always speak favorably of St Thomas', that is, Thomas Aquinas.[18]

DESCARTES REMAINED at La Flèche until 1615. If he, like so many of his relatives, was going to have a place in civil administration, he would need a degree in law. This meant matriculating in a university faculty. Thus that year – again just like his brother Pierre – he began attending lectures at the University of Poitiers, where his paternal great-grandfather Jean Ferrand I had been a rector fifty years earlier. He formally enrolled in May 1616, and that November he was granted a Bachelor's degree and, essential for teaching (should he be so inclined), a licentiate in civil and canon law. His public defence of forty theses – dedicated to his maternal uncle René Brochard, king's counsel in Poitiers, on topics of testaments and inheritance – was delayed, however, and not held until December.[19]

A legal career, perhaps as counsel or magistrate, and the comfortable living it afforded was now on the horizon. No doubt this is what his family expected of him. Descartes, however, had other ideas.

> From my childhood I have been nourished upon letters, and because I was persuaded that by their means one could acquire a clear and certain knowledge of all that was useful in life, I was extremely eager to learn them. But as soon as I had completed the course of study at the end of which one is normally admitted to the ranks of the learned, I completely changed my opinion. For I found myself beset by so many doubts and errors that I came to think I had gained nothing from my attempts to become educated but increasing recognition of my ignorance.[20]

The 'learning' afforded by an education in classical syllogisms not only contributed nothing to the search for truth but had a deadening effect on independent thinking, since it did not encourage original inquiry.

> That is why, as soon as I was old enough to emerge from the control of my teachers, I entirely abandoned the study of letters. Resolving to seek no knowledge other than that which could be found in myself or else in the great book of the world, I spent the rest of my youth travelling, visiting courts and armies, mixing with people of diverse temperaments and ranks, gathering various experiences, testing myself in the situations which fortune offered me, and at all times reflecting upon whatever came my way so as to derive some profit from it.[21]

Enough of books, lessons and rote exercises. It was time for a
real education. By 1618 Descartes had decided that much more
was to be learned through first-hand experience than by reading
dry Scholastic texts or poring over Galenic treatises in medicine.
A journey to other lands, especially, would, he believed, better
allow one to 'raise his mind above the level of mere book learning
and become a genuinely knowledgeable person'.[22]

TWO

'The great book of the world'

n early 1618 Descartes was a young man in search of adventure and unsure of his life's calling. His eclectic studies – at school and on his own – in science, mathematics, philosophy, law and even mysticism had left him somewhat adrift intellectually, hungry for knowledge but still in need of direction.

The first stop on Descartes' edifying itinerary in 'the great book of the world' was the United Provinces of the Netherlands, or the Dutch Republic. This was a natural destination for someone of his ambitions and curiosity. Despite its ongoing battle for independence from Spain, the Republic – at this point less a sovereign nation than a federation of seven provinces, each with its own executive and legislative body – had become a major European centre of trade, science and culture. A laissez-faire attitude towards commerce and a relatively tolerant intellectual and religious environment (albeit with differences from one province to the next) had allowed Holland, Utrecht, Zeeland, Groningen, Gelderland, Overijssel and Friesland, along with the territory of Drenthe and the so-called Generality Lands, quickly to grow into what was perhaps Europe's most progressive and cosmopolitan society.

The Republic had several universities: in Leiden, Franeker and Groningen, all important institutions of humanistic scholarship. Decades of innovative engineering had allowed the Dutch to build up their urban centres and expand the rural landscape, in part by reclaiming vast tracts of land from the sea. A powerful military, especially the navy, held its own against the superpowers of the era (Spain, France and England). Above all, the Dutch economy flourished through prolific domestic industries, such as textiles, sugar refining and beer, and a far-flung network of maritime and overland trade. To be sure, the so-called Golden Age was not golden for everyone. There was a significant population in the provinces living in poverty and struggling to put food on the table. And throughout the first half of the seventeenth century, the Dutch economy depended on morally abhorrent colonial practices, particularly in its treatment of indigenous peoples and the transportation of enslaved Africans. While the possession of enslaved people was technically illegal in the Republic, unscrupulous individuals and businesses profited from the slave trade between Europe, Africa and the Western hemisphere. The improbable success of the fledgling nation, impressive as it was, was not an entirely innocent enterprise.

Amsterdam, though still in its early years of expansion, was already a vibrant and diversely populated entrepôt. Bulk and luxury goods of all kinds from around the world – sugar, spices, wood, grains, fabrics – passed through its wharves and warehouses, while people of many nationalities (French, German, English, Italian, Polish, Russian, North African, even Spanish and Portuguese Jews, some of whom did in fact own enslaved people), on business or pleasure, walked the streets along its canals and filled the markets, cafés and taverns. For someone in the seventeenth century intent on studying 'the great book of the world' – not to mention applied and theoretical sciences, finance, mathematics, manufacturing, medicine and engineering – there was no better place to start than the Dutch Republic.

Descartes, however, did not pick the best time to go there. The Twelve-Year Truce with Spain, signed in 1609, was still in effect when the Frenchman landed in Breda, a fortified town near the border with the southern Netherlandish provinces, which were still loyal to the Spanish Habsburg crown. But the religious and political world of the United Provinces was in turmoil and about to undergo one of its periodic, usually brief but sometimes violent upheavals.

Just a few months after Descartes' arrival, the leaders of the Dutch Reformed Church convened the Synod of Dordrecht (Dort), a seminal event of early modern Dutch history. The gathering of ministers met from November 1618 to May 1619 to consider what to do about a heresy they believed to be breeding among their ranks. They were troubled by the followers of Jacob Arminius, a theology professor at the University of Leiden. In 1610 these liberal preachers had issued a 'remonstrance' in which they set forth their unorthodox views on a variety of sensitive theological questions. The Arminians, or 'Remonstrants', as they were called, rejected the strict Calvinist doctrines of grace and predestination. Where more orthodox theologians insisted that no one living after the Fall could possibly do good or achieve eternal blessedness without God's freely given and unearned grace, distributed to the elect independent of merit, the Remonstrants believed that a person had the capacity to contribute through good actions to his or her own salvation. They also favoured a separation between matters of faith and conscience (which should be left to individuals) and matters of politics (to be managed by civil authorities), and they distrusted and feared the political ambitions of their conservative Calvinist opponents. Like many reformers, the Arminians saw their crusade in moral terms. In their eyes, the true liberating spirit of the Reformation had been lost by the increasingly dogmatic, hierarchical and intolerant leaders of the Dutch Reformed Church.[1]

One of the chief political partisans of the Remonstrant camp was Johan van Oldenbarnevelt, the advocate or adviser of the

States of Holland, the province's governing body, composed of representatives from the cities and towns. Because of the size and importance of Holland, whoever was the leader of that province's states essentially held the most powerful office in the Republic after the stadholder, an appointed office traditionally given to a member of the House of Orange-Nassau and whose authority extended across several provinces. The stadholder was also the commander-in-chief of all Dutch military forces and, to many, a symbol of Dutch unity.

With Van Oldenbarnevelt's intervention, what was initially a doctrinal dispute within the Calvinist church and the theology faculties in the universities quickly became political. The States of Holland, urged on by Van Oldenbarnevelt, supported the liberalizing demands of the Remonstrants, which antagonized the ecclesiastic opponents to the Remonstrant cause and their own secular allies. The Counter-Remonstrant theologians, led by the Leiden professor Franciscus Gomarus, accused the Arminians of being covert papists, loyal more to Rome than to the United Provinces, while Van Oldenbarnevelt's political enemies saw in his support for the liberals an opportunity to label him a traitor working on behalf of the Republic's Catholic enemies.

In this way, the Remonstrant/Counter-Remonstrant battle over theology overlapped with conflicting views on domestic affairs and foreign policy. The opposing camps disagreed on whether civil authorities had the right to exercise control over the Dutch Reformed Church and its activities in the public domain. They also differed on how to conduct the ongoing struggle with Spain and how to respond to recent Protestant uprisings in France. With the Truce soon to expire, the Remonstrants sought a negotiated peace with the Spanish crown and wanted to stay out of French affairs, while the Counter-Remonstrants, always looking to undermine Catholic influence, were in favour of continuing the war with Philip III without compromise and aiding their Huguenot co-religionists by all available means. There was frequent, and sometimes quite brutal, persecution of Remonstrants in a number of Dutch cities, and many Arminian sympathizers were stripped of their offices and perquisites. By 1617 Holland's stadholder, Prince Maurits of Nassau, had entered the fray on the Counter-Remonstrant side. This was a shrewd political move by the prince. He hoped to successfully oppose Van Oldenbarnevelt's policies, especially any peaceful overtures to Spain, as well as to gain support from orthodox religious leaders for his domestic agenda, thereby increasing his own authority across the Dutch provinces and centralizing political power in the Republic.

When the delegates to the Synod of Dordrecht met in late 1618, they reiterated their commitment to freedom of conscience in the Dutch Republic, enshrined in Article Thirteen of the Union of Utrecht: 'Every individual should remain free in his religion, and no man should be molested or questioned on the subject of divine worship.' The Counter-Remonstrants controlled the gathering, however, and made heavy-handed use of their advantage. They confirmed the dogmas of the Reformed Church concerning grace and atonement – also known as the Five Points of Calvinism – and they succeeded in passing a resolution that restricted public worship and office holding to orthodox Calvinists. There was a purge of Remonstrants in the church and municipalities at all levels. Meanwhile, Van Oldenbarnevelt's enemies ruthlessly prosecuted him. In the spring of 1619 he was convicted of treason and beheaded.

Thus, just as the Catholic Descartes arrived in the Dutch Republic to broaden his horizons, the generally tolerant young, not-yet-formally-sovereign nation was seeing an increase in religious and intellectual intolerance.

SOON AFTER DISEMBARKING in the Low Countries, Descartes,
like many other young French noblemen, enlisted in the army
of Maurits of Nassau, now also Prince of Orange. This son of
Willem of Orange (Willem the Silent), the original leader of
the Dutch Revolt, was also a brilliant military man. When he
assumed the stadholdership of Holland, he began introducing
modernizing reforms into the Dutch armed forces and turned
them into a professional soldier corps with the latest in field
discipline and engineering. Maurits was particularly interested
in what science could do for his army, and so this was a good
opportunity for Descartes to study such things as military planning and the physics of moving bodies, especially projectiles.

While stationed in Breda, Descartes met a slightly older man
named Isaac Beeckman (1588–1637). Though it was a chance
encounter, Beeckman would turn out to be one of the most con-
sequential acquaintances of Descartes' life. He was a Calvinist
preacher of Counter-Remonstrant persuasion (with a theology
degree from the University of Leiden), a medical doctor (with
a *doctorat* from the University of Caen) and an accomplished

Adriaen Pietersz van de Venne (follower of), *Prince Maurits Accompanied
by His Two Brothers, Frederick V, Elector Palatine and Counts of Nassau on Horseback,*
c. 1625, oil on canvas.

mathematician. As Descartes' early biographer, Adrien Baillet, writing in 1670, tells the story, the two men got to know each other while standing in front of a poster proposing to all and any a mathematical problem to be solved:

> Beeckman was presently in the town of Breda, when someone unknown posted on the streets a problem of mathematics to offer it to the learned for them to solve. The problem was written in Dutch, such that M. Descartes, who was only recently arrived from France and thus unable to understand the language of the country, could at least see that it was a problem posed by an unnamed mathematician who thought to gain some glory in this way. Seeing passers-by congregating by this poster, he asked the first person standing next to him to translate into Latin or French the substance of its content. The man to whom, by sheer accident, he addressed this request was willing to give him this satisfaction in Latin, but only on the condition that he [Descartes] promised to give him the solution to the problem, which he thought to be very difficult.[2]

Baillet relates that not only did Descartes understand the problem, but, much to Beeckman's surprise, 'the young army cadet' solved it 'promptly and with much ease'. The two men quickly bonded over shared interests in mathematics and science. They challenged each other with a variety of problems in arithmetic, algebra, geometry and physics. Their meetings and correspondence from late 1618 into the early months of 1619 covered such topics as inertia, the acceleration of falling bodies (Beeckman challenged Descartes to demonstrate how far a body of some magnitude falling x distance in one hour will fall in two hours[3]), the notorious navigational difficulty of determining longitudinal position and a variety of pure mathematical problems, including cubic equations and what Descartes calls 'the famous problem of dividing an angle into any number of equal parts'.[4] Descartes also kept Beeckman informed of his progress in studying drawing, military architecture and, most difficult of all, Dutch. 'You will soon see what progress I have made in this language.'[5]

Among Beeckman's essential contributions to Descartes' philosophical development, well before Descartes knew anything of Galileo's work – to which, in fact, Beeckman would later introduce him – was the idea that mathematics could profitably be applied to problems in physics, thereby constituting a hybrid science that they referred to as *physico-mathematica*. Moreover, the physics they both favoured was a corpuscularian one, an anti-Aristotelian doctrine according to which all bodily phenomena could be explained solely by the motion and interaction of minute particles of matter no different in nature from the macroscopic bodies they composed. Beeckman, with his interest in music, also inspired Descartes to compose his first written work, a *Compendium musicae*. In this treatise, which remained unpublished in his lifetime, Descartes not only addressed in mathematical terms such topics as the nature and diversity of sound and 'the intervals of harmonies, scales and discords [*dissonantiarum*]',[6] but took up the aesthetic question of the 'purpose [*finis*]' of music, which, he claimed, is 'to delight us and move various affects in us'.[7]

Perhaps Descartes' most important breakthrough in this early period under Beeckman's tutelage is the idea of a 'completely new science [*scientia penitus nova*]',[8] one that will 'provide a general solution of all possible equations involving any sort of quantity, whether continuous or discrete, each according to its nature'. What he seems to have in mind here is an algebraic approach to a variety of mathematical problems, whether in arithmetic (with its discrete quantities), geometry (continuous quantities) or any other discipline dealing with units or shapes.

I hope I shall be able to demonstrate that certain problems involving continuous quantities can be solved only
by means of straight lines and circles, while others can be
solved only by means of curves produced by a single
motion, such as the curves that can be drawn with the new
compasses . . . and others still can be solved only by means
of curves generated by distinct independent motions
which are surely only imaginary, such as the notorious
quadratic curve. There is, I think, no imaginable problem
which cannot be solved, at any rate by such lines as these.
I am hoping to demonstrate what sorts of problems can
be solved exclusively in this or that way, so that almost
nothing in geometry will remain to be discovered.[9]

What these remarks, limited as they are at this point to
mathematics, represent is an early, embryonic manifestation of
Descartes' lifelong determination to come up with a single
method for resolving problems of any type or to establish an
all-encompassing, quantitatively grounded science. This ambition will inform, in a general way, Descartes' later projects, from
the *mathesis universalis* of the 1620s – which he calls a 'general science that explains everything that it is possible to inquire into
concerning order and measure, without restriction to any particular subject-matter'[10] – to the mathematico-mechanistic
programme in physics of the 1630s and '40s, a systematic natural
philosophy that will provide explanations for everything in the
cosmos.

Descartes and Beeckman deveoped a warm friendship over
a short period of time. At one point, Descartes tells Beeckman
that 'you ought not to think that all I care about is science; I care
about you, and not just your intellect – even if that is the greatest
part of you – but the whole man.'[11] He ends another letter by
recalling their 'unbreakable bond of affection'.[12] Descartes

acknowledges his debt to the Dutchman and is well aware of how their relationship stimulated his intellectual development.

> It was you alone who roused me from my state of indo-lence, and reawakened the learning which by then had almost disappeared from my memory. And when my mind strayed from serious pursuits, it was you who led it back to worthier things. Thus, if perhaps I should pro-duce something not wholly to be despised, you can rightly claim it as all your own; and I for my part shall send it to you without fail, so that you may have the benefit of it, and correct it into the bargain.[13]

Alas, the comity did not last. Despite Descartes' assurance that there 'will surely be a lasting friendship between us', things would sour in a few years over Descartes' suspicion that Beeckman did, in fact, take up the offer to 'claim it all as your own'. He will accuse Beeckman of taking undue credit for his, Descartes', ideas – in particular, the treatise on music. In a 1630 letter to a friend in Paris, he expresses his hope that Beeckman 'will learn not to deck himself out in someone else's feathers'.[14] This kind of falling-out with friends or colleagues would be something of a minor pattern throughout Descartes' life.

SHORTLY AFTER BEECKMAN returned home to Middelburg (he would later take up a position as vice principal at the Hieronymus grammar school in Utrecht), Descartes resumed his travels and departed for Copenhagen, then down to the German lands. From mid-1619 until the spring of 1622 he wandered through-out the principalities, electorates and bishoprics of the Holy Roman Empire, staying in Frankfurt, Prague, Ulm, Neuburg and other towns. He may also have served some time in the

Catholic army of Maximilian I, Duke of Bavaria – 'drafted', he would later say, 'because of the wars that are still being waged there'.[15]

It was an eventful three years, with Descartes present in Frankfurt at the coronation of a Holy Roman Emperor, the Catholic Ferdinand II, and possibly witnessing the Battle of White Mountain of 1620, which ended in the defeat of Ferdinand's rival, the Protestant Frederick V, Elector Palatine and (briefly) king of Bohemia. By the time Descartes returned to France by way of Poland and Friesland, in 1622, he had seen a good part of Central Europe, experienced war as a soldier (although we do not know if he actually participated in any battles), made significant progress as a mathematician and probably learned some German on top of his Dutch.

Still, Descartes remained restless. A couple of years after his return to France, which he spent in Poitou, Paris and Brittany, Descartes was off again to continue his geographical and intellectual wanderings. He wrote to his older brother Pierre in March 1625 to announce his plans to travel to Italy, 'a voyage beyond the Alps [being] of great utility for learning about business, acquiring some experience of the world, and forming some habits . . . not had before'. If such a trip did not make him richer, he added, 'at least it would make [me] more capable.'[16] Before departing his home in Châtellerault, he sold off some of his inherited properties, including a house in Poitiers and several farms. He clearly had no interest in managing any lands or taking up the social position to which he was entitled, and the money the sale brought would go far towards financing whatever independent path in life he ended up choosing.

'Throughout the following nine years,' he later wrote, 'I did nothing but roam about in the world, trying to be a spectator rather than an actor in all the comedies that are played out there.'[17] Descartes first went to Italy through Switzerland, taking only a couple of weeks in the spring of 1625 to explore what was for him an exotic land.[18] As Baillet describes the journey,

> It would have been easy for him to find in Basel, Zurich, and other cities philosophers and mathematicians capable of talking with him. But he was more curious to see the animals, the waters, the mountains, and the air of each region, with its weather, and generally whatever was furthest from human contact, in order better to know the nature of those things that seem the least known to ordinary scholars [*au vulgaire des sçavans*].[19]

Baillet, who has Descartes going to Rome and Florence, is making a lot of this up. Descartes was in Turin, and possibly Loreto, to which he had pledged to make a pilgrimage. 'I intend to go there on foot from Venice, if this is feasible and is the custom.'[20] He appreciated the intellectual life of Italy, particularly its scientific communities, although he did not get to meet Galileo, whom he would later describe as 'philosophizing much better than most, in that he abandons as much as he can the errors of the Schools and tries to examine physical matters through mathematical reasoning'.[21] He did not like the Italian climate, however. The heat and humidity of the Mediterranean country in the warm months did not suit this northern Frenchman. Writing to his friend Guez de Balzac in 1631, he said: 'I do not know how you can be so fond of Italy, where the air is so often pestilent, the heat of the day always unbearable and the cool of the evening unwholesome, and the darkness of night a cover for thieves and murderers.'[22]

There was another friend, also a Frenchman, whom Descartes had recently got to know in Paris and who would soon be undertaking his own trip to Italy. The theologian, mathematician and musical theorist Marin Mersenne was at the centre of a broad intellectual network, running his own international province within

the larger Republic of Letters. From his quarters in Paris, where he was a friar in the austere order of Minims, he corresponded with philosophers, theologians, mathematicians and scientists across the Continent and England. Mersenne was an acquaintance of, and collaborator with, some of the greatest minds and leading personalities of the first half of the seventeenth century – Galileo, Blaise Pascal, Pierre Gassendi, Antoine Arnauld, Thomas Hobbes and Constantijn Huygens, among many others.

Mersenne would later function as a kind of midwife to much of Descartes' thought. In addition to providing encouragement, Mersenne helped to edit and usher his writings into print. He was, in effect, Descartes' Paris-based philosophical manager and advisor, and as his literary agent and sentinel Mersenne often ran interference with correspondents, critics and publishers. He also enjoyed a fine intellectual fracas and was quite good at

Claude Duflos, *Marin Mersenne*, before 1727, engraving.

stirring up debates. This included inciting others to raise their objections to Descartes' theories.

Descartes needed the irreplaceable Mersenne in good form, and so when, years later, he heard that the priest would soon be heading south, he warned him to take care in terms that recall the report he had given Balzac. Italy, he said, is 'a country that is very unhealthy for the French. Above all, one should eat very little there, for their meats are too nourishing.'[23]

After his sojourn in Italy, Descartes returned to France by way of the mountainous Piedmont region.[24] While going over the Suse Pass near the French border during the spring thaw, he witnessed an avalanche. Writing in his 1637 treatise on meteorology about the nature of thunder in storms, he said:

> I remember having seen sometime ago, in the Alps, around the month of May, when the snows were warmed and made heavier by the sun, the slightest movement of the air was sufficient to cause a great mass suddenly to fall, which was called, I believe, avalanches, and which, echoing in the valleys, closely imitated the sound of thunder.[25]

Descartes was back in Paris by the summer of 1625, where he stayed – aside from another brief sojourn in Brittany – until late 1628. He had come a long way from the Jesuit-trained but aimless young man with a law degree. He was still unsure as to how he would make his living – his inheritance and income from the sale of properties was not sufficient to ensure a long-term livelihood – and he may yet have been considering a position as a counsellor in royal service.[26] But by the mid-1620s Descartes did at least have a better sense of his true vocation.

THE 'REVELATION' – this is what Descartes calls it – came to him one night early in his travels, in November 1619, when he was holed up, alone, in a warm room sheltering from the cold. He was still in Germany, either Neuburg or Ulm,

> where I had been called by the wars not yet ended there. While I was returning to the army from the coronation of the Emperor, the onset of winter detained me in quarters where, finding no conversation to divert me, and fortunately having no cares or passions to trouble me, I stayed up all day in a stove-heated room [*poële*], where I was completely free to converse with myself about my own thoughts.[27]

As to what happened that night, all we have from Descartes himself is the cryptic statement that 'I had a dream involving the Seventh Ode of Ausonius, which begins *Quod vitae sectabor iter* [What path of life shall I follow]?'[28] Baillet, on the basis of a now-lost Latin manuscript notebook by Descartes, provides further details of this dream and two others.[29]

In the first dream, Baillet reports, Descartes was walking along a road when some shadows or spirits (*fantômes*) frightened him and forced him to head to the left rather than continue to the right along his path, 'because he felt a great weakness on his right side'. Suddenly, a strong gust, a kind of whirlwind (*tourbillon*), spun him around three or four times on his left foot. He was in danger of falling when he saw an open gate leading to a college, which he entered to take a rest and heal his infirmity. As he was heading to the college's chapel to pray, he saw someone he knew but failed to acknowledge him. When he turned around to go back and make up for his incivility, the mighty wind returned and blew him aside. At the same time, he saw another person who called out to him by name 'in a friendly and welcoming manner' and gave him

something that looked like a melon from a foreign country to take
to some 'Monsieur N.' What was especially surprising was that
the wind that had caused Descartes so much trouble did not seem
to disturb the other people now around him, 'who stood up straight
and firm on their feet'. At this point Descartes woke up, and was
afflicted with a strong pain that he attributed to 'the operation of
some evil genius [*mauvais génie*] seeking to beguile him'.

After a couple of hours lying awake and reflecting on the
goods and evils of the world, Descartes fell back asleep and had
a second dream. This time he dreamt that he heard a sharp, loud
sound, 'which he took for a thunderclap'. This woke him up,
whereupon he saw many sparks flying about the room. This was
not unusual, Baillet relates Descartes as saying, as he was used
to waking up in the middle of the night with 'sparkling eyes',
and so it did not trouble him much.

No sooner had he fallen back asleep 'in a fairly great calm'
than Descartes had a third, quite different dream. Rather than
being alarming, this third vision seemed to Descartes to bear
providential significance. In the dream, he came upon a book,
un Dictionnaire, lying on a table. He was pleased by this, since 'he
hoped it could be useful to him.' However, the dictionary suddenly
disappeared and was replaced by another volume, a collection of
poems by a variety of authors from antiquity. When he opened
the book, it went right to a page with a verse that read *Quod vitae
sectabor iter?* (What path of life shall I follow?). An unknown man
then appeared, offering him a piece of paper with a poem on it
that began with the words *Est & Non* (It is and it is not) and recommending it to him highly. Descartes replied that he was familiar
with the piece, that it was one of the *Idylls* of the Latin poet
Ausonius. He wanted to show the stranger that it was, in fact, in
the collection he was now holding, which he thought he knew
well, but had some trouble finding it. The man asked Descartes
how he happened to possess that book, but Descartes could not

tell him. He finally found Ausonius poems in the book, but not the one that began with *Est & Non*. He told the man that there is an even 'more beautiful' poem by Ausonius that begins with *Quod vitae sectabor iter?* Descartes tried to find this poem in the book, but instead came upon several engraved portraits. He explained that the book was not the same edition as the one he was familiar with. Suddenly, the books and the man all disappeared.

Baillet says that Descartes, still asleep and in a new dream state, set to interpreting the last dream. The disappearing dictionary was, he believed, 'all the sciences brought together', while the poetry anthology represented 'a collection of philosophy and wisdom'. As for the poem beginning *Quod vitae sectabor iter?*, it was the 'good counsel of a wise person, or even moral theology'.

Once he was finally awake, Descartes continued with his interpretation of the 'sweet and very agreeable dream': the poetry in the volume represented 'revelation and enthusiasm, of which he did not despair of seeing himself favored'. The piece *Est & Non*, a Pythagorean verse, stood for truth and falsehood in human knowledge and the sciences. The upshot, he concluded (in Baillet's words), was that 'the spirit of truth, by means of this dream, wanted to open up for him the treasures of all the sciences.' It was an omen as to what the rest of his life held in store if only he chose the right path (*iter vitae*). The first two, rather unpleasant, dreams, however, were warnings against a life of passivity – no doubt what Socrates would have called 'an unexamined life'.

In his extant note, Descartes says only that 'in the year 1620, I began to understand the fundamental principles of a wonderful discovery.'[30] Baillet, providing only a bit more clarity, describes what was revealed through the dreams as 'the foundations of an admirable science'.[31] These foundations, it will later emerge, lay not in the reading of books or the wandering of foreign byways, but through careful reflection on the nature of knowledge and a scrutiny of the capacities of the human mind as it tries to understand both abstract realities (the 'eternal truths' of mathematics) and the natural world. In his later review of this period of his life, Descartes recalls that 'after I had spent some years pursuing these studies in the book of the world and trying to gain some experience, I resolved one day to undertake studies within myself too and to use all the powers of my mind in choosing the paths I should follow.'[32]

It is unclear whether what Descartes seeks at this point is simply a reliable method for resolving all manner of mathematical and scientific problems; substantive first principles that will ground knowledge generally; or, as we find in his writings over three decades, both. Descartes' ultimate goal was truth – in as many theoretical and practical domains as possible, and in the search for which 'I found myself as it were to become my own guide.'[33] Such a project is not to be undertaken casually, through a reliance on custom and habit, haphazard experience or raw introspection, but systematically, under the guidance of proven rules of inquiry. Only then, Descartes notes, can he be sure of 'attaining the knowledge of everything within my mental capacities'.

By the mid-1620s Descartes, at nearly thirty years old, was secure in his choice of vocation. It was a certainty that never wavered. Again, in hindsight, from the vantage point of his first published treatise, he says that

> I consider myself very fortunate to have come upon certain paths in my youth which led me to considerations and maxims from which I formed a method whereby, it seems to me, I can increase my knowledge gradually and raise it little by little to the highest point allowed by the mediocrity of my mind and the short duration of my life.

His success so far has only boosted his confidence, and he expects even greater results in the future.

> [W]hen I cast a philosophical eye upon the various activities and undertakings of mankind, there are almost none which I do not consider vain and useless. Nevertheless, I have already reaped such fruits from this method that I cannot but feel extremely satisfied with the progress I think I have already made in the search for truth, and I cannot but entertain such hopes for the future as to venture the opinion that if any purely human occupation has solid worth and importance, it is the one I have chosen.[34]

PARIS IN THE SEVENTEENTH CENTURY was unsurpassed as a centre of philosophical and scientific activity. The Dutch Republic, and especially Amsterdam, as we have seen, had its attractions for the intellectually curious; it is not hard to understand why the young Descartes thought to begin his pursuit of wisdom there. But the much larger Parisian scholarly community benefited from established institutions, abundant resources and high-level support. Despite occasional efforts at repression by the city's *parlement*, often at the urging of theologians at the Sorbonne ever on guard against freethinking and subversive ideas, the innovative pursuit of new knowledge flourished in the city's colleges, university faculties, academies and salons.

Paris held great allure for the period's philosophers, mathematicians, physicists, astronomers, engineers and chemists, not to mention poets, dramatists and humanist scholars. Throughout the century, the city attracted such important foreign philosopher-scientists as Thomas Hobbes from England, Christiaan Huygens from the United Provinces, Gottfried Wilhelm Leibniz from

Germany and Giovanni Cassini from Italy. With the support of royal and private patronage, and as the base for the far-reaching networks of Mersenne and others, Paris – like Rome, Florence, Bologna, London, Oxford, Leiden, Salamanca and other great epicentres of traditional learning and new inquiry – was home to a flourishing intellectual milieu. Indeed, as the century progressed, and certainly by the 1670s, everyone who was anyone in philosophy and the sciences wanted to be there.

It was during his return to France between 1625 and 1628, as he settled into the fertile and creative environment of Paris, that Descartes was finally able to devote serious and sustained attention to mathematical projects, both general (such as how to use arithmetical equations to solve geometrical problems) and particular (finding proofs for specific theorems). He also set to work on theoretical and empirical topics in optics, including a formulation of the law of refraction and experiments to determine the physical nature of light. (Much of this material would appear in the treatises *Geometry* and *Dioptrics*, published along with the *Discourse on Method* in 1637.) At the same time, Descartes could apply himself to elaborating that foundational method he was so sure would lead to philosophical and scientific knowledge.

This was also the period when Descartes developed a clearer conception of what truth itself must look like. Baillet, our source once again, tells a story of Descartes attending a gathering in Paris, in either 1627 or 1628, of 'learned and inquisitive persons' at the home of the Papal Nuncio, Cardinal Guidi di Bagni, to hear a lecture by a scientist named Nicolas de Villiers, Lord of Chandoux.[35] According to Baillet's narrative – which is based on a 1631 letter from Descartes to Étienne de Villebressieu and a lost manuscript by Descartes' friend Claude Clerselier – Chandoux, no less than other modern thinkers, 'sought to escape from the yoke of [medieval] Scholasticism' and argued on behalf of a 'new philosophy …established on unassailable foundations'. His presentation was

roundly applauded by the assembled company, which included
Cardinal Pierre de Bérulle, founder and head of the French
Congregation of the Oratory, a Catholic community of priests
and lay brothers. The guests approved of Chandoux's refutation
of the sterile and uninformative 'philosophy ordinarily taught
in the Schools'. The lone holdout in the audience was Descartes.
When one of Descartes' friends noticed his reticence and asked
him why he did not join the others in praising the lecturer,
Descartes replied that while he appreciated Chandoux's attack
on Scholastic philosophy, he was not pleased by the man's will-
ingness, despite his claim to have found 'unassailable foundations',
to settle for mere probability in the quest for knowledge.

> He added that when it was a matter of people easy-going
> enough to be satisfied with probabilities, as was the case
> with the illustrious company before which he had the
> honour to speak, it was not difficult to pass off the false
> for the true, and in turn to make the true pass for the false
> in favour of appearances. To prove this on the spot, he
> asked for someone in the assembled group to take the
> trouble to propose whatever truth he wanted, one among
> those that appear to be the most incontestable.

Someone stepped up to the challenge, Baillet says, whereupon
Descartes, 'with a dozen arguments each more probable than
the other', proved to the assembled company that the proposition they all thought true was false. Then, with equally plausible
reasoning, Descartes demonstrated that a proposition that they
were convinced was false is true.

> [Descartes] then proposed a falsehood of the sort that is
> ordinarily taken to be most evidently false, and by means
> of another dozen probable arguments, he brought his

hearers to the point of taking this falsehood for a plausible truth. The assembly was surprised by the force and
extent of the genius that M. Descartes exhibited in his
reasoning, but was even more astonished to be so clearly
convinced of how easily their minds could be duped by
probability.

When asked whether he knew of some other, better means
for avoiding sophisms and error and arriving at truth – that is,
real, absolutely certain knowledge and not mere probability –
Descartes replied that he knew none more infallible than the one
he had himself been using, adding that 'he derived it from the
foundations of mathematics.' He claimed that there was not any
truth that he could not clearly demonstrate with 'a knowledge
and certainty equal to that produced by the rules of arithmetic'
using only the principles of his own method, 'for all kinds of
propositions of any nature and any kind there can be'.[36]
    What that method or 'art of reasoning well' involved, at least
in these Paris years, is explained in Descartes' first philosophical
treatise, the *Rules for the Direction of the Mind* (*Regulae ad directionem
ingenii*). The *Rules* contains a method for 'directing the mind
with a view to forming true and sound judgements about whatever comes before it'.[37] The work is, in effect, a manual for how
to achieve absolutely certain knowledge in any discipline. Its principal idea – one that informs all of Descartes' writings – is that
few things are beyond the grasp of the human intellect as long as
the mind is well guided and not merely engaging in 'aimless and
blind inquiries'.
    At the core of Descartes' method are reliable rules for em-
ploying the intellectual operations that he calls 'intuition' and
'deduction'. Intuition is the mind's grasp of a relatively simple,
self-evident and indubitable truth, whether it be a single fact or
concept or the necessary connection between two concepts or

propositions. One intuits, for example, that one exists, that one is thinking and what a triangle is, as well as any relatively simple mathematical, logical or conceptual relations between just a few items, such as '$1 + 1 = 2$' or 'p implies q'.

> By 'intuition' I do not mean the fluctuating testimony of the senses or the deceptive judgement of the imagination as it botches things together, but the conception of a clear and attentive mind, which is so easy and distinct that there can be no room for doubt about what we are understanding . . . Intuition is the indubitable conception of a clear and attentive mind which proceeds solely from the light of reason.[38]

The certainty of intuition lies in its immediacy. In intuition, something is taken in 'at one glance'. Deduction, however, is a train of reasoning that consists in multiple steps of intuition. It is 'the inference of something as following necessarily from some other propositions which are known with certainty'. So long as one proceeds in the sequence from one proposition to the next via intuition and thereby grasps the necessary connections between them, then, no matter how many steps are involved, deduction preserves the certainty of its constituent intuitions. If one intuits that p implies q, that q implies r and that r implies s, then one deduces that s follows from p.

> Even if we cannot take in at one view all the intermediate links on which the connection depends, we can have knowledge of the connection provided we survey the links one after the other, and keep in mind that each link from first to last is attached to its neighbor. Hence we are distinguishing mental intuition from certain deduction on the grounds that we are aware of a movement or a

sort of sequence in the latter but not in the former, and also because immediate self-evidence is not required for deduction, as it is for intuition.[39]

A deduction can, in fact, be reduced to an intuition. All it takes is running through the series of intuited necessary connections often enough so that one can hold them all in a single mental act, 'passing from the first to the last so swiftly that memory is left with practically no role to play, and I seem to intuit the whole thing at once'.[40] With enough practice, one can eventually intuit that *s* follows from *p*.

Intuition and deduction play a primary role in mathematics, which represents the paradigm of absolutely true knowledge given its method of starting with clear and distinct first principles (in mathematics, these would be axioms and definitions) and proceeding by lucid demonstrations to indubitable proofs of theorems ('certain and evident cognitions'). Descartes notes that 'of all the sciences so far discovered, arithmetic and geometry alone are . . . free from any taint of falsity or uncertainty.' This is because 'the deduction or pure inference of one thing from another can never be performed wrongly by an intellect which is in the least degree rational.' Arithmetic and geometry are 'much more certain than other disciplines' in that 'they alone are concerned with an object so pure and simple that they make no assumptions that experience might render uncertain; they consist entirely in deducing conclusions by means of rational arguments.'[41]

Descartes is confident, however, that other sciences – in fact, all of 'human wisdom' – can, through his method, acquire the same degree of certainty as mathematics, well beyond the mere probabilities provided by other modes of reasoning. Early in the *Rules*, he introduces the term *mathesis universalis* (universal mathe- matics), essentially a science of proportions.[42] It is not mathematics per se but rather an extension to other disciplines of the kind of methodical and symbolic reasoning on discrete and continuous quantities that is so successful in arithmetic and geometry. 'Ordinary mathematics is far from my mind here, it is quite another discipline I am expounding . . . this discipline should contain the primary rudiments of human reason and extend to the discovery of truths in any field whatsoever.' Arithmetic and geometry, but also astronomy, music, optics and mechanics are all disciplines of *mathesis* because they deal with 'questions of order or measure, and it is irrelevant whether the measure in question involves numbers, shapes, stars, sounds or any other object whatsoever'.[43] As he would later put it, regarding 'all the special sciences commonly called "mathematics"', it is clear that 'despite the diversity of their objects, they agree in considering nothing but the relations or proportions that hold between these objects.'[44]

The method that Descartes endorses in the *Rules* and that informs any proper *mathesis* is simply a matter of proceeding through intuitions and deductions according to an order proper to the subject at hand.

By 'a method' I mean reliable rules which are easy to apply, and such that if one follows them exactly, one will never take what is false to be true or fruitlessly expend one's mental efforts, but will gradually and constantly increase one's knowledge till one arrives at a true understanding of everything within one's capacity.[45]

The first step in the method involves breaking down complex problems into simpler constituent problems, and these into yet simpler ones, until one arrives at some basic elements that are accessible to intuitions. These most basic elements are typically what Descartes calls 'simple natures', and include such things as thought, extension or matter, motion or rest, and power. Then, reversing the order, one starts from the intuition of the simple natures and uses them to resolve the questions at the next level up, and so on, until one finally arrives at a resolution of the original complex question.

One of Descartes' early achievements in optics, for example, was his discovery of the 'anaclastic', or the curve of a line which, through refraction, will focus incoming parallel rays of light so that they intersect at a single point. A crucial matter for the proper construction of lenses, it requires knowing the relation between the angle of incidence and the angle of refraction as light passes across the boundary between two different media (for example, from air to water) – that is, the law of refraction.[46] But knowing this relation depends upon knowing how a ray of light is bent or refracted as it crosses the boundary between media, which in turn depends on knowing the way light as a natural power passes through transparent media, which presupposes knowing something about light as a natural power, which, finally, requires one to know what a natural power is. Once one grasps, via intuition, the nature of natural power and how it is manifest in the action of light, progress is possible in understanding why light behaves the way it does when passing through this or that medium, and this will eventually allow for the derivation, in mathematical terms, of the law of refraction and the anaclastic curve.[47]

Another feature of the method involves translating the elements of a problem – numbers or geometrical concepts, physical bodies, relationships of various sorts – into concrete, two-dimensional quantities. To take a simple case, the number 1 would be represented by a single line segment of length x, and the number 2 as two line segments each of the same length, and thus the sum of 1 + 2 would clearly appear as three distinct line segments. The advantage of this symbolic representation is that it is easier to make 'simple and straightforward comparisons' and draw conclusions from visualized magnitudes (points, lines, shapes) than from abstract concepts or ordinary empirical phenomena. The imagination plays a key role here, as it is the faculty that depicts things in simplified form as 'bare figures'. This allows for commensurability among diverse items. By putting things of different natures into the same quantitative format, the equalities, differences and proportions can be more distinctly perceived. Through such figurative modelling, difficult problems in physics, for example, can be handled by the more tractable processes of addition, subtraction, multiplication and division.

> The preceding rules show us how to abstract determinate and perfectly understood problems from particular subjects and to reduce them to the point where the question becomes simply one of discovering certain magnitudes on the basis of the fact that they bear such and such a relation to certain given magnitudes.[48]

Descartes worked on the *Rules* for nearly a decade – putting it aside, picking it up again to make revisions and additions – and it shows. The text is a bit of a puzzle, and it is difficult to identify the strata of composition and the various, not always coherent, strands of thought.[49] Descartes himself eventually saw the limitations of the project and gave it up. He abandoned the incomplete manuscript and it was never published in his lifetime.[50] He was perhaps eager to get on with actually pursuing his research and elaborating a philosophical system. But his epistemological concern with a reliable method for discovering truth and certainty in the sciences remained a lifelong project and informs many of his later philosophical writings.

THREE

A Fabulous New World

oon after Descartes' death in Stockholm in 1650, inventories were made of his manuscripts and other items, both those he had taken with him to Sweden and those left behind in Holland.[1] Among the notebooks, draft papers and correspondence listed in Stockholm by his friend Pierre Chanut (1601–1662), the French ambassador to the Swedish queen's court, are several abandoned or unpublished works, including the *Rules for the Direction of the Mind* and the treatise on music. There are three pages titled 'On the Constituent Parts of the Lower Stomach', a sheet of parchment labelled 'The Remedy and Virtue of Medicaments' and a note on irrational numbers.

What is *not* in Chanut's catalogue is the manuscript of Descartes' first serious approach, from decades earlier, to laying out his philosophical system of nature.[2] Several fair copies of the work, which Descartes never published, were circulating in the 1650s, in France and elswhere. The original, however, was not with the philosopher's belongings in Sweden. It may have been among the items he had entrusted to his Dutch friends for safekeeping, or perhaps it was simply lost.

DESCARTES SAYS THAT during the years that he was working on the *Rules*, in the 1620s, he made a concerted effort at conventionality, 'appearing to live like those concerned only to lead an agreeable and blameless life, who take care to keep their pleasures free from vices, and who engage in every honest pastime in order to enjoy their leisure without boredom'. But the public life of leisure was only a cover for more private and ambitious interests. All the while he never stopped 'pursuing my project, and I made perhaps more progress in the knowledge of truth than I would have if I had done nothing but read books or mix with men of letters'.[3]

Paris may have held many attractions for a philosopher, but the city was not very conducive to Descartes' project. Nor would anywhere else in France be much better. In his native milieu, with its family obligations (including what must have been pressure from his father and brother to find himself a respectable occupation) and interruptions – from friends, colleagues, even inquisitive strangers – there were too many distractions for a scientist intent on making progress in the knowledge of nature. Reflecting back many years later, he wrote:

> As many people know, I lived in relative comfort in my native country. My only reason for choosing to live elsewhere was that I had so many friends and relatives whom I could not fail to entertain, and that I would have had little time and leisure available to pursue the studies which I enjoy and which, according to many people, will contribute to the common good of the human race.[4]

Descartes felt he had no alternative but to leave his homeland once again and go abroad. His departure from France in 1629 was thus motivated not by curiosity and wanderlust but by a desire for peace and quiet, and above all for the intellectual freedom to pursue his research undisturbed. His destination, as it had been ten years earlier, was the United Provinces of the

Netherlands. Writing in the *Discourse on Method* a few years later, while living in Amsterdam, he says that

> as I was honest enough not to wish to be taken for what
> I was not, I thought I had to try by every means to become
> worthy of the reputation that was given me. Exactly eight
> years ago this desire made me resolve to move away from
> any place where I might have acquaintances and retire to
> this country, where the long duration of the war has led
> to the establishment of such order that the armies main-
> tained here seem to serve only to make the enjoyment of
> the fruits of peace all the more secure.

It was not only the order and security of the Dutch Republic that made it an attractive locale for Descartes. The small territory, still fighting for independence, was among the most densely populated of Europe; and waterlogged Amsterdam, where Descartes lived for a time, while much smaller than Paris, was a fairly congested and hectic city. The difference was that the Dutch, among whom Descartes had few acquaintances, were, he says, so focused on going about their own business that they had little interest in the doings of a French intellectual abroad.

> Living here, amidst this great mass of busy people who
> are more concerned with their own affairs than curious
> about those of others, I have been able to lead a life as
> solitary and withdrawn as if I were in the most remote
> desert, while lacking none of the comforts found in the
> most populous cities.[5]

Descartes simply wanted to be left alone and devote as much of his time as possible to his work, and that was exactly what he could do among busy Dutch neighbours.

His voluntary exile turned out to be permanent. Descartes never again made his home in France, and he rarely returned there, making only a few short visits. He ended up spending most of his adult life in the Netherlands, with his residence alternating between cities and the countryside. The commercial bustle of a city afforded him the anonymity and freedom from everyday disruptions by family and friends that he greatly desired but that he could not enjoy in Paris. While living in Amsterdam, he noted that

> in this large town where I live . . . everyone but myself is engaged in trade, and hence is so attentive to his own profit that I could live here all my life without ever being noticed by a soul. I take a walk each day amid the bustle of the crowd with as much freedom and repose as you could obtain in your leafy groves, and I pay no more attention to the people I meet than I would to the trees in your woods or the animals that browse there. The bustle of the city no more disturbs my daydreams than would the rippling of a stream.[6]

During his early years in the Republic, Descartes changed address frequently. After a brief stay in a castle in Franeker, a university town in the far north, he lived in Amsterdam for six months, then in Leiden for two months (perhaps because it was home to the leading Dutch university), then, one year later, back in Amsterdam until the summer of 1632. This was followed by almost two years in Deventer, a town in the eastern province of Overijssel. In March 1634 he moved back to Amsterdam, settling for a year in a house on the Westermarkt.

To protect his privacy throughout these moves, he asked Father Mersenne back in Paris not to reveal his location to anyone. 'I do not so much care if someone suspects where I am, just as long as he does not know the exact place.'[7] He even suggested that

Mersenne engage in a little deception to put would-be visitors off his trail. 'If someone asks you where I am, please say that you are not certain because I was resolved to go to England.'[8]

The subterfuge worked, at least for a while, and Descartes found the 'time and leisure' he sought to immerse himself in research. Having left purely methodological topics behind, he was able to make great progress on an ambitious scientific treatise in which he hoped to provide an account of 'all of nature', including the heavens, the earth and even the human being, body and soul. He was ready to publish part of the work in 1633 and sent a copy to Mersenne for his review. However, something scared him off. In the end, he decided to abandon the project. It would not appear in print until fourteen years after his death.

What was it that had so alarmed Descartes that he was willing to write off many years of labour that he believed would lead not just to a better understanding of the universe – its origins, its constituent bodies, its rich variety of phenomena – but to the transformation of philosophy itself?

THE CHURCH OF SANTA MARIA sopra Minerva in Rome sits close by the Pantheon, in the district of the city known as the Campus Martius (Field of Mars). Its name comes from the fact that the earliest Christian church on the site was built over (*sopra*) the ruins of a temple believed at the time to have been dedicated to the Roman goddess of wisdom. The plain, even austere facade of Santa Maria sopra Minerva belies the ornate gothic interior, with its soaring vault and richly coloured arches and ceiling. Construction began in 1280, but the building was not completed until the mid-fifteenth century, under the direction of Cardinal Juan de Torquemada, the uncle of history's more familiar Torquemada, Tomàs, Spain's notoriously brutal Grand Inquisitor who would stop at nothing in his campaign to root out heresy.

By the early seventeenth century, the Dominican convent attached to Santa Maria sopra Minerva was regularly providing its own service to the intellectual purification of the Roman Catholic domain. It was the local headquarters of the Supreme Sacred Congregation of the Roman and Universal Inquisition, also known as the Holy Office. The members of this august and fearsome authority were charged with not only policing doctrinal matters but pursuing any perceived threats, theological or otherwise, to the Catholic faith. In the spring of 1633 they were once again meeting in the convent's rooms, this time to decide the fate of a seventy-year-old scientist from Florence.

One year earlier Galileo Galilei had published his *Dialogue Concerning the Two Chief World Systems*. Sponsored by the Lincean Academy in Rome and dedicated by Galileo to his Medici employer – his official title was 'Philosopher and Chief Mathematician to the Most Serene Grand Duke of Tuscany' – this work was, despite diplomatic and disingenuous disclaimers by Galileo, an extended brief on behalf of the Copernican heliocentric model of the cosmos. It was also, therefore, part of the case against the Ptolomaic geocentric model, which the Catholic Church had been defending with increasing vigour in the light of recent astronomical discoveries and new debates about the relationship between the Bible and scientific truth. Galileo went ahead with the publication of this work despite the fact that he had been warned by the Church many years earlier not to teach or defend the Copernican theory.[9]

The 'Galileo Affair' cannot be reduced to a single famous event – the 1633 trial and conviction of a scientist by the Catholic Church. Rather, it is a complex series of episodes stretching over two decades and involving a varied cast of characters and a host of philosophical, theological, philological and religious issues. It was not simply a clash between two competing views of the nature of the universe, but included profound theoretical differences over the relationship between science and religion, the status of

Scripture as a source of knowledge and the proper method for interpreting the holy texts. Even the nature of truth itself was in question, as well as who had the authority to decide what was a matter of faith and what was a matter of reason. All of this conflict was exacerbated by social and political factors both within the Church hierarchy and in its relationship to secular authorities, domestic and foreign.[10]

It all began in 1610 when Galileo published *The Starry Messenger* (*Sidereus nuncius*). In this short book, he reveals some of the remarkable discoveries he had made with (as the title page proclaims) 'the aid of a spyglass lately invented by him' – that is, by means of a refracting telescope that he had constructed himself and that was a significant improvement over earlier models. Galileo describes the 'variety of elevations and depressions' that he saw on the surface of the moon, which are especially visible around the boundary between the moon's illuminated and dark sides. These are taken as evidence that, contrary to the prevailing theory that celestial bodies are made of a different and more perfect matter from terrestrial ones, the lunar surface is in fact composed of ordinary matter and, like the surface of the earth, is rough, with mountains and valleys. Galileo also argues that the weak illumination often seen on the dark side of the moon ('the moon's secondary light') does not shine out of the moon itself; nor does it come directly from the sun or Venus. Rather, it is the sun's illumination of the moon's bright side being reflected back on to the moon's dark side by the earth, and it varies according to how close the moon is to the sun. Perhaps most stunningly, Galileo also describes how, over the course of several nights, he observed three 'starlets' around Jupiter that appear to change their position relative both to the planet and to each other. These, he concludes, are moons that orbit Jupiter – he names them the Medicean Planets, in honour of his patron – just as the moon revolves around the earth.

These discoveries do not amount to demonstrative proof of the truth of the Copernican system, as Galileo well knew. But he did see them as compelling evidence in favour of that theory, in part because they cause difficulties for both the Ptolomeic alternative and the Aristotelian assumptions about the nature of the heavens that support it. The 'earthshine' on the moon, Galileo notes, counts 'against those who argue that the earth must be excluded from the dancing whirl of stars . . . We shall prove that the earth is a wandering body,' just like the others.[11] Similarly, the moons around Jupiter show that the earth is not unique in terms of being the centre of orbit of other bodies. This, Galileo says, should be a 'fine and elegant argument for quieting the doubts' of those would-be partisans of the Copernican system who were nonetheless reluctant to accept that there should be only one celestial body that has an orbiting satellite while going through an annual revolution around the sun. 'Now we have not just one planet rotating about another while both run through a great orbit around the sun; our own eyes show us four stars which wander around Jupiter as does the moon around the earth, while all together trace out a grand revolution about the sun in the space of twelve years.'[12]

Later that year, Galileo added even more evidence to the Copernican brief when he discovered with his telescope that Venus goes through phases, just as the earth's moon does. These changes in the planet's illumination all but confirmed that it revolves around the sun, not the earth. While this would be consistent with the planetary system defended by the late sixteenth-century Danish astronomer Tycho Brahe – according to whom the planets revolve around the sun while the sun, the moon and the fixed stars revolve around the earth – it cannot be accounted for under the standard Ptolomaic model.

In *The Starry Messenger*, Galileo calls the sun 'the center of the universe',[13] and suggests some of the advantages of the Copernican system, though he is still cautious about calling it anything other than an 'hypothesis'. At the very least, it does a better job of accounting for the observable phenomena in the heavens. Just three years later, though, when he published a series of letters under the title 'History and Demonstrations Concerning Sunspots and Their Phenomena', Galileo unequivocally and publicly endorsed the heliocentric account of the cosmos as the *true* one. His Aristotelian opponents knew from their own observations about the dark spots that appear to be on the surface of the sun. They argued, however, hoping to preserve the perfection and immutability of this brightest of heavenly bodies, that these were in fact small planetary objects between the earth and the sun. Galileo countered with conclusive evidence that the spots were not like planets at all: that they are either 'contiguous with' the surface of the sun or separated from it by a very small distance (much like the earth's clouds).[14] Moreover, the changes and apparent motions in the spots show that the sun rotates on its axis and they are carried around with it.

Galileo now had no scruples about proclaiming that all of this data 'harmonizes admirably with the great Copernican system, to the universal revelation of which doctrine propitious breezes are now seen to be directed towards us, leaving little fear of clouds or crosswinds'.[15] Indeed, in his 1615 letter to the Grand Duchess Christina, he can tell her that 'as to the arrangement of the parts of the universe, I hold the sun to be situated motionless in the center of the revolution of the celestial orbs while the earth rotates on its axis and revolves about the sun.'[16]

There was growing concern within the Catholic Church's congregations charged with purity of faith and doctrine over new publications in favour of Copernicanism and the contentious debates they were generating. The cardinals were willing to accept the use of the Copernican system as a 'hypothesis' useful for practical purposes, such as navigation and calendrical calculation.

But, wedded as the Church was to the Aristotelian-Ptolomaic system, they were not willing to tolerate campaigns on behalf of the *truth* of any contrary theory. This commitment was based both on philosophical and theological reasons and on Scripture. Many dogmas of Catholicism set by the Council of Trent (1545–63), including some of its most important sacraments (such as Eucharistic transubstantiation), were grounded in principles of Aristotelian physics and metaphysics; thus any novel scientific claims that threatened to undermine those philosophical principles was taken to be a threat to Catholic theology as well.

The geocentric account of the cosmos also appeared to the guardians of Catholic orthodoxy to be unambiguously propounded by Holy Scripture. The Psalms were read to endorse geocentrism when they describe the sun as 'like a groom coming out of his chamber; It rejoices like a strong person to run his course,' and relate how God 'established the earth on its foundations so that it shall never totter' (104:5). The author of Ecclesiastes says that 'the earth remains forever,' while 'the sun rises and the sun sets' (1:4–5). The most famous passage, and the one most often used by the Ptolomeists, comes from the Book of Joshua (10:12–13). The Israelites have the upper hand in battle against the Amorites, and Joshua wants the day to be extended so there will be more time to finish off the enemy. He directs his plea to God:

> 'Sun, stand still at Gibeon,
> And moon, at the Valley of Aijalon!'
> So the sun stood still, and the moon stopped,
> Until the nation avenged themselves of their enemies
> . . .
> And the sun stopped in the middle of the sky and did
>   not hurry to go down for about a whole day.

How could Copernicans possibly make sense of such texts if the sun does not in fact move across the sky in a diurnal orbit around the earth?

The immediate aggravating factor that, in 1616, finally prompted the Holy Office to take action was not so much Galileo's writings – although its officers were aware of his views and gave his letters on sunspots a close examination – but a treatise by Paolo Antonio Foscarini titled *A Letter Concerning the Opinion of the Pythagoreans and of Copernicus About the Mobility of the Earth and the Stability of the Sun*. Foscarini's goal was to show that the Copernican system is consistent with both the Bible and Catholic theology, and he made use of Galileo's recent discoveries to bolster the case for the truth of the heliocentric account.

This was too much for the Inquisition and its sister body, the Congregation of the Index of Prohibited Books. The Holy Office condemned Copernicus' theory. Its assessors determined that the proposition that 'the sun is the center of the world and completely devoid of local motion' is 'foolish and absurd in philosophy, and formally heretical', while the proposition that 'the earth is not the center of the world, nor motionless, but it moves as a whole and also with diurnal motion . . . receives the same judgment in philosophy, and in regard to theological truth it is at least erroneous in faith'.[17] They judged these cosmological claims to be contrary both to divine Scripture and to the true Christian faith. Foscarini's book was condemned and placed on the Index, along with Copernicus' *On the Revolution of the Celestial Spheres* and other works supportive of the heliocentric account, 'to prevent the emergence of more serious harm throughout Christendom'.[18]

Galileo was treated more gently. He was given a private warning by the powerful Cardinal Robert Bellarmine, who was conveying an ultimatum from the pope. Galileo was ordered 'to abandon completely the aforementioned opinion that the sun stands still at the center of the world and the earth moves, and henceforth not to hold, teach, or defend it in any way whatever, either orally or in writing'.[19] That is, he must not present Copernicanism as a true theory; if he must discuss it – and it is unclear whether he is permitted to discuss it at all – he must treat it only as a 'hypothesis' that can account for the observed phenomena in the heavens. Galileo promises to obey, although he and the Inquisition's judges will later disagree over what were in fact the terms to which he agreed.

This is where things stood, more or less, when Galileo brought out his *Dialogue* in 1632. In this new book, Galileo publicly goes further than ever before. The *Dialogue* describes, in great detail, the essential elements and structure of a Copernican cosmos; and if Galileo had in fact been forbidden by Bellarmine from even discussing the theory, then the work is certainly a violation of the 1616 order. But in the *Dialogue* Galileo is no longer considering heliocentrism merely 'hypothetically'. He is clearly arguing *for* it. Over the course of the four-day conversation that takes place between Salviati, Sagredo and Simplicio, the reader is treated to an extensive and compelling case on behalf of the new planetary system, one which employs all the evidence that Galileo had been compiling over two decades.

In the guise of Salviati, Galileo reprises arguments from his earlier works – on sunspots, the phases of Venus, the moons of Jupiter, the mountains on the surface of the moon and so on – against an Aristotelian cosmology and in favour of Copernicanism. He now claims to be able to 'deduce', from astronomical observations and with the help of some fundamental principles of physics (including the law of inertia), that the sun and not the earth is the centre of the 'celestial revolutions'. Equally damaging to the old system, Galileo's telescopic results also confirm that the heavens are not eternal and incorruptible, given the appearance of new stars and spots that come and go on the face of the sun.

Galileo (Salviati) also addresses various objections raised against the heliocentric view – for example, using his physics to explain why bodies do not go flying off an earth that is spinning, and why an object falling from a tower does not land far to the west from the base of the tower being carried along eastwards by the earth's rotation.

On the dialogue's Fourth Day, Galileo presents what he regarded as the most direct and persuasive evidence in favour of the diurnal motion of the earth. He reprises material from a text that he had written, as a private letter, in 1616, and has Salviati argue that the only plausible explanation for the daily changes of sea level with the tides is the motion of the earth. The planet's rotation causes the water to surge back and forth, just like the water in a container in motion.

The cardinals were stunned that Galileo would have the audacity to violate the presumed terms of his agreement with Bellarmine (who had died in 1621). After reports on the *Dialogue* were commissioned by the Inquisition, Galileo was summoned to its chambers in Rome for interrogation. The Florentine astronomer insisted on the 'purity of my intention' and protested that 'I neither did hold nor do hold as true the condemned opinion of the earth's motion and the sun's stability.'[20] He offered the incredible disclaimer that he in fact meant to refute the Copernican system, not to teach or defend it (although he admits he can understand why an innocent reader might have come away with that impression).

His judges were not persuaded. On 22 June 1633, they issued their ruling. Galileo, they declared, 'has rendered [himself] vehemently suspected of heresy, namely, of having held and believed a doctrine which is false and contrary to the divine and Holy Scripture; that the sun is the center of the world and does not move from east to west, and the earth moves and is not the center of the world'. He was ordered to 'abjure, curse, and detest the aforementioned errors and heresies, and every other error and heresy contrary to the Catholic and Apostolic Church'. Moreover, they sentenced the elderly scientist to imprisonment, although this was subsequently commuted to house arrest. As for the *Dialogue on the Two Chief World Systems*, the Inquisitors proclaimed it to be 'prohibited by public edict'.[21]

Galileo's fate would have serious repurcussions for Descartes' plans finally to publish something.

SOON AFTER LANDING in the Dutch Republic in the spring of 1629, Descartes began working on a variety of topics in natural philosophy. For the next four years, he would be occupied both with questions as general as the origin of the cosmos, the nature of matter and the laws of motion, and with detailed causal explanations for particular phenomena, including such mysterious effects as gravity, magnetism and the tides. He would also address a number of problems in optics and the science of light and achieve some expertise in anatomy and understanding the workings of the human body – what he calls 'all the main functions in man'.

The initial impetus for this broad set of investigations was an unusual atmospheric event that Descartes heard about that first summer in the Netherlands. Two luminous spots had recently been witnessed on opposite sides of the sun, looking like secondary suns sitting on a ring or halo around the sun itself. Intrigued, Descartes asked Mersenne in Paris to send him another description of the parhelia, which had been first reported in Rome. He was set on determining what this strange occurrence was and why it should happen. In October he wrote to Mersenne that 'I was investigating the cause of the phenomenon which you write about in your letter. Just over two months ago one of my friends showed me a very full description of the phenomenon and asked me what I thought of it.'[22] Descartes believed, though, that he could not respond to this query until he had a deeper understanding of the nature of light, its behaviour as it passes through various media and a host of other optical and atmospheric effects. Indeed, he tells Mersenne, 'before I could give him my answer I had to interrupt my current work in order to make a systematic study of the whole of meteorology.'

Thus the beginning of what Descartes called 'a little treatise on the topic', one that will have the additional benefit of offering readers 'a specimen of my philosophy'. This work on optical and atmospheric questions would deal not just with the constitution and action of light, but with a wide variety of luminous phenomena. Subsequent letters to Mersenne mention the corona seen around the flame of a candle, the apparent colours of bodies and – since it was also to be a work of meteorology, broadly construed to include some of what now falls under astronomy – sunspots, the luminescence of clouds, the formation of rainbows and the brightness of light emanating from stars and the moon relative to their position on the horizon. Descartes even planned to investigate 'how the whiteness of bread remains in the Blessed Sacrament' after the miracle of Eucharistic transubstantiation – when the bread has been changed into the body of Christ – since it is an example of how colour is a matter of the way in which light is reflected off the surface of a body and received by the eyes.[23]

One thing led to another, however, and already by November the project had grown significantly in scope, expanding well beyond merely a 'discourse on colors and light'. Descartes informed Mersenne that he was now intent on providing an exhaustive account of 'all sublunary phenomena in general', and that his book would be delayed by at least a year. 'Rather than explaining just one phenomenon I have decided to explain all the phenomena of nature, that is to say, the whole of physics.'[24] With a new title in hand, Descartes was now investigating for 'my *Physics*' the acceleration of falling bodies, employing a rudimentary concept of inertia ('the motion impressed on a body at one time remains in it for all time unless it is taken away by some other cause'[25]), as well as related topics in ballistics ('whether a stone thrown with a sling, or a ball shot from a musket, or a bolt from a crossbow, travels faster and has greater force in the middle of its flight than it has at the start').[26] Still, he continued to refer to the project in April 1630 as 'the little treatise I have begun', and even suggests to Mersenne that it will be 'a discourse which will be so short that I reckon it will take only an afternoon to read'.

By November 1630, though, Descartes had come to terms with the fact that this still only 'half finished' project would be much longer and take more time than he had estimated. He anticipated having a complete draft in three years, and hoped Mersenne would then carefully review it, making any necessary corrections, and place it with a publisher.[27] 'My little treatise' and 'my *Physics*' is now 'my *World*'. The new working title better captures the global scope of its subject-matter. What he had earlier referred to as 'the discourse explaining the nature of colours and light' is now just one part of a grandly ambitious work that, years after Descartes' death, will be published as *Le Monde*.

The expansion of the project and the extension of its timeline was due to the fact that Descartes decided that, beyond optics, even beyond terrestrial physics, he needed to discuss cosmology, astronomy, animal physiology, the human body and even the human soul. Reflecting back on the origins of this project some years later, he notes that 'fearing that I could not put everything I had in mind into my discourse, I undertook merely to expound quite fully what I understood about light.' But the phenomena of nature, all composed of the same matter and obeying the same sets of laws, are not so discrete. Thus, while the nature and behaviour of light continued to be a unifying topic,

I added something about the sun and fixed stars, because almost all light comes from them; about the heavens, because they transmit light; about planets, comets and the earth, because they reflect light; about terrestrial bodies in particular, because they are either coloured or transparent or luminous; and finally about man, because he observes these bodies.[28]

Descartes was wavering about whether and how to include a discussion of living bodies, and especially human beings. In June 1632, writing from Deventer in the province of Overijssel, he tells Mersenne that he is finished with everything he has to say about inanimate bodies, and now 'I have been trying to decide whether I should include in *The World* an account of how animals are generated.' He has resolved at this point not to, 'because it would take me too long'.[29] Still, he feels he needs to say something about living beings, since the operations of merely animate bodies – that is, living bodies that are not also endowed with souls – are not fundamentally different from those of inanimate bodies; they are all made of the same matter and function according to the same kinetic principles.

With human beings, things are a bit more complicated. On the one hand, the human body itself is just another animate (living) body, and so what Descartes says about living bodies in general will apply as well to the human body. On the other, human physiology is especially complex and, for obvious reasons, important; Descartes has a great interest in medical matters and in the aetiology and treatment of disease. Then there is the fact that the human body is also united with a soul, an immaterial substance that does not operate according to the principles of physics, even when it interacts with the body. Thus, when Descartes tells Mersenne in June that 'I have finished all I had planned to include in [my treatise] concerning inanimate bodies. It only remains for me to

add something concerning the nature of man,' it is unclear whether
he is talking only about the human body and its purely physical
operations, or about the complete human being – a mind–body
union. It is also unclear where exactly the discussion of 'the nature
of man', whatever it may include, belongs in his *World*.

Just a few months later, Descartes had reached a little more
clarity on all of this. He told Mersenne in November 1632 that

> my discussion of man in *The World* will be a little fuller
> than I had intended, for I have undertaken to explain all
> the main functions in man. I have already written of the
> vital functions, such as the digestion of food, the heart
> beat, the distribution of nourishment, etc., and the five
> senses. I am now dissecting the heads of various animals,
> so that I can explain what imagination, memory, etc.,
> consist in.[30]

Descartes seems to have decided that the discussion of the human
being will form a separate treatise (or, possibly, a pair of treatises)
within the larger project of *The World*. First, he will deal the human
body merely 'as a machine',[31] distinct from the treatment of light
and the ways it affects and is affected by inanimate bodies, and
will show 'what structure the nerves and muscles of the human
body must have' in order to function as it does.[32]

Then there is the question of the human soul and its relationship to the human body. His discussion should include both
effects in the soul caused by its connection to the body (pains,
pleasures and sensory perceptions such as colour, taste and sound)
and effects in the body caused by the soul (voluntary motions of
bodily parts). Also at stake is the problem of how to determine
when a body is in fact endowed with a soul and when it is only a
material automaton, animate in the sense of living but composed
of matter alone, such as is the case with vegetative matter and

non-human animals – as Descartes will later put it, 'how we can know the difference between man and beast'.[33]

Finally, there is the soul itself and its purely intellectual or rational functions: that is, its nature, existence and operations as a substance ontologically distinct from and independent of the body. That Descartes was at work on such purely spiritual and metaphysical topics, and even drafted an essay on them to include in *The World*, either as the final element in the second part of the treatise or as a separate essay, is evident from the summary of his 1632 labours that he later offers in the *Discourse on Method*. He recalls that 'I described the rational soul, and showed that, unlike the other things of which I had spoken, it cannot be derived in any way from the potentiality of matter, but must be specially created.'[34] He says that he explained in what he wrote how the soul is not 'lodged in the human body like a helmsman in his ship', but rather is intimately joined with the body, although separable from it, as it must be in order to enjoy immortality after death.

In the end, what Descartes had by early 1633 was a two-part dissertation. Part One, eventually to be called *Treatise on Light* (*Traité de la lumière*), would use the phenomenon of light to lead an investigation of inanimate bodies in the celestial and terrestrial realms solely according to the principles of his physics, including an account of the origin and structure of the cosmos. Part Two, *Treatise on Man* (*Traité de l'homme*), concerned 'animals, and in particular men', and it was devoted to showing how the human body (like any animal body) operates on purely mechanical principles, without any functions that may be related to mind or thought.[35] The discussion of 'the rational soul', both by itself and in its relation to the human body, initially intended for a Part Three, would appear only in several of his later works: the *Meditations on First Philosophy*, the *Principles of Philosophy* and especially the *Passions of the Soul*.[36]

THE DOCTRINES IN *The World* are informed by a new theory of nature and a new approach to understanding the phenomena of the heavens and the earth. It is a vastly different kind of science than the Aristotelian variety that had dominated schools across Europe for centuries up to Descartes' era and that still enjoyed ecclesiastic support from both Catholic and Protestant authorities. Its partisans therefore had to tread carefully.

For Aristotelians, the proper objects of scientific inquiry were what they called 'substances'. They sought especially to understand the properties that substances have and the changes they undergo. A substance, which in its primary sense is simply any particular existing individual (a rock, a tree, a horse, a human being), is a compound 'hylomorphic' entity consisting of matter (*hyle*) and form (*morphē*). The matter gives the substance its materiality and its 'thisness', its numerical and spatial discreteness with respect to other substances. The form, however – an immaterial, soul-like item that unites with the matter – gives the substance its 'what-ness', its identity as a being of such and such a kind. The form, which is the more active constituent of the substance, is causally responsible for all the qualities by which a thing is what it is and for all the characteristic behaviours it exhibits. When a parcel of matter is informed by the form 'horse', for example, the result is a particular horse that looks and acts in horse-like ways. Its shape, its tendency to trot or gallop, its whinnying, are all generated by the form.

Forms are distinguished as substantial or accidental according to whether the properties and activities they ground are essential or accidental to the substance. The substantial form of human being imposes on the particular matter it informs just those properties essential to being a human: animality and rationality.[37] The other features or powers belonging to an individual that distinguish it from other members of the same species – in a human being, these would be hair, eye and skin colour, height and so on

– result from any number of accidental forms also informing the same matter.[38]

Under an Aristotelian hylomorphic metaphysics, moreover, any account of how a substance undergoes alteration and even a complete change of nature necessarily involves specifying determinate forms. Because the forms are responsible for the substance being what it is and acting as it does, a change or alteration in a substance occurs when that substance loses or acquires some form(s) or another. (In substantial change, whereby a thing is transformed into something of another kind altogether, the material substratum loses one substantial form and gains another. In the more common case of alteration, the substance remains what it is essentially but undergoes some change in one or more of its accidental properties – its colour or shape – through the loss and gain of accidental forms.)

This general model of explanation is also at work in Aristotelian physics and informs the Scholastic account of the dynamic behaviour of bodies in motion and rest. Aristotle had identified four species of fundamental elements or primary bodies, out of which all the matter of physical bodies is composed: fire, air, water and earth. Each of these four elements is in turn generated from a combination of two out of four primary qualities – heat, cold, dryness and moisture – which determine the nature of that element. Fire, for example, is made up of heat and dryness. As the primary qualities combine in various proportions in the elementary bodies and thus in the macroscopic physical bodies for which those elementary bodies provide the matter, they account in part for the observable behaviour of things in the world. The properties and effects of ordinary fire – its power to burn or dry other bodies – are explained by the preponderance in it of the element fire and thus of that element's primary qualities of heat and dryness.

This was the general metaphysical and physical schema of Thomas Aquinas and other medieval Aristotelians. In late Latin

Scholasticism of the sixteenth and early seventeenth centuries
– in works by Francisco Suarez, Eustachius a Sancto Paulo and
the Jesuit authors of the Coimbrian Commentaries on Aristotle
(so called because they were produced at the University of
Coimbra in Portugal) – one still finds an unwavering commitment to the hylomorphic doctrine of substance and the theory
of elements and qualities. At the same time, there is an expansion
in the number of primary qualities from four to six, with the addition of two motive qualities – heaviness (*gravitas*) and lightness
(*levitas*) – as well as an increase in the use of additional 'sensible'
qualities to explain natural phenomena. These were all called
'real qualities' and 'virtues', and practically every sensible and
insensible property or behaviour in bodies was to be explained in
terms of a body's possession of the relevant form or quality. The
forms and qualities, endowed with active powers, were regarded
as the efficient causes of their respective visible and invisible
effects. Thus the real quality 'heat' (*calor*) begets sensible warmth
in a body or that body's power of warming another body, and
the quality 'dryness' (*siccitas*) begets sensible dryness or the power
to dry. A swan is white (*albus*) because of the presence of 'whiteness' (*albedo*) in it, while gold is yellow because its matter is
informed by the quality 'yellowness'.

Even so-called occult powers such as magnetism and gravity,
whose operations are undetectable, are amenable to this kind of
explanatory schema. The lodestone affects iron the way it does
because it has the 'attractive quality' or 'magnetic virtue'.[39] A heavy
body falls towards the earth because it is endowed with the
form 'heaviness'. As the Coimbrian commentators put it, 'since
heavy and light things . . . tend towards their natural places,
there must be some means present in them . . . by the power of
which they are moved. This can be nothing other than their
substantial form and the heaviness and lightness which derives
from it.'[40]

A model of science that operated by infusing bodies with spiritual forms and qualities defined by the phenomena they are supposed to explain easily lent itself to critique and ridicule. Progressive early modern philosophers, including Descartes, found such explanations trivial and useless. It is totally uninformative to be told that the reason why a body fell was because it was 'heavy', or that an object was white because it contained 'whiteness'. The Scholastics, he notes,

> have all put forward as principles things of which they did not possess perfect knowledge. For example, there is not one of them, so far as I know, who has not supposed there to be weight in terrestrial bodies. Yet although experience shows us very clearly that the bodies we call 'heavy' descend towards the centre of the earth, we do not for all that have any knowledge of the nature of what is called 'gravity', that is to say, the cause or principle which makes bodies descend in this way.[41]

In other words, the explanations offered by Aristotelian Scholastics are no explanations at all. They simply take the property to be explained ('heavy') and make it part of the explanation ('heaviness'). A famous parody of this technique was offered by Molière in his 1673 play *Le Malade imaginaire*. When Thomas, a candidate in medicine, is asked at his degree disputation to explain why opium causes sleep, he responds: 'Because it has the dormitive virtue, which makes one sleep.' The chorus of examiners enthusiastically applaud him and welcome him into 'our learned body'.[42]

Despite these explanatory shortcomings, the philosophical paradigm of late Scholasticism remained orthodoxy within the colleges and universities in the first half of the seventeenth century. Scholars continued to defend neo-Aristotelian views in metaphysics and traditional (not to mention religiously safe) doctrines of nature in their lectures and textbooks designed to mould young minds, such as the students at La Flèche. While there was no shortage of anti-Aristotelians, *novatores* (innovators) critical of the old way of doing things, they needed to keep a low profile lest they fall afoul of the academic, ecclesiastic and civil authorities. In 1624 four Parisian scholars were in fact condemned for their disparaging treatment of Aristotelian philosophy in a placard announcing an upcoming disputation. Among other things, they critiqued the hylomorphic makeup of physical bodies. The Parlement of Paris forced the scholars to cancel the event, and the theology faculty at the Sorbonne declared their proposed theses heretical and forbade them from ever teaching again. In the wake of their trial, the University of Paris formally banned all anti-Aristotelian discussions. (Descartes' friend Mersenne took the side of Aristotle in this affair and condemned the would-be disputants as 'charlatans'.[43])

This event had a chilling effect on philosophical discourse in the university's faculties for some time, but it did not stop the promotors of more progressive thinking from pursuing their researches. Theoreticians and experimentalists continued to oppose sterile medieval theories as they sought a clear, illuminating and pragmatic understanding of phenomena. Descartes himself was already partial to the mechanistic, corpuscularian conception of nature during his time with Beeckman, and it informs his discussion of the body's role in sensation and imagination in the *Rules for the Direction of the Mind*. But it is only in *The World* that we first find a broad elaboration of his natural philosophy.

In Descartes' universe, there are no soul-like or spiritual entities such as forms or real qualities inhering in natural bodies. Writing some years later, he reminds Mersenne that 'I do not suppose there are in nature any *real qualities* which are attached to substances, like so many little souls to their bodies.'[44] There are human souls united with human bodies, but everything else – including the human body itself – is pure matter. Moreover, the matter that composes bodies, celestial and terrestrial, is homogeneous throughout the cosmos. There are not basic elements differing in nature from each other, and gone is the 'quintessence' or fifth element that, in the medieval cosmological system, made up the universe beyond our earthly realm. There is only one kind of material stuff, and it is simply three-dimensional extension. Cartesian matter does come in different sizes and volumes, and Descartes refers to 'elements' of the first, second and third kind, a purely quantitative designation that depends on the degree of rarefaction and 'subtlety'. (Matter of the first kind is the smallest and most fluid; matter of the second kind is 'middling' in size; and matter of the third kind is larger and moves more slowly.) But it makes no difference whether it is the matter of the heavens or the matter of our world; it is all just extension. There are no phenomena of nature that cannot be explained solely by the motion, rest, collision, conglomeration and separation of microscopic and visible parts of this universal matter.

> If you find it strange that, in explaining these elements, I do not use the qualities called 'heat', 'cold', 'moisture' and 'dryness' – as the philosophers do – I shall say to you that these qualities themselves seem to me to need explanation. Indeed, unless I am mistaken, not only these four qualities but all the others as well, including even the forms of inanimate bodies, can be explained without the need to suppose anything in their matter other than the motion, size, shape and arrangement of its parts.[45]

In *The World*, Descartes asks us to imagine God in the beginning creating a single, undifferentiated mass of matter extended indefinitely in all directions. When God then introduces motion into that extension, it gets broken up 'into as many parts and shapes we can imagine . . . wholly in the diversity of the motions'. Initially these parts are vortices or 'swirls' of matter, each circulating around a centre. Some vortices are massive, and constitute the heavens that carry around planets; others are quite small, and belong to the sublunary realm. Individual bodies of whatever size are parcels of matter whose parts are 'so closely joined together that they always have the force to resist the motions of the other bodies'.[46] (One implication of the identification of matter with extension is that there are no voids, no spaces without matter; what appears to be empty space is, by virtue of being extended in three dimensions, a body, even if it is not a visible body. This is an aspect of his physics that Descartes only hints at here. He says: 'I do not wish to insist that there is no vacuum at all in nature. My treatise would, I fear, become too long if I undertook to explain the matter at length.'[47] However, he will explicitly argue for the impossibility of a vacuum in a later work.)

According to this schema, God does not actually create anything in particular other than the matter and motion or introduce any order or arrangement to things. But because the operations of an eternal and immutable God are themselves eternal and immutable, the quantity of matter and motion in the universe must remain constant; neither matter nor motion can suffer any increase or decrease. There must also be a certain regularity to the ways in which the parts of matter, once established, interact. Thus, the world will be governed by three general laws:

(1) A law of inertia, which states that 'each particular part of matter always continues in the same state unless collision with others forces it to change its state.'
(2) A law governing the transfer of motion in collision between bodies, whereby no body can give to another body any motion except by losing as much of its own motion at

the same time; nor can it take away any motion from another body unless its own motion is increased by the same amount. (3) A law of rectilinear motion, according to which all tendency to motion in a body is to continue moving in a straight line, even if the body, because of the impingement of other bodies, is forced to move in a circular pattern.

With these laws of nature in place, the motions of matter are, Descartes insists, 'sufficient to cause the parts of this chaos to disentangle themselves and arrange themselves in such a good order that they will have the form of a quite perfect world – a world in which we shall be able to see not only light but also all the other things, general as well as particular, which appear in the real world'.[48] In short, God's role in creation is scaled back considerably. Most of what we find in the world around us – the bodies we see and their ongoing interactions – is the consequence only of matter, motion and laws. The visible universe was generated by and operates on purely mechanistic principles, with all phenomena explained solely by the motion and contact of parts of matter of varying sizes and shapes.

Thus celestial bodies move around the centre of their heaven not because of some attractive power operating over great distances, but because they are swept along by the vortex of finer matter within which they are embedded ('just as boats that follow the course of a river'). And the falling of a body to the ground is explained not by a spiritual occult form or quality in the body that moves it towards its natural resting place; nor does it happen by some mysterious force acting on the body over empty space. Rather, gravity is the result of a downward pressure exerted on terrestrial bodies by the smaller, quicker and therefore upward-moving microscopic bodies – the 'more subtle matter' – of the first element of the heaven surrounding the earth. As for light, the topic that initiated the undertaking of the treatise, it is only an impulse that the rotational motion of a body composed of the first element (such as the sun) communicates through the minute corpuscles of a material medium. When that impulse finally reaches the human eye, it is communicated to the brain by way of the optic nerve, and subsequently translated by the soul into a luminous perception.

Another central tenet of the Aristotelian philosophy was that all knowledge ultimately has an empirical source and derives either immediately or mediately through sense experience. 'There is nothing in the intellect that was not first in the senses' was a common Scholastic refrain. And for the Aristotelian, the world revealed by that experience was pretty much as the senses reported it to be. The colours and other sensible properties that bodies appear to have are really in those bodies ('whiteness', 'redness', 'warmth'). For Descartes and other mechanists, however, the evidence of the senses is unreliable. They do not reveal the world as it truly is. The colours we perceive and the warmth we feel are just the soul's response to motions (stimulations) in the brain caused by external bodies. In the bodies themselves, colour is nothing but the way in which the size and shape of the outermost corpuscles of a body form a texture that reflect the impulses of light in a particular way, affecting the trajectory and spin of the medium's corpuscles. What we feel as warmth is, in the body itself, merely an increased motion of the minute corpuscles composing it.

A mechanistic explanation of sensible qualities and their perception in the human mind through the motion of imperceptible bodies is certainly not new with Descartes. The doctrine goes back to the ancient atomism of the Epicureans. In Descartes' time, Galileo argued in his 1623 treatise *The Assayer* that while most people believe that 'heat is a real phenomenon or property or quality that actually resides in the material world by which we feel ourselves warmed', in fact

those materials that produce heat in us and make us feel
warm . . . are a multitude of minute particles having certain shapes and moving with certain velocities. Meeting
with our bodies, they penetrate by means of their extreme subtlety, and their touch as felt by us when the pass
through our substance is the sensation we call 'heat.'

Heat as a feeling, colour as a visual experience and many other
sensible qualities, Galileo insisted, have 'no real existence save
in us'.[49]

Because the topic of sensation concerns the human being,
Descartes reserves most of his discussion of this for the second
treatise composing of *The World*, the *Treatise on Man*. Much of this
work is taken up with the most basic functions of a living human
body, those that occur whether or not that body is united with a
soul.

In the Aristotelian philosophy, while only human beings had
a rational soul, the organic internal processes and basic motions
of the human body were explained through the introduction of
lower-level souls (forms) into the body's matter. Generation,
growth, the circulation of the blood, the digestion of food and so
on depended on the vegetative soul, which was present in all living
things, whether animal or plant. Sensory perception and the active
movement of the body were a function of the sensitive soul, which
informed the bodies of all animals, human and non-human.
Descartes, continuing his attack on substantial and accidental
forms, and hylomorphism generally, dispenses with all such non-
rational souls. The human body he describes is no less a kind of
machine than other animate and inanimate bodies. In its ordinary operations, it is simply a collection of material parts moving
and interacting with each other and with other bodies according
to the laws of nature.

We see clocks, artificial fountains, mills and other similar machines which, even though they are only made by men, have the power to move of their own accord in various ways. And, as I am supposing that this machine [the human body] is made by God, I think you will agree that it is capable of a greater variety of movements than I could possibly imagine in it, and that it exhibits a greater ingenuity than I could possibly ascribe to it.[50]

Through empirical investigation involving dissection and other modes of experimentation, supplemented by logical reasoning – including, presumably, 'intuition' and 'deduction' – Descartes carefully determined the structure of the human skeleton, musculature and organs and the actions of its circulatory, respiratory, nervous and digestive systems.

Key to practically all of the body's functioning – the internal motions that regularly maintain it, its passive and active responses to external stimuli, and its interactions with the soul – are what Descartes calls 'animal spirits'. These are 'a very fine wind, or rather a very lively and very pure flame' – they are not spiritual at all, but a highly rarefied vapour produced from the blood by the separation of its finer parts. The spirits are transported throughout the body by the channels that contain and protect the nerves, which are simply tiny fibres connecting the extremities of the body to the brain. The body moves when the muscles are inflated by the spirits sent there by the brain or deflated as the spirits depart. In instinctive motions – for example, flinching at the sight of a threat – the spirits are stimulated in a purely mechanical manner, as their minute parts are pushed in this or that direction by other bodily parts in motion, which in turn are responding to the impression caused by an external body. The human body in this case acts similarly to that of a sheep that flees at the sight of a wolf; the sheep's turning around and running away is a purely mechanical response, a matter of motions in muscles generated by the image of the predator in the sheep's optical apparatus.

Descartes compares the role of the animal spirits in the human body to the air that is forced through the pipes of an organ by a bellows, or to the water that, through a hydraulic system, moves animated statues such as those in the French king's estate at Saint-Germain-en-Laye.

> You may have observed in the grottoes and fountains of the royal gardens that the force that drives the water from its source is all that is needed to move various machines, and even to make them play certain instruments or pronounce certain words, depending on the particular arrangements of the pipes through which the water is conducted.[51]

Of course, the human being is more than a machine operating on strictly mechanical principles. The human body is united with a soul.

> I hold that when God unites a rational soul to this machine, as I intend to explain later on, He will place its principal seat in the brain and will make its nature such that the soul will have different sensations depending on the different ways in which the nerves open the entrances to the pores in the internal surface of the brain.[52]

The animal spirits are, in fact, always responding to or affecting one particular part of the brain: the pineal gland, which Descartes locates right at the brain's centre. It is the position and motion of this gland that directs the spirits that flow through it into the pores of the brain that are the endings of the nerve channels, and through these into the limbs and sense organs.

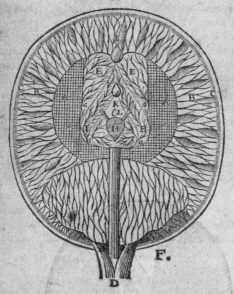

Notez aufli que lors que ie dis que les Efprits en for-
tant de la glande H, tendent vers les endroits de la fu-
perficie interieure du cerueau, qui leur font le plus di-
rectement oppofez, ie n'entens pas qu'ils tendent toû-
jours vers ceux qui font vis à vis d'eux en ligne droite;
mais feulement vers ceux, où la difpofition qui eft pour
lors dans le cerueau les fait tendre.

Or la fubftance du cerueau eftant molle & pliante, L X V.
fes concauitez feroient fort étroites, & prefque toutes Quelle dif-
ferenie il y

I ij

Interior of the brain, with nerve endings and the pineal gland in the centre, from
Traité de l'homme (1664).

faire en cette machine des mouuemens tout femblables
à ceux aufquels nous fommes naturellement incitez,
lors que nos fens font touchez en mefme forte.

Comme par exemple fi le feu A fe trouue proche du
pié B, les petites parties de ce feu, qui fe meuuent comme vous fçauez tres-promptement, ont la force de
mouuoir auec foy l'endroit de la peau de ce pié qu'elles
touchent; & par ce moyen tirant le petit filet c, e, que
vous voyez y eftre attaché, elles ouurent au mefme in-
ftant l'entrée du pore d, e, contre lequel ce petit filet
fe termine; ainfi que tirant l'vn des bouts d'vne corde,

D ij

The sensation of heat, from *Traité de l'homme*.

In sensory awareness – whether through sight, touch, smell, hearing or taste – other bodies impinge, either directly or through a medium, on the exterior of the human body. The motions caused on the surface of the human body constitute a kind of kinetic isomorphic image of that external body. The image is communicated by the spirits in the nerve channels to the brain, where they impress the image on the brain's interior surface by causing its pores to open or close in that same pattern. Spirits flowing to this pattern on the brain's interior surface from the pineal gland maintain the image as they cause the gland to move in this or that way, which in turn stimulates the soul to have this or that sensation or idea. This is how we perceive things and have other kinds of sensations in their presence. Thus, in tasting salt, 'the tiny fibres that make up the marrow of the nerves of the tongue and which serve as the organ of taste in this machine' are easily moved in different ways by the particles of salt, whose shape and size affect the tongue differently from particles of brandy.[53] When those motions terminate in the brain and, by means of the animal spirits, determine the particular movement of the pineal gland, we experience the salty sensation.

It is crucial to Descartes' account of human experience that, as much in the case of a salty or sweet taste as in the perception of red or blue or the sound of a musical note, there is no resemblance whatsoever between 'our sensations and the things that produce them'. He reminds us, right at the beginning of *The World*, that 'words . . . bear no resemblance to the things they signify, and yet they make us think of those things'; likewise, 'why could Nature not also have established some sign which would make us have the sensation of light, even if the sign contained nothing in itself which is similar to this sensation?'[54] The motions in the brain (pineal gland) are a kind of natural sign that, on the occasion of their occurrence, stimulate the mind to 'interpret' them and produce the appropriate qualitative sensory experience.

There are many other topics of physics, cosmology and human physiology addressed in the two treatises constituting *The World*: the origin and arrangement of stars (including the sun), the revolutions and rotations of planets and their moons, the paths of comets, the tides (which for Descartes are an effect of the moon's position), the beating of the heart, the breaking down of food in digestion, the structure of the eye and the perception of distance, emotions like joy and sadness, memory, and even dreams.

The Cartesian universe as described in the two treatises composing *The World* functions like a grand mechanical structure. Its various parts – animal, vegetable and mineral – all operate, actively and passively, according to basic and perspicuous physical principles that can (in theory) be captured in mathematical, or at least quantitative, terms. This general picture of nature, in one form or another, grounds all of the great and progressive philosophy and science of the seventeenth century, from Galileo's physics to Robert Boyle's corpuscular chemistry to John Locke's theory of knowledge to the later mechanics of Christiaan Huygens, Gottfried Wilhelm Leibniz and Isaac Newton.[55]

THERE ARE VARIOUS OTHER topics that Descartes had envisioned including in 'my treatise on physics'. He wrote to Mersenne in 1630 to say that 'I shall discuss a number of metaphysical questions,' including a doctrine that would stir up a good deal of controversy.

The abstract, necessary and universal truths of logic, mathematics, metaphysics and even ethics were long regarded by philosophers and theologians as 'eternal'. They were said to have an independent, uncreated existence, not unlike what Plato attributed to his ethereal 'Forms'. The laws of identity and non-identity, the essence of a triangle and the geometric truths that follow from it, and (at least according to many philosophers) the nature of justice – all of these were typically assumed to be eternally true, independent not only of human beliefs and desires but of the will of God as well. God, no less than human beings, could not violate the law of non-contradiction; nor could God give a triangle more than three sides. Descartes, by contrast, insisted that such truths, like the laws of nature and other contingent truths about existing things in the world, were established by God at creation. He tells Mersenne that

> the mathematical truths which you call eternal have been laid down by God and depend on him entirely no less than the rest of his creatures. Indeed, to say that these truths are independent of God is to talk of him as if he were Jupiter or Saturn and to subject him to the Styx and the Fates. Please do not hesitate to assert and proclaim everywhere that it is God who has laid down these laws in nature just as a king lays down laws in his kingdom.[56]

Though created, the laws in question remain eternal because God's will, though absolutely free and undetermined, is itself eternal and immutable and thus does not change.

For Descartes, such a doctrine was essential to safeguarding divine omnipotence, 'the greatness of God'. If the eternal truths were independent of God, then they would represent a limitation on God's power by subjecting God to a kind of external rational necessity. God would be just as bound by the laws of mathematics or metaphysics as we are. In a follow-up letter to Mersenne a month later, he further defends his view by arguing that the relationship between the will and the understanding in God is not at all what it is in human beings. In finite rational creatures, the will and the understanding are distinct faculties of the mind. The role of the will is to provide a judgement – either an affirmation or rejection – of the ideas that the understanding puts before it.

A person believes that $1 + 1 = 2$ when his will, faced with that proposition, assents to it. The simplicity of God's nature, however, does not allow for distinct faculties. The 'mind' of an infinite being bears no resemblance whatsoever to the human mind. Thus in God will and understanding are one and the same thing, and for God to understand that $1 + 1 = 2$ is for God to will that $1 + 1 = 2$. 'In God, willing and knowing are a single thing in such a way that by the very fact of willing something he knows it and it is only for this reason that such a thing is true.'[57]

Mersenne, naturally, was puzzled by this strange view. 'You ask me', Descartes wrote to his friend, 'by what kind of causality God established the eternal truths. I reply: by the same kind of causality as he created all things, that is to say, as their efficient and total cause . . . You ask also what necessitated God to create these truths; and I reply that he was free to make it not true that all the radii of the circle are equal – just as he was free not to create the world.'[58]

Descartes remained committed to this unorthodox doctrine throughout his philosophical career. He was also aware of the trouble it might have caused him. After all, in what sense can a metaphysical or moral truth be necessary if it is created and therefore contingent? Thus, while he encourages Mersenne 'to assert and proclaim everywhere that it is God who has laid down these laws in nature just as a king lays down laws in his kingdom' and 'to tell people as often as the occasion demands', he adds: 'provided you do not mention my name'.[59] In the end, he did not include it in *The World*.

Another metaphysical topic that Descartes had promised to address in *The World* but that does not appear in the extant version – nor is it obviously the subject of any of the manuscripts in the Stockholm inventory – is 'the rational soul'. As we have seen, according to his remarks in the *Discourse on Method*, he did indeed write that projected third part.[60] This treatise on the soul, though, is long lost. So is the 'little treatise of Metaphysics' that, in a letter from late 1630, Descartes tells Mersenne 'I began when in Friesland [that is, Franeker, mid-1629], in which I set out principally to prove the existence of God and our souls when they are separate from the body, from which their immortality follows.'[61] However, much of what Descartes apparently had put in these essays about God and the soul do appear in his later works, especially the *Meditations on First Philosophy*. Such spiritual questions would come to occupy more and more of Descartes' attention in the coming years, as he sought to offer not just explanations of particular natural phenomena but secure metaphysical foundations for his entire philosophical and scientific enterprise.

FOUR

Rebuilding the House of Knowledge

ven after settling for good in the United Provinces, Descartes never gave up his peripatetic ways. Between 1629 and 1632 he changed domicile often, moving between at least six different cities and towns. When he began work on material related to *The World*, he was living in Franeker, where he matriculated in the Arts Faculty at the university. By the time he was ready to see the treatise in print, in late 1633, and after several relocations – including a short stay in Leiden and three separate residencies in Amsterdam – he had been dwelling for a couple of years in the countryside outside Deventer, another university town, where his friend Henricus Reneri was newly appointed to the chair in philosophy. Over the next ten years, seeking to maintain the solitude he desired for his work, he would rarely stay in the same place for more than two years.

IT WAS NOW, in the early 1630s, over a decade since the truce with Spain had expired. Though the Dutch Republic enjoyed de facto sovereignty, it had not yet been granted formal independence; this would have to wait until 1648, with the Peace of Westphalia and the signing of the Treaty of Münster, which ended the Thirty Years War. Meanwhile, Philip IV, who had inherited the Spanish and Portuguese thrones from his father, was still eager to regain his family's rebellious northern territories. The resumption of hostilities in 1621, and especially the reimposition of Spanish embargoes against Dutch shipping, had sent the Dutch economy (and national morale) into an extended slump. The cost of fighting was enormous – both the army and the navy had to be increased – and a substantial drain on the Republic's coffers.

Nonetheless, the Dutch managed to hold their own militarily and would soon recover economically. Moreover, the domestic political situation had grown less fraught since 1625, when stadholder Maurits of Nassau died and was replaced by another son of Willem I, Frederik Hendrik. The new stadholder was not only a more tolerant and cultivated person than Maurits, but politically more astute. He did not share his half-brother's Counter-Remonstrant fervour. Indeed, Frederik Hendrik was known to be friendly to the Arminian camp and was willing to provide it some protection, up to a point. He knew to walk a fine line between bringing Remonstrants in from the cold and not antagonizing their more orthodox theological opponents. Under his shrewd leadership, the councils of a number of cities – including Amsterdam – were soon back in Remonstrant hands. The Counter-Remonstrants were not happy about this, but there was little they could do. Religious friction continued, as it would for most of the rest of the century, with the fortunes of each camp rising or falling in part according to how well the country fared in its various wars with Spain, England and France. But by the early 1630s things had certainly quieted down.

Along with a degree of domestic peace, Frederik Hendrik's stadholdership also opened a period of cultural blossoming. The arts, both visual and literary, flourished, not least under patronage from the stadholder's court in The Hague, with the tasteful guidance of the prince's wife, Amalia van Solms. 'History' paintings (depicting stories from the Bible, mythology and ancient and recent history), portraits, landscapes, marine scenes and genre pictures were being produced at an extraordinary rate by artists

catering to both wealthy and middle-class patrons. The recent
recession had not been without some effect on the art world,
especially the size, prices and even the subjects of paintings. As
one historian puts it, while canvases and panels became smaller
and the chromatic range more limited, 'the elegant "garden parties"
and "Merry Companies" of the Truce era receded, to be replaced
by battle views, skirmishes, and genre scenes featuring soldiers
in taverns, brothels and guardrooms.'[1] Still, despite the economic
contraction, there really was no significant decline either in the
demand by Dutch burghers for pictures to hang in their homes,
businesses and meeting halls or in the ability of Dutch artists to
adapt to changes in that demand.

The literary scene, too, fared well under the new regime.
There was a relatively high level of literacy in Dutch society, and
poetry and drama by such celebrated writers as Jacob Cats, Pieter
Cornelisz Hooft[2] and Joost van den Vondel – none of whom
shied away from political themes – kept readers entertained and
edified. Meanwhile, the bookshops of Amsterdam and some of
the province's other cities, taking advantage of the more lenient
– or, better, 'don't ask, don't tell' – policy in Holland, teemed with
works in many languages that were unavailable elsewhere. Dutch
publishers flooded the European market with literature that had
been or would be banned by civil and ecclesiastic authorities in
France, England, Spain and the German and Italian states. Authors
of radical political works, of tracts promoting religious dissent,
atheism and libertinism, and of erotic novels all took advantage
of the relative freedom of the press in the Republic. Even treatises
of natural science that broke with the reigning Aristotelian paradigm were available at printer-booksellers such as Hondius,
Blaeu and the famous Leiden house of Elzevir.[3]

The climate of relative toleration did not mean that one
should not be careful, and Descartes knew this. He was justifiably
concerned about how his novel theories in *The World* would be

Michiel Jansz. van Mierevelt (workshop of), *Frederik Hendrik, Stadholder of Holland*, c. 1632, oil on canvas.

received by those who were less open-minded in such matters, especially religious authorities. As he speculated on the origin of the cosmos, he risked being drawn into treacherous debates about whether the universe is created or eternal, finite or infinite. By rejecting Aristotelian metaphysics and the modes of explanation employed in its physics, he was also ruling out ways in

Michiel Jansz. van Mierevelt (copy after), *Amalia van Solms*, c. 1632, oil on panel.

which theologians had long accounted for various doctrines of the faith. Scholastic theories that used the forms and qualities of Arisotelian hylomorphism to explicate Church mysteries – such as the Incarnation and the transubstantiation of the Eucharistic host – had practically become as much a part of Catholic dogma as the mysteries themselves. For this reason, Descartes considered publishing the treatise anonymously. 'I wish to do this principally because of theology, which has been so subordinated to Aristotle that it is almost impossible to explain another philosophy without it seeming initially to be contrary to faith.'[4]

To Descartes' conservative religious contemporaries, however, the most striking and problematic feature of *The World* – had he published it – would have been his rejection of the geocentric model of the universe in favour of Copernican heliocentrism. There is no mistaking the cosmological arrangement in the work. The sun sits squarely at the centre of the vortex that contains, and causes the revolutions of, the earth and other planets that move around it. Nor is it the only luminous body that has orbiting planets.

> Even though all [the planets] tend towards the centres of the heavens containing them, this is not thereby to say that they could ever reach those centres. For as I have already said, these are occupied by the sun and the other fixed stars . . . Thus, you see that there can be different planets, at varying distances from the sun . . . The matter of the heaven must make the planets turn not only around the sun but also around their own centre.[5]

Descartes knew that he was treading on dangerous ground. The heliocentrism is, in part, the reason why he decided to present his overall account of the universe in purely hypothetical terms, 'as if my intention were simply to tell you a fable'.[6] He says in the treatise that he is not describing this actual world, the one that the Bible tells us God created. Rather, he is talking about 'another world – a wholly new one which I shall bring into being before your mind in imaginary spaces'.[7] He hoped that by presenting his Copernican cosmology as a counterfactual fiction – the way a cosmos *might* be constructed – he would be afforded some protection from theological critics who would otherwise attack him for expounding a doctrine that was regarded by the Catholic Church as 'contrary to Holy and Divine Scripture'. Besides, did not the Catholic Church allow the discussion of heliocentrism, so long as it was considered merely a 'hypothesis' and not presented as the truth?

Descartes' faith in his ruse was shaken when, in November 1633, as he was about to send *The World* to Mersenne for publication 'as a New Year's gift', he learned about the recent condemnation of Galileo. He was already somewhat familiar with Galileo's general theories in physics, although it is unlikely that at this point he knew any of the Italian's works at first hand. Just a year before, in late 1632, he had remarked to Mersenne that 'what you tell me about the calculation which Galileo has made concerning the speed at which falling bodies move . . . bears no relation to my philosophy.' Mersenne, benefitting from the wide European intellectual network of which he was the centre, apparently *had* read Galileo's new treatise soon after its publication that year. He explained to Descartes Galileo's view that all bodies fall at the same rate regardless of their material or weight (and assuming their fall is not affected by the friction of any medium). Descartes insists that this cannot be right. 'According to my philosophy there will not be the same relation between two spheres of lead, one weighing one pound and the other a hundred pounds, as there is between to spheres of wood, one weighing one pound and the other a hundred pounds . . . he [Galileo] makes no distinction between these cases, which makes me think that he cannot have hit upon the truth.'[8]

Descartes' interest was sufficiently piqued, however, and he wanted to know what Galileo had to say about the ebb and flow of the tides, which he knew (from Mersenne) is also discussed in the *Dialogue on Two Chief World Systems*. But in his rural retreat, outside Deventer, the work was not so easily obtainable. This may explain why it was not until a year later that he went to look for a copy. It was quite a revelation when he learned why he could not find one.

After searching in vain in bookstores in Amsterdam and Leiden, he was told that Galileo's book had been burned in Rome and that Galileo had been convicted by the Catholic Church of heresy and punished. Descartes was shocked by the news. He told Mersenne that 'I was so astounded at this that I almost decided to burn all my papers or at least to let no one see them. For I could not imagine that he – an Italian and, as I understand, in the good graces of the Pope – could have been made a criminal for any other reason than that he tried, as he no doubt did, to establish that the earth moves.' Descartes concedes that if that view is false, then 'so too are the entire foundations of my philosophy'. The heliocentric model 'is so closely interwoven in every part of my treatise that I could not remove it without rendering the whole work defective'.[9] Moreover, Descartes reminded his friend, Galileo himself had used the manoeuvre of presenting that model as a mere hypothesis; if that did not save a Florentine who was friendly with the pope, it was unlikely to save Descartes. Rather than incur the wrath of the Church, Descartes decided not to publish *The World* after all. 'I have decided to suppress the treatise I have written and to forfeit almost all my work of the last four years in order to give my obedience to the Church, since it has proscribed the view that the earth moves.' Many years later, he would remind Mersenne that 'the only thing that has stopped me publishing my Philosophy up to now is the question of defending the movement of the earth.'[10]

This was not so much an act of faithful obedience by a devoted Catholic as a safe and self-interested tactic within Descartes' general strategy to preserve his 'repose and peace of mind'.[11] It is unlikely that the Church's censors would have been taken in by Descartes' rhetorical strategy anyway. His remark in *The World* that, though he has couched his narrative as a fiction, 'the truth will not fail to manifest itself sufficiently clearly' made it fairly transparent what he was doing.[12]

BY EARLY SPRING 1634, after two years in Deventer, Descartes was on the move again. There was a year in Amsterdam, then several months each in Utrecht and Leiden. Finally, Descartes settled in for two and a half years near Alkmaar, just north of Haarlem, possibly in one of the several villages of Egmond (Egmond-Binnen, Egmond aan den Hoef or Egmond aan Zee). He apparently liked being near the North Sea, and would make his home along the Dutch coast for much of the rest of his life.

Despite the close call in 1633, Descartes continued preparing his research for publication. Now, however, he was separating detailed empirical investigations of particular phenomena from the grander, and more contentious, physical and theological principles and cosmological speculations that, in *The World*, provide their foundations. 'I thought it convenient for me to choose certain subjects which, without being highly controversial and without obliging me to reveal more of my principles than I wished, would nonetheless show quite clearly what I can, and what I cannot, achieve in the sciences.'[13] The result was a series of essays that presented his work in geometry and his findings in optics and meteorology. He published these in 1637, accompanied by a substantial introductory treatise in which he reviewed his overall philosophical and scientific project.

The first of these essays, called simply *Dioptrics* (*La Dioptrique*), is essentially both a truncated and an expanded version of the *Treatise on Light*. Whereas in *The World* Descartes' discussion of the constitution and behaviour of light and related questions was set in the framework of ('deduced' from) more general physical principles – the nature of matter, its division into 'elements', the laws of motion and rest and so on – in the *Dioptrics* he asks his reader simply to accept certain assumptions about what light is and how it acts. In a letter to Mersenne, Descartes says, 'You ask if I regard what I have written about refraction as a demonstration. I think it is, in so far as one can be given in this field without a previous demonstration of the principles of physics by metaphysics – which is something I hope to do some day but which has not yet been done.' But he reminds his correspondent that, in general, 'people are satisfied if the author's assumptions are not obviously contrary to experience and if their discussion is coherent and free from logical error, even though their assumptions may not be strictly true.'[14] To be sure, Descartes does believe that his conditional assumptions *are* true; he just does not want to stir up any hornets' nests at this point.

> I have called them 'suppositions' simply to make it known that I think I can deduce them from the primary truths I have expounded; but I have deliberately avoided carrying out these deductions in order to prevent certain ingenious persons from taking the opportunity to construct, on what they believe to be my principles, some extravagant philosophy for which I shall be blamed.[15]

Descartes' most general assumption or hypothesis in the *Dioptrics* is, of course, a mechanistic one, identical to the theory of light in *The World*: light is an impulse travelling from a luminous body through a material medium. Its properties are now presented,

however, through a series of mundane analogies. Just as the motion
at one end of a walking stick is directly and immediately conveyed
to the other end, so the impulse that is light passes through the
corpuscles of a medium instantaneously. And like the wine that
moves through a vat of grapes being crushed, flowing freely along
certain determinate paths until it exits through holes at the bottom
of the barrel, so goes the propagation of light.

> Thus, all the parts of the subtle matter that are in contact
> with the side of the sun that we are looking at, tend in a
> straight line towards our eyes at the same instant that
> we open them, without some hindering others, and even
> without being hindered by the larger parts of matter of
> transparent bodies that are between the two [the sun and
> the eye].[16]

None of this requires Descartes, at least at this point, to go into
much detail and establish anything certain about the physical
constitution of light and the media through which it passes.

> Thus, not having here any occasion to speak about light
> except to explain how its rays enter the eye and how they
> can be deflected by the diverse bodies they encounter,
> there is no need for me to try to say anything about its
> true nature. I believe it will suffice if I make use of two
> or three comparisons that will aid in conceiving it in that
> manner that to me seems most useful in explaining all of
> its properties that experience reveals to us, and for deduc-
> ing, subsequently, all the others that are not so easily
> noticed.[17]

Descartes' method here is clear. There are phenomena to be
explained. These include the reflection and refraction of light

and the perception of colours. Assume, then, a certain hypothesis about what light is and how it behaves, using familiar everyday processes (a blind man walking with a stick, crushing grapes in winemaking, tennis balls hit by rackets) to make that hypothesis perspicuous. Then show how, given that hypothesis, the phenomena are in fact explained with great clarity. Even better if the hypothesis allows for predictions of additional observations that are borne out through controlled experiments. This lends experiential support to, and even confirms, the truth of the hypothesis – in this case, an assumption about the corpuscular nature of light and the mechanics of its propagation. In one of the other 1637 essays, *Meteors* (*Les Méteores*), Descartes concedes that

> It is true that, since the knowledge of these things depends on general principles of nature, which, as far as I know, have not yet been well explained, I need at the beginning to make use of some suppositions, just as I did in the *Dioptrics*. But I will try to make them so simple and so easy that you will have practically no difficulty in believing them, even if I have not demonstrated them.[18]

The theory about light that informs the *Dioptrics* may not have the demonstrable certainty that it would have were it deduced from 'first principles' of metaphysics and physics. But Descartes has, at this point, decided to scale back his theoretical ambitions in order to present his scientific findings to the public.

Having stipulated some general features of light, Descartes then goes on to show how explanatorily rich his hypothesis is. Once he provides a demonstration of the geometrical principles of reflection and refraction and elucidates the structure of the eye and the mechanisms of perception, he can explain the ways in which hyperbolic and elliptical lenses – like the lens of the eye itself – refract rays of light. This, in turn, is used in his description of how telescopes function. Descartes even provides an account of how properly to cut glass lenses.

In the *Meteors*, too, Descartes avoids grounding his account in more universal principles of nature. He told his friend, the French Jesuit priest Antoine Vatier, who taught at La Flèche and who had been reading the new essays, that

> I cannot prove a priori the assumptions I made at the beginning of the *Meteors* without expounding the whole of my physics; but the observational data which I have deduced necessarily from them, and which cannot be deduced in the same way from other principles, seems to me to prove them sufficiently a posteriori.[19]

The corpuscular 'assumptions' and optical theories of the *Dioptrics* inform Descartes' discussion of various atmospheric phenomena. These include clouds and other 'vapours and exhalations', which arise from the agitation of the fine material in terrestrial bodies by the sun or some other heat source, 'just as the dust in the countryside rises up when it is merely pushed and agitated by the foot of some passer-by'.[20] Similarly, wind is the agitation of the minuscule particles composing the air, which in turn are generated through the rarefication of water. When these particles condense and contract into larger, visible parts, they form mists and clouds. Snow, rain and hail occur when the size and weight of these parts exceed the resistance of the air corpuscles that keep them from descending to the earth.

One of the final chapters of the treatise deals with the rainbow: the atmospheric causes of its manifestation and of the arrangement of its colours. Descartes regards this as among his more exciting discoveries and promotes his explanation of 'so remarkable a wonder of nature' as proof that his method leads to 'knowledge not possessed by those whose writings we have'.[21] We see a rainbow

– whether in the sky or in the spray of a fountain – when light rays reach the human eye after multiple refractions and reflections through the water droplets suspended in the air. As for the different colours, Descartes concludes, after experimenting with a flask of water and a prism, that this is a function of differences in the ratio between rotation and tendency to rectilinear motion among the fine particles through which the impulse composing the rays passes.

> The nature of the colours . . . consists only in the fact that the parts of the subtle matter that transmits the action of the light tend to rotate with more force than move in a straight line, in such a way that those that tend to rotate much more strongly cause the colour red, while those that tend only a little more strongly cause the colour yellow.[22]

From a philosophical perspective, the most interesting of the publications of 1637 is the relatively short quasi-autobiographical and theoretical treatise that introduces the scientific essays. The original title Descartes envisioned was rather unwieldy: *The Plan of a Universal Science, which is capable of raising our nature to its highest degree of perfection, together with the Dioptrics, the Meteors and the Geometry, in which the author, to give proof of his Universal Science, explains the most abstruse topics he could choose, and does so in such a way that even persons who have never studied can understand them.*[23] In what he eventually called simply *Discourse on Method* (*Discours de la méthode*) Descartes narrates his intellectual itinerary as he rejected the science of probable conjectures that satisfied others and turned to the pursuit of truth in the form of absolutely certain cognitions. While the *Discourse* is a step back from the earlier, more ambitious treatise 'which certain considerations prevent me from publishing' – that is, *The World* – it nonetheless presents in summary form many of the ideas that Descartes had already broached in that work, as

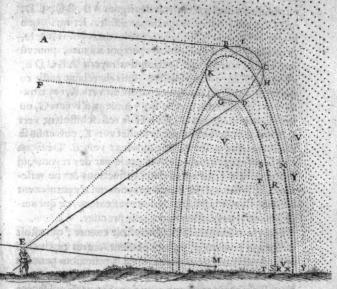

principal arcenciel.   Et enfin qu'en toutes les autres
gouttes marquées V il ne doit paroistre aucunes cou-
leurs. Examinant aprés cela plus particulierement en la
boule B C D ce qui faisoit que la partie D paroissoit rou-
ge, i'ay trouué que c'estoient les rayons du soleil qui ve-
nans d'A vers B se courboient en entrant dans l'eau au
point B, & alloient vers C, d'où ils se refleschissoient vers
D, & là se courbans derechef en sortant de l'eau , ten-
doient vers E: car sitost que ie mettois vn cors opaque

The rainbow, from *Les Météores* (1637).

well as in the *Rules for the Direction of the Mind.* He reviews the
guidelines of the method he had laid out many years earlier in
the *Rules.* He also summarizes the metaphysical, epistemological
and theological reflections that he has recently engaged in and
would in just a few years write up and publish as the *Meditations
on First Philosophy.*

His project, he claims, is analogous to that in which one rebuilds
a house. First you must tear down the old structure – in this
case, it means ridding the mind of its old and dubious opinions,
both the naive beliefs of ordinary common sense, some of which
may indeed be true but lack proper justification, and the more
sophisticated but false theories of Aristotelian Scholasticism.
Then, following a proper order of construction, one establishes
new, more solid foundations upon which to erect the edifice. If
that edifice is a body of knowledge, and if it is truly to be secure
and to have the absolute certainty of *scientia,* the foundations
upon which it rests must consist in epistemology – whereby one
discovers what knowledge is, and whether and how it is possible
– and metaphysics, which, for Descartes, includes knowledge of
God, the soul and the most general principles of reality. To clarify
what he has in mind, Descartes is willing to reveal some things in
the *Discourse* that he had previously kept to himself, albeit without
going too far. In a letter to Mersenne just before publication, he
reports that 'I have also inserted a certain amount of metaphysics,
physics and medicine in the opening *Discourse* in order to show
that my method extends to topics of all kinds.'[24]

Of course, he notes, while one is rebuilding a house 'you need
some other place where you can live comfortably while building
is in progress.' Thus in the *Discourse* Descartes recalls how, while
engaging in these abstract philosophical exercises, he also adopted
what he calls 'a provisional moral code', so as to continue functioning in the ordinary activities of life without disruption,
and – just as important – without drawing attention to himself.

This code, somewhat reminiscent of ancient Stoic philosophy, stipulates:

> First, to obey the laws and customs of my country, hold-
> ing constantly to the religion in which by God's grace
> I had been instructed from my childhood, and govern-
> ing myself in all other matters according to the most
> moderate and least extreme opinions . . . Second, to be as
> firm and decisive in my actions as I could . . . Third, to try
> always to master myself rather than fortune, and change
> my desires rather than the order of the world . . . And
> finally, I decided to review the various occupations which
> men have in this life in order to try to choose the best.

On this last point, Descartes decided that 'I could do no better than to continue with the very one [occupation] I was engaged in, and devote my whole life to cultivating my reason and advancing as far as I could in the knowledge of the truth, following the method I had prescribed for myself.'[25]

In the *Discourse*, as earlier, Descartes describes his growing frustration with both the traditional and antiquated learning of the Schools and the scepticism about the possibility for real knowledge adopted by many of his contemporaries. He especially emphasizes how important it is to 'raise the mind above things which can be perceived by the senses' and conceived by the imagination. As he has shown in the *Dioptrics*, sensory appearances are misleading as to the true nature of things. They have led ordinary people and, more seriously, philosophers to conclude quite naively that the properties that objects in the world *seem* to have really do belong to them – that the colours they see and the heat and cold they feel are real qualities in physical objects, rather than being merely sensory effects in the mind of the perceiver caused by the motions among the finer parts of material things. Knowledge about the world can, Descartes insists, come only by moving beyond the confused testimony of the senses, by ignoring what is obscure and confused in the raw visual, tactile, auditory and olfactory evidence with which we are constantly bombarded to get to a scientific core that is conceptually pure and composed only of 'clear and distinct' elements. This is achieved through the intellect and the proper and critical use of our reasoning faculties.

Descartes' emphasis on the intellect and reason, his quest for absolute certainty and his continued use of the term 'deduction' to describe an essential part of his method have given rise to the notion that he was a kind of arch-'rationalist' who rejected any appeals to experience and experiment as an aid to acquiring knowledge of the world. A not-uncommon mischaracterization of Cartesian science in popular literature, and even in some early scholarship, is that it is an entirely a priori affair – that not just the universal principles of nature but even the detailed explanations of particular phenomena are deduced (in the contemporary, strictly logical sense) from axiomatic starting points. On this reading, the senses and experience have no role to play in the scientific enterprise.

Descartes' methodological remarks in the *Discourse*, mostly summarizing how he proceeded in *The World*, clearly give the lie to such a caricature. It is true that Descartes' metaphysics – his account of the existence and nature of the soul, his proofs for the existence of God, even his demonstration of the most general laws of nature regarding motion and rest – proceeds strictly by logical deduction through concepts without any empirical input. Moreover, empirical results can never falsify those first principles and what follows immediately from them: the impossibility of a vacuum, for example, is established on metaphysical grounds according to the nature of matter, and is thus immune to experimental refutation. But Descartes makes it clear that, when it comes to the specific causal mechanism behind this or that phenomenon in the world, to the real details of nature, observation and experimentation are absolutely crucial. Here is the all-important passage from the *Discourse*:

> I noticed, regarding observations, that the further we advance in our knowledge, the more necessary they become. At the beginning, rather than seeking those which are more unusual and highly contrived, it is better to resort only to those which, presenting themselves spontaneously to our senses, cannot be unknown to us if we reflect even a little.

What this initial, uncritical gathering of data is supposed to do is provide one with a basic familiarity with things – that there are bodies, that they appear to have certain properties (some of which they may not in fact really have), that they relate to each other in certain ways – and thereby establish what there is to be explained. Such observations are 'common to all men' and appear to be nothing but the spur to inquiry. The method of investigation and explanation itself, however, begins at a more conceptual, even a priori level.

> First, I tried to discover in general the principles or first causes of everything that exists or can exist in the world. To this end I considered nothing but God alone, who created the world; and I derived these principles only from certain seeds of truth which are naturally in our souls. Next, I examined the first and most ordinary effects deducible from these causes. In this way, it seems to me, I discovered the heavens, the stars, and an earth; and on the earth, water, air, fire, minerals, and other such things which, being the most common of all and the simplest, are consequently the easiest to know. Then, when I sought to descend to more particular things, I encountered such a variety that I did

not think the human mind could possibly distinguish the forms or species of bodies that are on earth from an infinity of others that might be there if it had been God's will to put them there.

This is the point at which things turn empirical, at least in Descartes' telling (if not in his actual process of discovery).[26] First, careful observation and description is required to compile a catalogue of the phenomena in the visible world that require explanation. Because there are many different ways, consistent with the general principles, in which the observed phenomena might be brought about – many possible underlying causal mechanisms – one must appeal to experiments to discover the true causes of those 'effects', that is, to figure out just how these particular things connect with the more general things and be 'deduced' from (explained by) them.

Consequently, I thought the only way of making these bodies useful to us was to progress to the causes by way of the effects and to make use of many special observations. And now, reviewing in my mind all the objects that have ever been present to my senses, I venture to say that I have never noticed anything in them which I could not explain quite easily by the principles I had discovered. But I must also admit that the power of nature is so ample and so vast, and these principles so simple and so general, that I notice hardly any particular effect of which I do not know at once that it can be deduced from the principles in many different ways; and my greatest difficulty is usually to discover in which of these ways it depends on them. I know no other means to discover this than by seeking further observations whose outcomes vary according to which of these ways provides the correct explanation.[27]

What Descartes offers here is an approximation of the hypothetico-deductive method in modern science. On the background of established theoretical principles that constrain the kinds of entities and processes which can appear in explanations, one frames hypotheses that 'save the phenomenon'. Each hypothesis is then used to make predictions: if the proposed mechanism is the underlying cause of the phenomenon, then what other effects should be observed? These predictions are tested through controlled experiments. If the predictions do not bear out, then the hypothesis is falsified. Ideally, in the end all but one of the explanations – presumably the true one – will be eliminated.

Beyond questions of method proper and a summary of his epistemological and metaphysical speculations, Descartes also addresses an issue raised by his studies in anatomy. Because the human body operates on purely mechanical principles, being no less of a 'machine' than non-human animals, what distinguishes the human being from other creatures is the presence of a soul operating in and through that body. But how does one know that there is indeed a soul united to a body? Were one to come across an automaton built to resemble and move just like a human being, how could one determine that this was not a real, ensouled human being?

For Descartes, the problem of 'other minds' is settled through readily detectible linguistic habits.

> If any machine bore a resemblance to our bodies and imitated our actions as closely as possible for all practical purposes, we should still have two very certain means of recognizing that they were not real men. The first is that they could never use words, or put together other signs, as we do in order to declare our thoughts to others.

The machine in question might be able to utter single words, string them together into sentences and even respond to queries such as 'Does this hurt?' But, Descartes insists, 'it is not conceivable that such a machine should produce different arrangements of words so as to give an appropriately meaningful answer to whatever is said in its presence, as the dullest of men can do.' It is the flexible and creative use of language that indicates, not with absolute certainty but with at least a reliably high degree of probability, that we are in the presence of real human being and not a robot.

An additional consideration is the limited capacity of the automaton to respond to new and unforeseen circumstances through its behaviour. The machine can do only what it has been programmed to do, while a rational human being has the ability to act and respond in original and practically infinite ways.

> Even though such machines might do some things as well as we do them, or perhaps even better, they would inevitably fail in others, which would reveal that they were acting not through understanding but only from the disposition of their organs. For whereas reason is a universal instrument which can be used in all kinds of situations, these organs need some particular disposition for each particular action; hence, it is for all practical purposes impossible for a machine to have enough different organs to make it act in all the contingencies of life in the way in which our reason makes us act.[28]

These same criteria mark the difference between human beings and non-human animals. 'Magpies and parrots can utter words as we do, and yet they cannot speak as we do: that is, they cannot show that they are thinking what they are saying.'[29] This is supposed to prove not just that non-human animals lack reason, but that they do not have souls at all and are merely mechanical automata – natural machines, but machines nonetheless.

DESCARTES WAS CONCERNED about the reception awaiting the *Discourse* and its essays. He had a pretty good sense that they would not meet with universal approval. He told Mersenne, who was assisting in finding a publisher, 'I would rather not put my name on it.'[30] And the first edition was indeed published, in Leiden, without Descartes' name on the title page. Still, he wanted to make sure that these works were accessible and widely read, which explains his choice to compose them, like *The World*, in French rather than Latin. 'If I am writing in French, my native language, rather than Latin, the language of my teachers, it is because I expect that those who use only their natural reason in all its purity will be better judges of my opinions than those who give credence only to the writings of the ancients.'[31] Descartes' intention was 'to prepare the way and to test the waters' for his 'treatise on physics' – that is, a more complete presentation of his philosophical system, including the metaphysical and physical foundations that would take the particular explanations of natural phenomena now presented in a hypothetical manner and establish them with all due certainty.[32]

As it turned out, the treatises that appeared in 1637, Descartes' first publications, did succeed in bringing him to the attention of the learned world – for better and, in terms of the controversies that followed, for worse.

FIVE

'I think, therefore I am'

ife along the coast of the Netherlands suited Descartes quite well. Writing to Mersenne in 1638 from the village of Egmond-Binnen, he notes that,

> just between us, there is nothing more contrary to my designs than the air of Paris, with the infinite distractions [*divertissements*] that are inevitable there; and as long as I am allowed to live in my own way, I will always stay in the countryside, in some country where I cannot be disturbed by visits from my neighbors, as I do here in a corner of North Holland. It is this reason alone that made me prefer this country to my own, and I am now so accustomed to it that I have no desire to change it.[1]

A few years later, he tells his friend Claude Picot that he has found in Egmond 'a solitude . . . as peaceful and with as much sweetness as he has ever had'.[2] While the Republic may have lost some of the charm that originally brought him there, he admits to Picot, still, he could spend the rest of his life in this quiet part of the world.[3]

The solitude was especially good for Descartes' ongoing scientific investigations. As an experimentalist, he now had the leisure, space and means to pursue the observations in anatomy and botany he needed to help advance and confirm his theories.

He monitored the growth of plants in the garden of his small house. And because he was living in a rural community, he had ready access to animals, living and dead. Descartes worked with chickens and studied the formation of embryos in their eggs, and he performed vivisection on the heart of a rabbit to study the circulation of the blood.[4] He also arranged for local butchers to kill pregnant cows so that he could study the development of their foetuses. 'I arranged for them to bring me more than a dozen wombs in which there were small calves, some as big as mice, others like rats, and yet others like small dogs, in which I was able to observe many more things than in the case of chickens because their organs were larger and more visible.'[5]

Although his time in Egmond would be interrupted by moves to Santpoort, another coastal village that was close by Haarlem and where he lived from January 1639 to April 1640, a year-long residency in Leiden (from April 1640 to April 1641) and two years in Endegeest, back up near Alkmaar (from April 1641 to May 1643) – as well as several trips to Paris and Brittany to take care of family affairs – he would always return to the Egmond area. It was, Descartes had decided, the ideal setting for a natural philosopher who was more intent on serious scientific work than seeking a reputation and the honours conferred by polite society.

THE 'QUIETER AND MORE TRANQUIL LIFE' that Descartes found in the Republic and valued so highly, however, was now subject to frequent and often unwelcome distractions.[6] Despite publishing the *Discourse on Method* and its scientific essays anonymously, there was little secret as to who the author was. Descartes had copies sent to various academic, scientific and mathematical circles in the United Provinces and France in order to solicit comments. He also made sure that the texts were sent to French Jesuits, in the hope that they might see fit to adopt them in their schools as a replacement for the Aristotelian works in their curriculum. All this only ensured that Descartes would now, besides receiving the recognition for his discoveries that he craved, be inundated with correspondence from both partisans and critics. Then again, in the *Discourse* itself he asks 'all who have any objections to take the trouble to send them to my publisher, and when he informs me about them I shall attempt to append my reply at the same time, so that readers can see both sides together, and decide the truth all the more easily'.[7]

Among the first to respond was Libert Froidmont (Fromondus), a conservative philosopher and theologian in the southern Low Countries with anti-Copernican credentials who would soon be appointed to a chair in Bible Studies at the University of Louvain. In the autumn of 1637 Froidmont pressed Descartes on a number of issues, including his account of the circulation of the blood. Descartes was familiar with William Harvey's 1628 book *An Anatomical Exercise Concerning the Motion of the Heart and Blood in Animals*, in which Harvey argues that the heart has an intrinsic 'faculty' of beating, which causes the blood to move throughout the body. Descartes agreed with Harvey that the circulation of the blood is generated by the heart. In the *Discourse*, however, he claims that the beating of the heart is due not to some innate power in that muscle, but rather to the swelling of the blood that is heated by the heart (as a kind of 'fire'), which swelling causes the heart itself to expand. When that blood cools and contracts as it moves from one chamber to another, the heart, too, contracts.[8] Froidmont objected that Descartes' account was highly implausible. 'It would take the heat of a furnace to rarify the drops of blood sufficiently rapidly to make the heart expand.' He was also concerned that Descartes' elimination of substantial forms and reduction of the body's functions to mechanical operations, in both animals and humans, 'will perhaps open the way for atheists to deny the presence of a rational soul even in the human body'.[9]

Descartes' reply to Froidmont was perfectly courteous. Writing to their intermediary Vopiscus Fortunatus Plemp (Plempius), a Dutch physician in Amsterdam who was a friend of Descartes' – though they would later have a falling out – he expresses his appreciation for 'the care with which he [Froidmont] has read my book' and 'the judgement of a man so gifted, so learned in the topics I treated'.[10] Apparently, though, Froidmont found Descartes' responses to his objections a little testy. Descartes later tells Plemp that 'I am surprised that he should conclude from them that I was annoyed or irritated by his paper.'[11] He was only responding in kind to what he took to be the 'hard things' that Froidmont had said, having concluded that 'he liked that style of writing . . . I was afraid he might enjoy the game less if I received his attack too gently and softly.'[12]

Overall, Descartes seems not to have been prepared for the more vehement criticisms that came his way, and he did not accept them with much grace. The *Dioptrics*, for one, received harsh treatment from the French mathematician Pierre de Fermat. Mersenne had sent a copy of the work to Fermat, who deserves equal credit with Descartes for the development of analytic geometry and the use of algebraic equations to solve geometric problems. Fermat objected to Descartes' claim that the laws of motion apply in the same way to both the actual motion of bodies and their tendency to motion, which is central to Descartes' account of the behaviour of light. 'I doubt', Fermat says in a letter to Mersenne, 'that the inclination to motion must follow the laws of motion itself, since there is as much difference between the one and the other [that is, tendency to motion and motion] as there is between potency and act.'[13] He also found fault with Descartes' proffered demonstration of the sine law of refraction. And while he admired Descartes' directions on the cutting of lenses, he wished that 'the foundations on which they are established were better proven than they are. But I apprehend that they lack truth as much as proof.' Fermat's summary judgement of the *Dioptrics* is captured by his suggestion that Descartes was 'groping about in shadows'.[14]

Descartes was taken aback by this critique from someone he did not know. He accused Fermat of not understanding his arguments, and even of failing to 'listen to reason'. 'It cannot reasonably be doubted that the laws that govern movement, which is the actuality, as he says himself, must govern also the tendency to move, which is the potentiality of the same actuality.'[15] Meanwhile, Mersenne, who liked to stir up debates, sent Descartes a copy of Fermat's treatise *De maximis et minimis, et de inventione tangentium linearum curvarum* (On Maxima, Minima and on Finding Tangents of Curved Lines), to which Descartes replied that 'I would be happy to say nothing about the writing that you have sent me, in so far as I could not say anything that would be to the advantage of the person who wrote it.'[16] Nonetheless, he was able to point out 'manifest errors' in Fermat's calculations of the tangent to a parabolic curve.

Among those who came to Fermat's defence in this dispute was the formidable Gilles Personne de Roberval, holder since 1634 of the Ramus Chair of Mathematics at the Collège de France. Roberval insisted that Descartes failed to understand Fermat's method of calculating tangents in his treatise, and that therefore the objections which he sent to Fermat were 'absurd'. 'If Monsieur Descartes had well understood the method of Monsieur de Fermat . . . he would have ceased to admire how this method has so many defenders and would admire the method itself.'[17] Descartes in turn treated Roberval with condescension. In a letter to Mersenne in July 1638, Descartes calls Roberval 'as vain . . . as a woman who attaches a ruby to her hair in order to appear more beautiful'. As for Fermat, he says in the same letter that 'I am completely disgusted with his discussion; I find nothing reasonable in anything he says.'[18] Referring to both Fermat and Roberval, Descartes confessed to the French mathematician Claude Mydorge that

'I despise those who intend to denigrate my Geometry without understanding it.'[19] He resented the way they had criticized his work in mathematics and optics, and blamed their attacks on malice and jealousy.

> As for M. [Fermat], his way of treating me confirms entirely my opinion that I have had from the start, that he and those in Paris have conspired together to try to discredit my writings as much as they could; perhaps

Rolland Lefebvre (Lefevre), *Pierre de Fermat*, 1640–75, oil on canvas.

because they were afraid that, if my Geometry became
fashionable [*estoit en vogue*], then whatever little they learned
from the Analysis of Viete [the mathematician François
Viète] would be mocked.[20]

Descartes, perhaps regretting his tone, soon wrote somewhat
apologetically to Fermat, by way of Mersenne, requesting for-
giveness on the grounds that he did not know who he was. 'I ask
him very humbly to forgive me and to believe that I did not know
him.'[21] Descartes would also patch things up somewhat with
Roberval in the early 1640s during one of his visits to Paris. The
truce was short-lived, however, and the two would be at loggerheads again within a few years.

Despite encouraging others to send him their objections to
his work – something Descartes would do throughout his career,
usually through the mediation of Mersenne or another confidant
– he clearly did not take criticism well. He had thin skin, but also
an arrogance and brutal honesty that he was not shy about exposing
in public. In the *Discourse* he notes that

> I have already had frequent experience of the judge-
> ments both of those I held to be my friends and of some
> I thought indifferent towards me, and even of certain
> others whose malice and envy would, I knew, make them
> eager enough to reveal what affection would hide from
> my friends. But it has rarely happened that an objection
> was raised that I had not wholly foreseen, except when
> it was quite wide of the mark. Thus I have almost never
> encountered a critic of my views who did not seem to be
> either less rigorous or less impartial than myself.[22]

Writing to Mersenne soon after receiving Fermat's objections,
he says that 'I am happy when I see that the strongest objections

that are made to me are not worth the weakest ones that I have made to myself.'[23]

DESCARTES' VIEW of many of the objections that he received to his 1637 writings was that they were based on an inadequate understanding of his philosophy. He attributed the mistakes of his critics to their ignorance of the physical and metaphysical foundations of his scientific work. He knew, of course, that he bore most of the responsibility for this by withholding *The World* from publication. But, he often insisted, had his critics been able to read that treatise and understand the bigger picture, they would have recognized how well grounded his theories were. Unfortunately, aside from the brief summary that he offers in Part Four of the *Discourse* concerning the metaphysical reflections he had been engaging in for some years – and he admits to Father Vatier that what he wrote there was 'obscure' and 'the least worked out section of the whole book', but 'the publisher was becoming impatient'[24] – the readers of the essays on optics and meteorology could not possibly see how the assumptions in the scientific essays were capable of being confirmed by being systematized with first principles. After telling Vatier that he could not prove a priori the assumptions he had made at the beginning of the *Meteors* 'without expounding the whole of my physics', he reassures his friend that 'I could deduce them in due order from the first principles of my metaphysics.' However, he continues, 'as concerns the publication of my *Physics* and *Metaphysics*, I can tell you briefly that I desire it as much or more than anyone, but only under certain conditions, without which I would be foolish to desire it.' He suggests that 'if [my *Physics*] ever sees the light of day, I hope that future generations will be unable to doubt what I say.'[25]

If among those 'certain conditions' clearing the way for publication was the Church changing its mind on heliocentrism,

then they would not obtain for some time. Nonetheless, others continued to press Descartes to publish what he had to say concerning the 'first principles of my metaphysics'. Two of his closest friends, Mersenne and Constantijn Huygens, secretary to stadholder Frederik Hendrik, were among the more insistent. (Descartes had sent to Huygens a copy of the *Discourse* and essays immediately after their publication, so that he might pass them on to the Prince of Orange.) Writing to Descartes in November 1637, Huygens 'begs to inspire you to continually share your

Jan Lievens, *Constantijn Huygens, c.* 1628–9, oil on panel.

writings with the world'.[26] Two years later, he beseeches Descartes
to 'bring *The World* into the world [*mettre le Monde au monde*]'.[27]
Even Descartes' critics wanted to see what Descartes was holding
back. Jean-Baptiste Morin, a professor of mathematics at the
Collège de France, admired Descartes' mathematical work but
had problems with a number of details in his theory of light. For
one thing, Morin, who was relatively sympathetic to the mechanistic doctrine, did not accept Descartes' characterization of the
'subtle matter' through which light was transmitted. Nor did he
think that the motion of luminous bodies could travel through
that medium as far as our eyes in order to cause us to see light.[28]
He even wonders how Descartes could not have anticipated the
harsh treatment that his 'hypothetical' physical writings would
receive.

> In what concerns mathematics, men will only admire the
> subtlety of your mind, and as for physics, I think that you
> will not be surprised if there are people who contradict
> you. For having reserved the knowledge of the univer-
> sal principles and notions of your new Physics (whose
> publication is passionately desired by all the learned)
> and grounding your reasonings only on comparisons, or
> suppositions, whose truth is at least dubious, this is to
> sin against the first precept of your method.[29]

ULTIMATELY, ALL THE PLEADING worked. By 1640 Descartes
realized that it was time to return to the 'little treatise' that he
had begun soon after arriving in the Dutch Republic and in which,
he had said at the time, he was 'able to discover the foundations
of physics . . . and prove metaphysical truths in a manner which
is more evident than the truths of geometry'.[30] After expanding
the treatise in light of his studies in the intervening years, filling

out the arguments and preparing for the inevitable objections, he was finally ready to present to the public the foundations of his philosophy. Coy until the very end, Descartes would not let even friends know about his plans. He said to Huygens in July 1640 that 'I am astonished that you have been told that I was going to publish something on metaphysics . . . your information must be quite inaccurate.'[31] Nonetheless, just a few months later, Descartes wrote to Mersenne to tell him that 'I am sending you my work on metaphysics . . . so that I can make you its godfather and leave the baptism to you.'[32] It was the Minim priest's duty to bring the manuscript to the printer and shepherd it through the publication process.

Just as Galileo had played an incidental role in Descartes' decision to suspend his plans regarding *The World*, one wonders whether he may also have unwittingly contributed to Descartes' decision now to publish both the metaphysical treatise and, a few years later, a textbook of his entire philosophical system. In late 1638 Descartes read Galileo's new work, *Discourses and Mathematical Demonstrations Concerning Two New Sciences*. The Italian scientist's courage to continue with his work, despite being under house arrest and once again contesting philosophical orthodoxy, may have inspired Descartes to put aside his fears. He tells Mersenne that

> I find he [Galileo] philosophizes much more ably than is usual, in that, so far as he can, he abandons the errors of the Schools and tries to use mathematical methods in the investigation of physical questions. On that score, I am completely at one with him, for I hold there is no other way to discover the truth.

Still, he remained quite critical of many of Galileo's findings in mechanics and his calculations regarding falling bodies. The problem, he notes, is that 'he [Galileo] has not investigated matters in an orderly way, and has merely sought explanations for some particular effects, without going into the primary causes in nature; hence, his building lacks a foundation.'[33]

Descartes was not going to make the same mistake; his building would rest on solid ground. As he informs Mersenne, 'these six Meditations contain all the foundations of my physics,'[34] and with the help of his friend he would make sure that the international philosophical community was well informed as to what these were. Published in Paris in 1641, the Latin treatise that for a long time Descartes called simply 'my Metaphysics' was now *Meditations on First Philosophy* (*Meditationes de prima philosophia*). It would, over time and along with the *Discourse on Method*, become his most widely read work.

What Descartes understood by 'the foundations of my physics' was twofold. First, there is epistemology, the task of which is to establish what exactly true knowledge is and whether and how it is possible. Descartes wanted to show that an absolutely certain understanding of the world can, in principle, be achieved and the means by which it is best pursued. The epistemological endeavour of the *Meditations* must therefore address the challenge of scepticism, or the view that absolutely certain knowledge is *not* possible by creatures such as we are, with limited cognitive faculties and subject to varied conditions in a world that is constantly in flux. According to many sceptics of Descartes' time, the best we can hope for in science and even ordinary life are probabilities.[35]

Scepticism first flourished as a philosophical school in antiquity. It enjoyed a comeback in the sixteenth century with the rediscovery and translation of the *Outlines of Pyrrhonism*, in which the Greek thinker Sextus Empiricus (second century CE) presented a wide variety of arguments to undermine confidence in our ability to acquire objective knowledge of the world and certainty in the abstract sciences. Optical illusions (a stick that is straight appears bent when half-submerged in water); familiar variations in, and errors of, sense and reasoning; disagreements between people over matters of taste; differences in mores across cultures – such considerations, ancient and modern sceptics suggested, should make us wary of any claims to absolute truth in empirical and intellectual affairs. Michel de Montaigne (1533–1592), for one, in the longest of his essays, the 'Apology for Raymond Sebond', rehearsed these various 'tropes' of scepticism for the purpose of dulling the allure of dogmatism and encouraging self-examination and humility in human affairs. By the early seventeenth century, this 'Pyrrhonian' revival – so called after the ancient sceptic Pyrrho of Elis – was growing in popularity among European intellectual circles in France, England and elsewhere.[36]

Beyond addressing sceptical concerns about the possibility of knowledge, Descartes intended the six parts of the *Meditations* also to serve as a progressive exercise that draws us away from a reliance on the senses for knowledge of the way the world really is. While science – even, as we have seen, of the Cartesian variety – cannot succeed without experimentation, its starting point must, he insisted, lie in the intellect alone. The epistemology of the *Meditations* is thus, in effect, a counter to the naive confidence in sense experience found among the unphilosophical masses and the more sophisticated empiricist methodology of Aristotelian-Scholastic science.

Second, the foundation of Descartes' physics includes metaphysics. In the strict sense, for Descartes, this is an investigation of spiritual matters, namely God and the soul, the ostensible main topics of the *Meditations*.[37] After all, the subtitle of the first edition of the work states 'in which the existence of God and the immortality of the soul is demonstrated'. But Descartes also considers some very general principles about body and the physical world. All of this constitutes the real content of 'first philosophy'. As he explains to Mersenne, 'I do not confine my discussion to God and the soul, but deal in general with all the first things to be discovered by philosophizing.'[38] Descartes wants to show what he, using reason alone and his own method of inquiry, can discover about mind, matter and their Creator, and how the most basic understanding of such general things can lead to other, even more useful knowledge. Once established, these certain and indubitable foundations for science – *his* science – will in turn ground a general theory of nature (physics in the broad sense) and particular scientific explanations of natural phenomena that constitute the individual sciences.

Writing a few years after the publication of the *Meditations*, Descartes employs the metaphor of a tree to explain how he sees the entire structure of human knowledge: 'The whole of philosophy is like a tree. The roots are metaphysics, the trunk is physics, and the branches emerging from the trunk are all the other sciences, which may be reduced to three principal ones, namely medicine, mechanics, and morals.'[39] In the *Meditations*, Descartes tends primarily to the roots of the tree of knowledge, 'which contains the principles of knowledge, including the explanation of the principal attributes of God, the non-material nature of our souls and all the clear and distinct notions which are in us'.[40]

Before these most basic truths can become evident and certain to Descartes, as he narrates his cognitive itinerary in the work, he must first undertake a kind of intellectual cleansing and reorientation. Descartes tells the reader in the 'Synopsis' that serves as a preliminary summary for the *Meditations* that one of his goals is to 'free us from all our preconceived opinions and provide the easiest route by which the mind may be led away from the senses'.[41] He wants, first, to empty the mind of all and any dubitable opinions and prejudices (some of which were acquired in childhood) that may hinder proper inquiry into nature, and then to redirect our attention from the confusing testimony of sense experience towards the clear and distinct ideas of the intellect.

The starting point of this process is the so-called methodical doubt. Progressing in a systematic manner, Descartes will consider all of his mind's contents, all of his beliefs and judgements, in order to see if there is something, anything, that is not merely a haphazardly acquired opinion (whether it be true or false) or ungrounded prejudice but real knowledge, an absolute certainty. His strategy in using the method of doubt is to play the sceptic to as radical a degree as possible – not for the sake of undermining human knowledge but in order to beat the sceptic at his own game. If Descartes can show that there are certain unassailable beliefs even for someone who is in the midst of an extreme sceptical crisis, where everything is subjected to the possibility of doubt, no matter how remote, then the reconstruction of the edifice of knowledge, especially scientific knowledge, can begin on a secure basis. Descartes was fond of comparing this procedure to more familiar sorts of activities. There is, as we have seen, the analogy of tearing down a house and rebuilding it from the ground up because its foundations were unstable. He also says it is like going through a barrel of apples to see if there are any that have gone bad whose rot might spread to the good fruit.

> Suppose [a person] had a basket full of apples and, being worried that some of the apples were rotten, wanted to take out the rotten ones to prevent the rot from spreading. How would he proceed? Would he not begin by tipping the whole lot out of the basket? And would not the next step be to cast his eye over each apple in turn, and pick up and put back in the basket only those he saw to be sound, leaving the others?

In the first stage of his project, Descartes will tip over the contents of his mind, to separate the false beliefs from the others, so as to prevent their contaminating the rest and making the whole lot uncertain. Now the best way they can accomplish this is to reject all their beliefs together in one go, as if they were all uncertain and false. They can then go over each belief in turn and re-adopt only those which they recognize to be true and indubitable.[42]

He concedes that this is not an easy thing to do. It requires an uncomfortable degree of reflection and critical self-examination. However, Descartes says at the beginning of the *Meditations*, it is something that must be undertaken at some point, if only to see what one does know and, more importantly, *can* know. 'I realized that it was necessary, once in a lifetime [*semel in vita*], to demolish everything completely and start again right from the foundations if I wanted to establish anything at all in the sciences that was stable and likely to last.'[43]

Descartes begins the First Meditation by noting that many things that people ordinarily and uncritically take to be certain can in fact be subjected to doubt. There are, for example, the simple (and easily resolvable) doubts about objects that arise when they are perceived under less than ideal circumstances. It is easy to mistake the size or shape of something when it is seen at a distance or through a fog. The lesson here is that the senses are not *always* to be trusted, that not everything they report about the external world is true. 'From time to time, I have found that the senses deceive, and it is prudent never to trust completely those who have deceived us even once.' These kinds of errors are not very serious, though, and one can guard against them through careful examination of what the senses are reporting and under what conditions.

Still, there are many other beliefs about the world that even the most careful and critical observer ordinarily accepts as certain.

These constitute some of the core beliefs of common sense, such as that one has a body, that there is an external world composed of many other bodies, and that things in that world are basically as they appear to be under optimal observational conditions. 'Although the senses occasionally deceive us with respect to objects which are very small or in the distance, there are many other beliefs about which doubt is quite impossible, even though they are derived from the senses – for example, that I am here, sitting by the fire, wearing a winter dressing-gown, holding this piece of paper in my hands, and so on.' What could be more certain than that there is a world out there made up of familiar objects?

And yet, Descartes continues, even these apparently certain beliefs can be put into doubt. It is a highly implausible doubt, to be sure, but for the sake of completeness every possibility must be examined. In this case, all that is required is to remember the deceptive character of dreams, in which fantasies are mistaken for reality. 'How often, asleep at night, am I convinced of just such familiar events – that I am here in my dressing-gown, sitting by the fire – when in fact I am lying undressed in bed!' Perhaps, Descartes suggests, he is only *dreaming* that he is sitting by the fire, holding a piece of paper, or even has a body. In this case it would all be an illusion and these most evident beliefs would in fact be false. The experiences of dream-life are so realistic, so much like what is ordinarily considered to be waking life, that one cannot tell whether one is awake or dreaming; thus, on any given occasion, what one takes to be a waking experience of independent reality may not be such. Or, to put the doubt another way, let it be granted that one knows when one is awake and when one is asleep. But because of the phenomenological, qualitative similarity – the experiential vividness, the composition of things, their shapes and colours, and so on – between dreams (which are known to be illusory) and waking life (which is believed to be veridical), how can one be certain that the appearances of waking life are not also illusory?[44] Dream experiences are not to be trusted, so why should any more credence be given to waking experiences, since the two kinds of experience are so much alike? The level of doubt thus deepens, and Descartes' confidence in the senses as a source of knowledge about the world diminishes as he continues his quest for something certain.

And yet, he notes, even if one's experiences are all dreams, or no more veridical than dreams, must there not at least be a world out there, an external realm of things that, if not exactly resembling the items presented in sensory experience, are none-theless sufficiently like them to serve as the basic materials out of which one's illusory perceptions are constituted? Where would the stuff of dreams come from if there were not at least *something* outside the mind that is their ultimate causal source?

> It surely must be admitted that the visions which come in sleep are like paintings, which must have been fashioned in the likeness of things that are real, and hence that at least these general kinds of things – eyes, head, hands, and the body as a whole – are things which are not imag-inary but are real and exist. For even when painters try to create sirens and satyrs with the most extraordinary bodies, they cannot give them natures which are new in all respects; they simply jumble up the limbs of differ-ent animals.[45]

Or perhaps, Descartes continues, there are not even such 'general kinds of things' in an external world, and maybe no external world at all. Even so, surely there can be no doubting the reality of 'even simpler and more general things', such as bodily nature in general, or extension, shape, size and number. These are the most basic and abstract items imaginable. Moreover, they do not require the existence 'in nature' of anything, since they seem to be only simple and objective concepts discovered by the understanding. So, Descartes says, let it be granted that all those sciences that depend on the actual existence of things in nature are now uncertain – 'that physics, astronomy, medicine, and all other disciplines which depend on the study of composite things are doubtful'. Still, he suggests, mathematics, at least, as well as other purely rational disciplines that require only such simple concepts as number and extension, 'which deal only with the simplest and most general things, regardless of whether they really exist in nature or not', would appear to remain true and certain. 'For whether I am awake or asleep,' Descartes says, 'two and three added together are five.'

However, if the project of the First Meditation is to be pursued thoroughly and consistently to the end, even these apparently most certain truths have to be put to the test in order to see if there might be any conceivable reason for doubting them. Are the principles of mathematics in fact real, objective and absolute truths, as they seem to be, or simply compelling fictions concocted by the mind? This is where Descartes takes the epistemological exercise to what he calls a 'metaphysical' level.[46] For he now entertains the radical possibility that, while he may have been created by an omnipotent God – and this is not yet certain either, but appears to be only 'a long-standing opinion' – still, because he lacks any firm knowledge about this God, he presently has no compelling reason to believe that his divine creator has not made him such that he regularly goes astray even in matters where he thinks he has 'the most perfect knowledge'. How, Descartes asks, can he be sure that he is not wrong 'every time I add two and three or count the sides of a square, or in some even simpler matter, if that is imaginable?' For all Descartes knows at this point, God, or whoever his creator may be, is malicious and thus has intentionally given him a faulty and deceptive mind, a rational faculty that, even when used properly and carefully, produces only false beliefs. Descartes may feel compelled to believe that two plus two equals four, because his intellect tells him it is so. But maybe, just because his intellect has its origin in an all-powerful and deceptive deity and therefore is systematically unreliable, that proposition is in fact *not* true.

Descartes suggests that this kind of doubt is even more compelling if the origin of my being lies not in the creative activity of some God but simply in the random forces of nature. Let us then assume, he says, 'that I have arrived at my present state by fate or chance or a continuous chain of events, or by some other means; yet since deception and error seem to be imperfections, the less powerful they make my original cause, the more likely it is that I am so imperfect as to be deceived all the time.'[47] It is immaterial whether Descartes was created by a God of unknown, and possibly vicious, character, or whether his being is the result of natural happenstance. Either scenario raises serious doubts about the reliability of his faculties, including reason itself. For all Descartes knows, he is deceived even with respect to those things that seem to him to be the most certain – such as his belief that there is an external world, or the truths of mathematics. Perhaps, because of his congenitally and inherently defective nature, nothing at all that Descartes thinks to be true, no matter how subjectively certain he may feel about it, really *is* true. 'I am finally compelled to admit that there is not one of my former beliefs about which a doubt may not properly be raised.'

By the end of the First Meditation, Descartes' descent into sceptical doubt is complete. Some of the doubts are generated by highly improbable and fantastic considerations. At one point, in order to reinforce the uncertainty engendered by the case of dreams – the force of habit is strong, he says, and it is hard 'not to slide back into my old opinions' – he even considers the possibility, reminiscent of Don Quixote's 'Evil Enchanter', that all of his sensory experiences are merely 'phantasms' and illusions generated by an all-powerful evil deceiver, a 'malicious demon [*genius malignus*]' intent on deceiving him.⁴⁸ Nonetheless, Descartes insists that these considerations, however unlikely, need to be taken seriously in this philosophical moment if he is to discover something that is absolutely certain and immune to any doubt whatsoever, for the purpose of re-establishing the edifice of knowledge on perfectly sound foundations. While there may certainly be, among the things that Descartes had believed, many that really *are* true, he needs to come up with some reliable way to distinguish these from what is false or doubtful.

BY THE END OF THE FIRST MEDITATION, the epistemic model of common sense, with its naive reliance on sense experience and unjustified confidence in reason, has been broken down. With the Second Meditation, the rebuilding begins. Even in the midst of radical sceptical doubt, Descartes immediately comes upon a first irrefutable truth. There is one thing that he can know with absolute certainty: 'I am, I exist [*ego sum, ego existo*].' (The more famous phrase, 'I think, therefore I am,' made its first appearance several years earlier, in French in the *Discourse* as 'je pense, donc je suis'; the familiar Latin rendering, 'ego cogito, ergo sum', comes later, in the *Principles* and in the 1644 Latin translation of the *Discourse*.) The belief in one's own existence is indubitable, completely immune to any sceptical suspicion whatsoever. One cannot possibly doubt one's own existence, no matter how hard one tries. In fact, the harder one tries, the more convinced one will be that one exists. The mere fact that I am thinking is sufficient to establish for myself that I am, regardless of *what* I happen to be thinking – even if I am thinking that I do not exist, and even if I am contemplating the possibility that I am being tricked by an evil demon.

But there is a deceiver of supreme power and cunning who is deliberately and constantly deceiving me. In that case I too undoubtedly exist, if he is deceiving me; and let him deceive me as much as he can, he will never bring it about that I am nothing so long as I think that I am something. So after considering everything very thoroughly, I must finally conclude that this proposition, *I am, I exist*, is necessarily true whenever it is put forward by me or conceived in my mind.[49]

At the same time, these reflections establish something essential about the 'I' who is thinking and who cannot but conclude that he exists. Through the 'I am, I exist' argument, Descartes realizes, also with absolute certainty, that he is a thinking thing, an individual who has a great variety of thoughts, beliefs, feelings, desires and so on. This, too, cannot be doubted. 'What then am I? A thing that thinks. What is that? A thing that doubts, understands, affirms, denies, is willing, is unwilling, and also imagines and has sensory perceptions.'[50] All of these are activities of his thinking. They are conscious states whose presence and whose status as *his own* cannot possibly be doubted. At this point, Descartes has no solid reason for believing that he is anything *but* a thinking thing. He does not yet know whether he also has a body, or whether it is in fact a body that is doing all this thinking; the existence of material and external things has not yet been re-established with any certainty, and his own essence is still unknown. But for now, he can be indubitably sure – even if his faculty of thought was created by an evil deceiver – that he is at least a thinking thing, or mind.

(This shows why 'I am being deceived, therefore I am' or 'I doubt, therefore I am' – *dubito, ergo sum* – is just as good an argument, and serves Descartes' purposes just as well, as 'I think, therefore I am': to be deceived or to doubt is to think. By contrast,

'I am in my bed, therefore I am' would not work: the premise of this argument has been rendered uncertain by the sceptical doubts of the First Meditation, and so the conclusion, even if it follows necessarily from the premise, must be equally uncertain. However, 'I think I am in my bed, therefore I am' or 'I believe I am in my bed, therefore I am' would work; the premise in each of these is absolutely certain, since one cannot possibly doubt that one is thinking or believing something.)

Now what makes his own existence so certain and indubitable, Descartes discovers, is that he perceives it with the utmost 'clarity and distinctness'. He can thus formulate the 'general rule' that 'whatever I perceive very clearly and distinctly is true.' Yet how can he be confident that this principle is correct? How can he know that his faculty for clear and distinct perception – that is, reason or intellect itself – is reliable and is the source not merely of some subjective feeling of certainty, but of real and objective *truth*? After all, what if that faculty was given to him by an evil deceiver? Descartes recognizes the psychological fact that when he is actively in the throes of perceiving something clearly and distinctly (such as '$1 + 2 = 3$'), he cannot bring himself to doubt it. But when he is no longer actually attending to the proposition and the demonstration in its favour, especially when the subject is a bit more complex than simple arithmetic – for example, the proof of the Pythagorean theorem – room for doubt creeps in. He may remember, quite correctly, that he once perceived the matter clearly and distinctly while going through the proof; but now, in the absence of that persuasive clear and distinct perception itself, he can wonder whether it is indeed an indubitable truth, since he can now doubt the veracity of his faculty for clear and distinct perception.

The next step in the argumentative progress of the *Meditations* is thus a crucial one. Descartes insists that the certainty of his own existence as a thinking thing leads, as well, to the absolute certainty of the existence of God. And once Descartes knows that he (along with his rational faculty) was in fact created by this true God – once he knows that the author of his being is an omnipotent and perfectly good and benevolent deity who would never want to see him be systematically led astray – he has established something of great epistemological and metaphysical importance.

Descartes offers several arguments for God's existence. All of them take their start – as they must, given Descartes' current epistemic situation – from something that he discovers indubitably to be in his mind, namely, the *idea* of God. While he can still, at this point, doubt whether there is anything in an external world corresponding to the thoughts he has, he cannot possibly doubt that he, as a thinking thing, has those thoughts. And among the many thoughts that Descartes is certain that he has is the idea of an infinite, all-perfect being. Moreover, the fact that a thinker has an idea of such a being is, like any fact, something that needs an explanation, a *causal* explanation that must be sufficient to account for every feature of the effect.

Descartes insists that a finite, created being such as himself could not possibly be the cause of the idea of an infinite, eternal being. This is because a being that is merely finite could not, through its own resources, be the origin of the notion of a being that is infinite. The proposed cause of an effect must, Descartes insists, 'contain as much reality' as the effect, since 'something cannot arise from nothing, and what is more perfect – contains in itself more reality – cannot arise from what is less perfect.' This is as true for the content of an idea as it is for an actually existing thing, since 'the mode of being by which a thing exists . . . in the intellect by way of an idea, imperfect though it may be, is certainly not nothing, and so it cannot come from nothing.'[51] Not only does a finite being not have enough reality in itself to bring an infinite being into existence, it does not have enough reality in itself to generate even the *idea* of a being that is truly

infinite. Descartes concludes that the only possible explanation
for the idea of God in his mind must be that there really *is* such
an infinite being who has all the attributes represented in the
idea and who, when creating Descartes, endowed his mind with
that clear and distinct idea, like 'the mark of the craftsman
stamped on his work'.

  Employing a version of the a priori 'ontological argument',
one that is quite different from that first used by Anselm of
Canterbury in the eleventh century, Descartes also argues that
it is impossible to clearly and distinctly conceive of God as *not*
existing. The idea of God – which is 'the most clear and distinct'
of all of the ideas that Descartes discovers in his mind – is the
idea of a supremely perfect being. But a supremely perfect being
must necessarily have all perfections (otherwise it would not be
the *supremely* perfect being). Existence, Descartes insists, is 'a
supreme perfection'. Therefore, the idea of God necessarily implies
the thought that God exists.

> It is quite evident that existence can no more be sepa-
> rated from the essence of God than the fact that its three
> angles equal two right angles can be separated from the
> essence of a triangle, or than the idea of a mountain can
> be separated from the idea of valley. Hence it is just as
> much of a contradiction to think of God (that is, a su-
> premely perfect being) lacking existence (that is, lacking
> a perfection), as it is to think of a mountain without a
> valley.[52]

In other words, to insist that 'God does not exist' is to put forward
a proposition that is as logically contradictory and inconceivable
as the proposition that 'a triangle does not have three angles.'

  Through these arguments, Descartes comes to realize that
the careful use of his rational thinking, working on the ideas he

indubitably finds within himself, leads him inexorably to the conclusion that 'I cannot think of God except as existing,' and that his, Descartes', being as a thinking thing has its origin not in some malicious demon or in the random forces of nature but in an infinitely perfect being. Even in the midst of the most radical sceptical doubts, Descartes cannot but conclude that God exists and that it is God who created him.

Moreover, he continues, God cannot be a deceiver. This is because God is necessarily wise and good. An infinitely perfect being must have *all* perfections, and wisdom and goodness are perfections. Thus an infinitely perfect being would never produce a creature whose rational faculties are so inherently faulty that he is systematically deceived whenever he uses them properly; nor would such a being interfere with the operation of those faculties so as to lead their owner astray. Such malicious intentions are 'impossible' for God, 'for in every case of trickery or deception some imperfection is to be found'.[53]

Descartes' intellect now has a divine guarantee. His faculty of clear and distinct perception has been vindicated. With the absolute certainty that he is a thinking thing who was created by an omnipotent and benevolent deity, the overwrought sceptical doubts of the First Meditation about his rational faculties and the beliefs they generate can be dismissed. Knowledge *is* possible. At the end of the Fifth Meditation, he says that

> I see plainly that the certainty and truth of all knowledge depends uniquely on my knowledge of the true God, to such an extent that I was incapable of perfect knowledge about anything else until I knew him. And now it is possible for me to achieve full and certain knowledge of countless matters, both concerning God himself and other things whose nature is intellectual, and also concerning the whole of that corporeal nature [extension

or spatial dimension] which is the subject matter of pure
mathematics.[54]

Descartes can now be confident that whenever he employs his
intellect properly he will not go wrong. As long as he proceeds
with sufficient care and attentiveness and affirms only what he
clearly and distinctly perceives to be true – only what he appre-
hends with such compelling evidence that his will cannot withhold
its assent – he will reach truth. Descartes concludes the Fourth
Meditation by saying:

> every clear and distinct perception is undoubtedly some-
> thing, and hence cannot come from nothing but must
> necessarily have God as its author . . . So today I have
> learned not only what precautions to take to avoid ever
> going wrong, but also what to do to arrive at the truth.
> For I shall unquestionably reach the truth, if only I give
> sufficient attention to all the things which I perfectly
> understand, and separate these from all the other cases
> where my apprehension is more confused and obscure.[55]

What Descartes learns from his epistemological foray, with reason
now validated by divine benevolence, is that the proper use of his
faculties can give him not just beliefs, but true and justified beliefs
– that is, knowledge. He no longer has any reason, however fantastic or unlikely, to doubt that one plus one really does equal
two. The most important rule is to avoid precipitate judgement
and give credence only to what one has irresistible, epistemically
justificatory reasons to believe. One can then be sure that what
one believes is not only subjectively certain in the sense of psychologically compelling, but objectively certain and true. Descartes
offers this principle as an essential guide to any philosopher or
scientist sincerely looking to make progress in his inquiries.

At the same time, he warns that atheists can never achieve the absolute certainty that is available to believers. This is because atheists cannot have the confidence in their rational faculties that comes from knowing that those faculties were created by an omnipotent, non-deceiving God.[56] The atheist will, like all people, believe many things that happen to be true, along with many things that happen to be false. But because the atheist denies the existence of God, he can never be *justified* in knowing that those beliefs are true, and thus can never have real knowledge.

Having done his epistemological groundwork, Descartes can now proceed immediately to discover a number of additional truths. Among the first things he can be certain of after the existence and veracity of God is a basic metaphysical fact, one that he knows will be essential to the foundations of his physics. There is, he now recognizes through clear and distinct concepts, a real and radical distinction in nature between mind and body. Mind is a simple, immaterial substance whose fundamental nature is thought or thinking; body is a composite, material substance whose fundamental nature is extension. The two substances have absolutely nothing in common, and the one can exist independently of the other.

> Simply by knowing that I exist and seeing at the same time that absolutely nothing else belongs to my nature or essence except that I am a thinking thing, I can infer correctly that my essence consists solely in the fact that I am a thinking thing ... I have a clear and distinct idea of myself, in so far as I am simply a thinking, non-extended thing; and on the other hand I have a distinct idea of body, in so far as this is simply an extended, non-thinking thing.

Because, Descartes notes, 'everything which I clearly and distinctly understand is capable of being created by God so as to correspond exactly with my understanding of it', he knows as well that if he can clearly and distinctly conceive of one thing without the other, he can justifiably conclude that 'the two things are distinct, since they are capable of being separated, at least by God.' Now thought or mind *can* be clearly and distinctly conceived without conceiving of body, and body or matter *can* be clearly and distinctly conceived without thought. Accordingly, he concludes, 'it is certain that I am really distinct from my body and can exist without it.'[57] From 'I exist' to 'I am a thinking thing' to 'I am a thinking thing that can exist without a body,' Descartes has made considerable metaphysical progress since the Second Meditation.

Mind and body differ not only in essence, but therefore in the kinds of properties of which each is capable. Because the nature of mind and the nature of body are mutually exclusive, the modifications or 'modes' of one cannot belong to the other. The modes of minds or thinking things are thoughts or ideas: perceptions and volitions, purely mental activities; minds do not, and cannot, have shape, size, spatial location or motion. Bodies or material things, however, because they are not minds or souls, cannot have thoughts; they lack mental life altogether. Bodies are non-thinking, extended (spatial) substances. Their properties include size and shape, motion and rest, and indefinite divisibility into parts.

Descartes is now, by the Sixth Meditation, also ready to put to rest the doubts of the First Meditation concerning the *existence* of bodies. He can be reasonably certain that there is in fact an external world. The non-deceiving God who created him has clearly given him a strong natural propensity to believe in such a world on the basis of the data of his senses. For example, he cannot help but judge that his visual experiences 'are produced by corporeal things', and that if he is awake and sees a tree it must be because there is a tree causing that perception. If there were no world of corporeal things actually and ordinarily producing such experiences, then a demonstrably benevolent God would, in giving him such a propensity, have led him astray, which (he insists) is absurd. 'I do not see how God could be understood to be anything but a deceiver if the ideas [of sense] were transmitted from a source other than corporeal things. It follows that corporeal things exist.'[58]

However, the external world whose existence has been reinstated by Descartes is not, qualitatively, the same external world in which he, in the persona of the philosophically naive meditator at the beginning of this long exercise, once believed. One of the things that Descartes has learned over the course of the *Meditations* is that the reports of the senses are not to be trusted regarding the true natures of things. The working assumption of *The World*, that the bodies that exist outside the mind do not really have the colours, sounds, tastes and other sensory qualities that they are ordinarily perceived to have, is now more than just a 'hypothesis'. Descartes shows in the *Meditations* that all that he perceives clearly and distinctly to belong to bodies, and to corporeal nature in general – and thus all that he, through the divine guarantee, is justified in attributing to physical things – are purely mathematical properties: shape, size, divisibility and mobility. This is because the clear and distinct idea of body or matter consists only in extension, or three-dimensional space. Since he is now to judge things only according to the clear and distinct ideas of the intellect and affirm only what he perceives with supreme, unimpeachable and irresistible evidence, he must look beyond the confused, obscure and misleading testimony of the senses and believe that external bodies consist in extension alone. All the other properties that *seem* to belong to bodies and that make up the richness of our sensory experience are – just like the pains and pleasures that bodies often cause in us – only perceptions in the mind brought about by the motions of matter.

Among those bodies in the external world, Descartes recognizes that there is one in particular to which he, as a thinking thing, is deeply related. With the uncertainty of the First and Second Meditations dispelled, he may now conclude that he does indeed have 'a body that is very closely joined to me'. Mind may be different from and independent of matter, but that does not preclude their being united in a human being. 'There is nothing that my own nature teaches me more vividly than that I have a body, and that when I feel pain there is something wrong with the body, and that when I am hungry or thirsty the body needs food and drink, and so on.' More than a simple and indifferent juxtaposition of two things, the mind's union with the body is a rather intimate one, or so 'nature' – Descartes' God-guaranteed propensities – leads him to believe:[59] 'Nature also teaches me, by these sensations of pain, hunger, thirst, and so on, that I am not merely present in my body as a sailor is present in a ship, but that I am very closely joined and, as it were, intermingled with it, so that I and the body form a unit.'[60] Somehow, despite their radical disparity, the mind and the body whose union constitutes a human being engage in an immediate and mutual causal relationship: some mental events cause motions in the body (such as the voluntary movements of a limb), and some motions in the body bring about events in the mind (for example, a sensation of pain). Descartes' best explanation of this fact is that the correspondence between the two substances is the result of a divine institution – God has so providentially created the nature of mind and body that certain motions do give rise to certain thoughts, and vice versa – and thus testimony to 'the power and goodness of God'.

THE METAPHYSICAL MIND—BODY distinction (which later
philosophers call 'dualism') so central to the *Meditations* can
certainly contribute to establishing the soul's immortality, as
promised in the work's original subtitle.[61] Descartes does not
really fulfil this promise in the text. Nonetheless, the groundwork has been laid. In response to Mersenne's concern about
the absence of any explicit discussion of the issue, he writes:

> You say that I have not said a word about the immortality
> of the soul. You should not be surprised. I could not prove
> that God could not annihilate the soul, but only that it
> is by nature entirely distinct from the body, and conse-
> quently is not bound by nature to die with it. This is all
> that is required as a foundation for religion, and is all that
> I had any intention of proving.[62]

In the *Meditations* itself, Descartes claims only that an immaterial
mind is not subject to the decay and decomposition that inevitably affects the material body, and so it is naturally capable of
surviving the latter's demise and existing without it. To Mersenne,
though, he goes further and concludes that 'the mind, in so far
as it can be known by natural philosophy, is immortal.' The only
reason why a soul would perish is if God chose to destroy it.

Descartes told his friend Guillaume Gibieuf (1591–1650),
a Catholic priest and theologian in France who he hoped would
help him secure for his new treatise the approval of 'the gentlemen of the Sorbonne' – the theological faculty of the University
of Paris – that 'it is the cause of God that I have undertaken to
defend.'[63] But Descartes' main concern in the *Meditations*, no more
than in the *Discourse* and its accompanying essays, is not Christian
apologetics; rather, it is science. His metaphysics empties the
bodily realm of all spiritual or mind-like elements. There are no
Aristotelian active, immaterial forms, qualities or powers in the

physical world. The *only* truly animated body in nature – the only body endowed with a soul (*anima*) – is the human body. Mind–body dualism thus does important work on behalf of Descartes' scientific project. The exhaustive and exclusive distinction of mind and body – *everything* is either mental or physical, and everything is *either* mental *or* physical – provides the right metaphysical foundation for the mechanistic picture of the world. Whatever takes place in the physical world is and must be explained by material principles alone.

SIX

Loss and Conflict

n the autumn of 1640 Descartes was putting the finishing touches on the *Meditations*. He would soon send the manuscript to Huygens in The Hague, who in turn would convey it to Mersenne in Paris. Descartes trusted Mersenne to bring the book to press, and even gave him carte blanche to do some editing. 'I am very much indebted to you for the care you are taking of my book of metaphysics,' he wrote in December 1640, 'and I give you a free hand to correct or change whatever you think fit.'[1]

He initially wanted to have only a small number of copies printed, as a preview run, to send to some theologians 'for their opinion of it'. What Descartes sought, in fact, was their approval, or at least to find out what they might find objectionable from a religious perspective. 'I have no fear that it contains anything that could displease the theologians, but I would have liked to have the approbation of a number of people so as to prevent the cavils of ignorant contradiction-mongers.' He was concerned, though, that copies of the book would end up in the hands of 'almost everyone who has any curiosity to see it; either they will borrow it from one of those to whom I send it, or they will get it from the publisher, who will certainly print more copies than I want'.[2]

In the end, Descartes asked Mersenne to circulate the manuscript among some 'learned critics', including philosophers and theologians with whom the Minim friar was personally acquainted

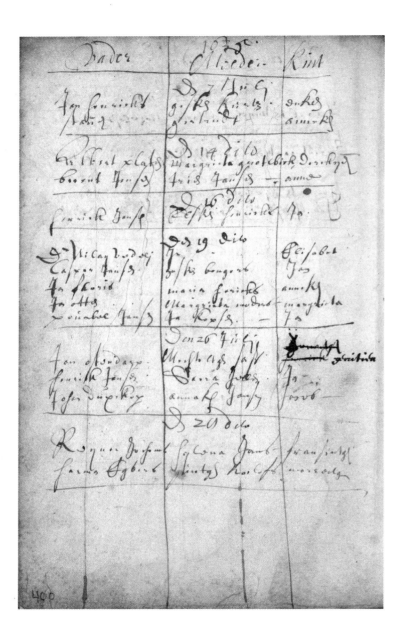

Record of the baptism of Descartes' daughter.

or at least knew by reputation. Mersenne was to collect their objections, especially – and despite Descartes' confidence that it contained nothing of which the ecclesiastics, Catholic or Reformed, might disapprove – on topics that could potentially be problematic. 'I will be very glad if people put to me many objections, the strongest they can find, for I hope the truth will stand out all the better from them.'[3]

Between receiving Descartes' manuscript of the *Meditations* in November 1640 and the publication in Paris of the first edition in August 1641, Mersenne took care to invite, collect and forward objections to this metaphysical and epistemological exercise. Descartes, for his part, was occupied with composing responses to them. It was in the midst of these preparations that Descartes was hit with the deepest tragedy of his life.

His daughter, only five years old, died.

While living in Amsterdam, from the spring of 1634 to the spring of 1635, Descartes had rented rooms in the home of Jacob Thomasz Sergeant. Sergeant, an Englishman who lived at 6 Wester-markt, close by the Westerkerk and just behind the present-day Anne Frank House, was a French teacher and bookseller. He had a servant named Helena Jansdr van der Stroom (d. 1683).[4] On 19 July 1635, most likely in Deventer, 21-year-old Helena gave birth to a girl. In the record of the baptism, which also took place in Deventer, the father is listed as 'Reyner Jochems' (René, Joachim's son) – that is, Descartes.[5] The child's given name was Fransintge, the Dutch diminutive of Francine. It is unclear how the baptism was arranged, since the Reformed Church typically did not baptize children born out of wedlock.

According to Baillet, Descartes was rather secretive about the whole affair. He says that Descartes refused to acknowledge publicly either his relationship with Helena or his fatherhood, and suggests that perhaps it was out of shame. 'The marriage of Monsieur Descartes is, for us, one of the most secret mysteries of the hidden life he led outside his country far from his relatives and friends. There is nothing more agreeable with the profession of a philosopher than the freedom of a celibate.'[6]

Despite Baillet's reference to a 'secret marriage' that was, he says, 'a stain on his [Descartes'] celibacy', we know that Descartes and Helena did not marry.[7] In fact, she would wed someone else in just a few years – a Jan Jansz van Wel, from Egmond – with Descartes acting as witness and providing a generous dowry of six hundred guilders for her.[8] Descartes, Helena and Fransintge do appear at least to have lived together from autumn 1637 until 1639, in Santpoort, near Haarlem. In a letter to an anonymous recipient of 30 August 1637, Descartes, writing from Egmond, says that 'I spoke yesterday with my hostess to see if she would accommodate my niece [that is, daughter] here and how much she wanted me to pay for that. She told me, without any delib-eration, that I should bring her whenever I wanted, and that we could easily come to some agreement as to price, since it was indifferent to her whether she had one child more or less to care for.' Apparently, he was hoping to bring Helena as well, and was setting up a position for her as servant to his hostess. 'It should be arranged for Helena to come here as soon as possible.'[9]

Baillet, a bit of a French chauvinist, also reports (probably wishfully) that Descartes was planning at some point to send his daughter to France, 'in order to procure for her a suitable educa-tion' and where she could live with some members of his family 'and be raised with piety under great exemplars'.[10] Alas, it was not to be. Fransintge died on 17 September 1640, while she and Helena were in Amersfoort. She succumbed to scarlet fever after three days. Though Descartes was in Leiden, seeing to preparations on the *Meditations*, he may have made it back in time. He was, Baillet says, heartbroken over the loss. 'He wept for her with a tenderness that showed him that the true philosophy does not extinguish the natural. He proclaimed that she, by her death, left him with the

greatest regret that he had ever felt in his life.'[11] Descartes seems
to have kept his mourning to himself, however. Even during
Fransintge's illness, just days before her death, he was preoccupied
with other matters. On 15 September, he was writing to Mersenne
from Leiden to thank him for the advice he had given him regarding
'my treatise of Metaphysics, in which I believe I have hardly omitted
anything necessary for demonstrating the truth', and responds to
some technical questions about fountains and other 'machines',
the speed of missiles and 'the subtle matter' surrounding the earth,
among other scientific topics.[12] There is no mention whatsoever
in the letter to his good friend regarding the child's condition. In
later correspondence, there is not a word about Helena, and only
one oblique, but touching, reference to the loss of his daughter.[13]
Writing in 1641 to Alphonse Pollot (1602–1668), a member of
the stadholder's entourage in The Hague who it seems had also
recently lost someone close (his brother), Descartes says

> I have just learned the sad news of your loss, and though
> I do not undertake to say anything in this letter which
> could have any power to soften your pain, I still cannot
> refrain from trying, so as to let you know at least that I
> share what you feel. I am not one of those who think that
> tears and sadness are appropriate only for women, and
> that to appear a stout-hearted man one must force one-
> self to put on a calm expression at all times. Not long ago,
> I suffered the loss of two people who were very close to
> me, and I found that those who wanted to shield me from
> sadness only increased it, whereas I was consoled by the
> kindness of those whom I saw to be touched by my grief.[14]

As far as we know, this is the only occasion in writing in which
Descartes shared his sorrow over Fransintge – as well as over
the death of his father, Joachim, who passed away just a month

after his daughter – with someone else. Descartes' grief was clearly a very private affair.

BY AUGUST OF 1641 the book was in print. This first edition, published by Michel Soly in Paris, included both the *Meditations* and six sets of objections and Descartes' replies, with the debate taking up considerably more space than the original text. The volume was prefaced by a flattering dedicatory letter to 'the Dean and Doctors of the sacred Faculty of Theology at Paris' – that is, the Sorbonne – whom Descartes calls 'the greatest tower of strength to the Catholic Church'. This was part of his continued effort to get what he calls their 'verdict' on the work, and especially their *approbation* and protection.

The objections that Descartes received from clerics and theologians focused mainly on his discussion of God. The author of the first set of objections was Johan de Kater (Caterus), a Catholic priest in Alkmaar. De Kater worried that Descartes' alleged proofs for God's existence do not succeed. He suggests that the a priori 'ontological' proof, based on the idea of God necessarily containing the perfection of existence, shows only that the two concepts ('God' and 'existence') are linked, not that 'the existence is anything actual in the real world' and, thus, that God truly exists.[15] The second set of objections, ostensibly from 'theologians and philosophers' but composed mostly by Mersenne himself, raise the question of why the presence of the idea of an infinite being (God) in a finite mind necessarily entails that that infinite being must exist as the cause of that idea. Could not an individual simply take the idea of 'some degree of perfection' and increase it 'an indefinite number of degrees and thus positing higher and higher degrees of perfection up to infinity' finally arrive at the idea of an infinite being? Furthermore, the objector (Mersenne) continues, considering Descartes' claim that God cannot be a deceiver, why might not deception be perfectly compatible with God's providential goodness? 'Cannot God treat men as a doctor treats the sick, or a father his children? In both these cases there is frequent deception though it is always employed beneficially and with wisdom.'[16]

By far the most important philosophical points, and the most contentious exchanges, occur in the third, fourth and fifth sets of objections, which came from three individuals who already were or soon would be major figures on the seventeenth-century intellectual scene. The English philosopher Thomas Hobbes (1588–1679) first met Mersenne in the mid-1630s, during his travels on the Continent. In late 1640 he ended up back in Paris, this time as a royalist exile during the English Civil War. (He would remain in the French capital until 1651.) As a member of Mersenne's circle, he received a copy of the *Meditations* with great interest. However, his response to the work was quite hostile. He took particular issue with Descartes' mind–body distinction. He grants that 'the thing that thinks is the subject to which mind, reason or intellect belong,' and that we cannot 'conceive an act without its subject . . . of knowing without a knower, or of thinking without a thinker'. But, he insists, 'it seems to follow from this that a thinking thing is something corporeal. For it seems that the subject of any act can be understood only in terms of something corporeal or in terms of matter.' Moreover, what Descartes calls 'ideas' are, Hobbes claims, in fact only concrete, material images in the brain. This is as true of the idea of God as of any external object, and we arrive at this idea only through construction and expansion on the basis of our sensory ideas of external objects.

There is little common ground between Hobbes and Descartes. They are both vigorous critics of Scholastic philosophy and partisans of the new mechanistic science. But where Descartes is committed to an unbridgeable ontological divide between mind and matter, Hobbes is a materialist who, in his own writings,

dismisses the notion of an immaterial substance (such as a soul). In his most important work, the political treatise *Leviathan*, he proclaims that '*substance* and *body* signify the same thing; and therefore, *substance incorporeal* are words which, when they are joined together, destroy one another, as if a man should say an *incorporeal body*.'[17] Hobbes is also an empiricist. He rejects Descartes' view that there are certain ideas 'innate' in the mind, whether as fully formed concepts or as native propensities to think certain things. 'Concerning the thoughts of man . . . the original of them all is that which we call *Sense*. (For there is no conception in a man's mind

John Michael Wright, *Thomas Hobbes, c.* 1669–70, oil on canvas.

which hath not at first, totally or by parts, been begotten upon the organs of sense.)'[18] Among Descartes' innate ideas is, of course, the idea of God. Hobbes denies not only the innateness of such a concept, but that there is anything like the idea that Descartes relies on in his proofs of God's existence. 'There is no idea or conception of anything we call *infinite*.'[19] Of Hobbes, Descartes says to Mersenne, 'I am very surprised that, although from the way he writes the author shows himself to be an intelligent and learned man, he seems to miss the truth in every single claim which he puts forward as his own.'[20] He soon decides, as he and 'the Englishman' are simply talking past each other, that 'the best thing would be for me to have nothing more to do with him, and, accordingly, avoid answering him. For if his temperament is what I think it is, it will be hard for us to exchange views without becoming enemies.'[21]

A more productive set of objections came from a freshly minted theologian in Paris. Antoine Arnauld (1612–1694) was the youngest of twenty children in a prominent family of the *noblesse de robe*. Various members of the family were deeply embedded in the Jansenist movement, an austere theological reform faction within French Catholicism. Inspired by the writings of Cornelius Jansen (1585–1638), a Flemish theologian and Bishop of Ypres, the Jansenists adopted a strong doctrine of efficacious grace, whereby God's salvific aid was freely distributed independently of individual merit or effort and could not be refused or misused. They also advocated a rather strict penitential discipline, including occasional deprivation of the sacraments, in response to what they saw as the lax morality of their archenemies, the Jesuits. Jansenists would suffer persecution from the French ecclesiastic establishment and secular authorities, as well as from Rome, for their 'unorthodox' views. Arnauld himself would eventually flee France and spend much of his adult life in exile in the southern Netherlands.

In early 1641 Arnauld was still working on his doctorate at the Sorbonne when he received the *Meditations* from Mersenne. This was no doubt a calculated move by Descartes' friend to gain an ally from within the theology faculty. The strategy would work, at least with respect to Arnauld, if not his colleagues.

Arnauld had one of the keenest analytic minds of his era, and it shows in his objections. He divides these into three sections. In the first, 'The Nature of the Human Mind', directed at the Second Meditation, he raises the problem of how it follows from the fact that one is unaware that anything else belongs to one's essence

Pierre Drevet, after Jean Baptiste de Champaigne, *Antoine Arnauld*, 1696, engraving.

that nothing else – like a body – really does belong to one's essence. The most that can be concluded with certainty from such a premise, Arnauld insists, is 'that I can obtain some knowledge of myself without knowledge of the body', but not that there is a 'real distinction in existence between mind and body'.[22]

In the section 'Concerning God', Arnauld objects to a particular premise in Descartes' proof for the existence of God in the Third Meditation. God, he says, cannot be regarded as 'self-caused' in the sense of standing to Himself as an efficient cause, since an efficient cause must be distinct from and prior to its effect. 'Since every effect depends on a cause and receives its existence from a cause, surely it is clear that one and the same thing cannot depend on itself or receive its existence from itself.'[23] God would have to exist before He existed in order to cause His own existence, which is absurd. The only meaningful sense in which God is self-caused, Arnauld insists, is a 'negative' sense, whereby God's being does *not* derive from something other than God.

Arnauld's most famous objection to Descartes' overall strategy in the *Meditations* – one that has generated an enormous amount of discussion in the scholarly literature – is the apparent circularity of using reason to prove God's existence and benevolence when God's existence and benevolence are required by Descartes, in his sceptical pose, to validate the use of reason in the first place, as a reliable guide to truth. Arnauld puts the point succinctly yet, it seems, fatally.

> I have one further worry, namely how the author avoids reasoning in a circle when he says that we are sure that what we clearly and distinctly perceive is true only because God exists. But we can be sure that God exists only because we clearly and distinctly perceive this. Therefore, before we can be sure that God exists, we ought to be able to be sure that whatever we perceive clearly and distinctly is true.[24]

Finally, in the section 'Points Which May Cause Difficulty to Theologians', Arnauld highlights a problem that later does, indeed, cause very serious difficulties to theologians. He is concerned that Descartes' theory of body and matter is inconsistent with the Catholic dogma of the Eucharist enshrined by the Council of Trent. The Council had ruled at its Thirteenth Session, in 1551, that 'by the consecration of the bread and wine a change is brought about of the whole substance of the bread into the substance of the body of Christ our Lord, and of the whole substance of the wine into the substance of his blood.'[25] Because Descartes has emptied the material world of sensible qualities such as colour, taste and smell, leaving behind only extension and its modes (shape, size, motion and rest), his philosophy appears to Arnauld to be incompatible with the standard explication of transubstantiation in the sacramental host. Catholic theologians since the Middle Ages had explained transubstantiation – whereby there is a 'real' and not merely symbolic presence of Christ in the sacraments – with the use of Aristotelian forms and qualities. On the account favoured by the followers of Thomas Aquinas, the substance of the bread of the host is, through God's miracle on the occasion of the priest's utterance of the words *hoc est corpus meus*, converted into Christ's body; on the account preferred by the followers of Johannes Duns Scotus, the substance of the bread is annihilated and replaced by Christ's body. In both cases, though the bread-substance is no longer there after consecration, the accidental forms or real qualities of the bread (its visual appearance, its odour, its flavour) remain. This is why, despite being Christ's body, the host *looks*, *smells* and *tastes* like bread. This Scholastic account, over time, became so intimately connected with the Catholic dogma itself that it practically became one of its tenets.[26]

On Descartes' metaphysics, however, such a real and independent existence of accidents without their original substance is ruled out in principle. The bread is nothing but a particularly shaped parcel of extension, minute particles of matter organized in a certain way. There is no appearance, smell or taste to be miraculously suspended without its underlying (bread) substratum.

Arnauld's questions on this point – and they appear only in the second edition of the *Meditations* – drew Descartes, reluctantly, into dangerous theological terrain. Dealing with 'truths of revelation' (as opposed to truths of reason) was something that he tried to avoid as much as possible. However, he recognized the force of Arnauld's point and needed to address the problem, especially if he was not to alienate the 'learned doctors of the Sorbonne'. Thus, after a half-hearted attempt to clarify that 'I have never denied that there are real accidents,' Descartes makes a bold effort to reconcile his metaphysics with the real presence of Christ in the host. What affects the senses in perception, he says, is only the superficies of a body – the texture formed by the outermost particles of matter, with all of its microscopic nooks and crannies. 'For contact with an object takes place only at the surface, and nothing can have an effect on any of our senses except through contact.' Therefore, in transubstantiation, if the substance of Christ's body is confined by God within material 'boundaries' or dimensions that exactly match those that had characterized the now-absent bread, 'it necessarily follows that the new substance [Christ's body] must affect all our senses in exactly the same way as that in which the bread and wine would be affecting them if no transubstantiation had occurred.'[27] Christ's body looks, smells and tastes like bread because it has taken on an extension identical to that of bread and so affects our senses as bread does.

Arnauld certainly did not intend to get Descartes into trouble, but ultimately that is what happened. Descartes would later, in a 1645 letter to the Jesuit priest Denis Mesland, offer a somewhat different account of transubstantiation. Just as the particles of bread that we ingest in ordinary eating become a part of *us* because they congeal with the parts of our body that are united with our souls – a kind of 'natural transubstantiation' in diges- tion, he calls it – so the miracle of the host occurs when the matter of the bread gets 'informed by his [Christ's] soul simply by the power of the words of consecration' and thereby becomes Christ's body.[28]

Descartes feared that this philosophical foray into revealed theology would be 'shocking', and he was right. It is fairly certain that when the Catholic Church placed Descartes' writings on its Index of Prohibited Books in 1663, 'until they are corrected [*donec corregantur*]', it was Descartes' attempt at explaining transubstan- tiation in a novel way that was the aggravating factor.[29] Arnauld himself, who simply wanted to have clarification on this matter, was not sufficiently reassured. The topic came up again several times in their subsequent correspondence. One thing that both- ered Arnauld is that if Christ's body takes on the exact extension of bread, then, given Descartes' identification of a body with its extension, it *is* bread! Descartes replied that he preferred not to answer this question in writing.[30]

Descartes' failure to satisfy Arnauld on this count did not diminish the Jansenist's enthusiasm for the new philosophy. While Arnauld believed that Cartesians were better off acknowledging the inexplicability of this mystery of the faith, he would none- theless go on to become one of the staunchest, if more cantankerous and controversial, defenders of Descartes' philosophy in the second half of the century.[31] Descartes, in turn, was impressed by the young *Sorbonniste*. He was generally disappointed by the quality of the objections he had received so far. He tells Mersenne that 'the objectors seem to have understood absolutely nothing of what I wrote.'[32] But of Arnauld he says that 'he has put me greatly in his debt by producing his objections. I think they are the best of all the sets of objections, not because they are more telling, but because he, more than anyone else, has entered into the sense of what I wrote.'[33] In a rare moment of humility, he concedes that he has changed several things in the *Meditations*, 'thus letting it be known that I have deferred to his judgement'.[34]

Descartes was less taken by the objections lobbed against him by another prominent philosopher. Pierre Gassendi (1592–1655) was a French Catholic priest from Provence. He was also, somewhat incongruously for a man of faith, a devotee of the Epicurean philosophy and contributed to the revival of that ancient system in the seventeenth century.[35] Gassendi was, like Hobbes, a member of Mersenne's intellectual coterie and a defender of the mechanistic philosophy of nature against the Aristotelians. Unlike Descartes, however, who insisted on the infinite divisibility of extended bodies and the identification of body with space (thus rendering a vacuum metaphysically impossible), Gassendi was, in keeping with his Epicureanism, an atomist. There were, he claimed, fundamental, invisible and indivisible particles of matter moving in a void; the collision, aggregation and separation of these 'atoms' explained the nature of bodies and the observable phenomena.

Much of Gassendi's assault on Descartes' *Meditations* is informed by his empiricist theory of knowledge. Gassendi had little confidence in the ability of the human intellect to discover the true essences of things. Rather, knowledge comes through the senses, and all we can really grasp through them are appearances. He thus accepts a mitigated sceptical stance towards our capacity to understand the world around us.[36] One can know how things *seem*, and on the basis of that pursue a probabilistic science devoted both to uncovering regularities in nature and to formulating and testing hypotheses about hidden corpuscular causes. Gassendi is confident that the best, 'most likely' explanatory theory of the way the world works is the atomist mechanistic one. But, given the limitations of our faculties, we

cannot know with absolute certainty how things really are in their innermost nature.

Unlike Hobbes, Gassendi was not a thoroughgoing materialist. He distinguished between a corporeal soul in human beings, composed of a very fine concatenation of atoms that accounts for our vegetative and sensory functions, and an incorporeal (and immortal) soul, which accounts for our higher cognitive powers. This did not prevent him from having serious reservations about the kind of mind–body dualism that he found in Descartes, primarily on epistemological grounds. In both his long set of objections to the *Meditations* and a later, even longer critique, the *Disquisitio*

Claude Mellan, *Pierre Gassendi*, c. 1637–8, engraving.

metaphysica (Metaphysical Inquiry, 1644), whose subtitle was 'Doubts and Instances Against the Metaphysics of R. Descartes and His Responses', Gassendi attacks Descartes' conviction that he has discovered the essence of the mind as an immaterial substance. He agrees that the mind or soul is a 'thinking thing'; this is evident through the testimony of introspection. But he is not willing to say that we can know what the *essence* or inner substance of the mind is. Nor does he see that Descartes has provided any real explanation of how the mind functions. What is missing is a perspicuous account of thinking substance that reveals what thinking really is.

> When you go on to say that you are a thinking thing, then we know what you are saying; but we knew it already, and it was not what we were asking you to tell us. Who doubts that you are thinking? What we are unclear about, what we are looking for, is that inner substance of yours whose property is to think. Your conclusion should be related to this inquiry, and should tell us not that you are a thinking thing, but what sort of thing this 'you' who thinks really is. If we are asking about wine, and looking for the kind of knowledge which is superior to common knowledge, it will hardly be enough for you to say 'wine is a liquid thing, which is compressed from grapes, white or red, sweet, intoxicating', and so on. You will have to attempt to investigate and somehow explain its internal substance, showing how it can be seen to be manufactured from spirits, tartar, the distillate, and other ingredients mixed together in such and such quantities and proportions. Similarly, given that you are looking for knowledge of yourself which is superior to common knowledge (that is, the kind of knowledge we have had up till now), you must see that it is certainly not enough for you to announce that you are a thing that thinks

and doubts and understands etc. You should carefully scrutinize yourself and conduct a kind of chemical investigation of yourself, if you are to succeed in uncovering and explaining to us your internal substance. If you provide such an explanation, we shall ourselves doubtless be able to investigate whether or not you are better known than the body whose nature we know so much about through anatomy, chemistry, so many other sciences, so many senses and so many experiments.[37]

It might seem easy to accuse Gassendi of making a category mistake here. After all, Descartes wants to say that, because of the essential differences between mind and body and thus the unbridgeable gap between mental and mechanical explanations, we cannot possibly provide a mechanistic or 'chemical' investigation of the mind's activities. But this would seem to miss Gassendi's point. What he is demanding from Descartes is not literally a mechanistic account of thinking. Rather, he wants an account of thinking that makes the essence of the mind and the generation of its properties as clear as a mechanistic or chemical account does for wine and its properties. Such an account of thinking need not be framed in terms of matter and motion, but it must do the same kind of explanatory work and incorporate the study of thought into the domain of the natural (but not necessarily the physical) sciences. It is an important challenge that Gassendi issues here, a request for the scientific basis of the mind's activities – perhaps an early expression of the so-called hard problem of consciousness[38] – and it is a shame that Descartes does not take it more seriously.[39] Of course, given Gassendi's sceptical stance, he is also certain that it is a request that Descartes, or anyone else, cannot possibly satisfy.

The best we can do, Gassendi believes, is to think of the nature of the mind by way of analogy with body. He is not claiming that the mind *is* a body or material thing. He is simply insisting that

Descartes has not proven that it is an *im*material thing. Although he argues elsewhere that reason can provide *probable* knowledge of the mind's immateriality, this is something we can know for certain only by faith.[40]

> Why is it not possible that you are a wind, or rather a very thin vapour, given off when the heart heats up the purest type of blood, or produced by some other source, which is diffused through the parts of the body and gives them life? May it not be this vapour which sees with the eyes and hears with the ears and thinks with the brain . . . You reach the conclusion that thinking belongs to you. This must be accepted, but it remains for you to prove that the power of thought is something so far beyond the nature of a body that neither vapour nor any other mobile, pure and rarefied body can be organized in such a way as would make it capable of thought.[41]

The problem of 'thinking matter' – whether a purely material system, properly structured, could either naturally give rise to thought or, at least, be endowed with thought by God – occupied philosophical minds in the seventeenth and eighteenth centuries. It is a question that intrigued Leibniz, Boyle and Locke, among others.[42] Gassendi thought that the corporeality of the mind is, if not impossible, rather unlikely. But his point in the Fifth Set of Objections to the *Meditations* is only that Descartes' arguments do not establish the human soul's immateriality. 'You still have to prove that being capable of thought is inconsistent with the nature of body.'[43]

Gassendi raises a number of other problems for Descartes' dualist metaphysics, some of which would prove to cause ongoing trouble for Cartesian philosophy. How, for example, are thoughts or ideas in an immaterial mind supposed to be able to represent and thus make known material bodies? Material images at least resemble the physical objects they represent. But there can be no resemblance whatsoever between a material body and an immaterial thought. 'If it [the mind] lacks parts, how will it manage to represent parts? If it lacks extension, how will it represent an extended thing?'[44]

Even more problematic is the question of mind–body interaction. There appear to be causal relations between motions in the body and thoughts in the soul. When the body is damaged, there is a feeling of pain; when one wills to move one's arm, the arm moves. But the only intelligible model of causality, Gassendi seems to assume, is the mechanical one, which requires local contact: bodies pushing other bodies. An immaterial soul, however, has no extension, no physicality and no motion, so how could it come into contact with the body and move it? 'Given that you move many of your limbs', Gassendi asks, 'how could you accomplish this unless you were in motion yourself? . . . Since it is you who cause [*sic*] your limbs to move, and they never assume any position unless you make them do so, how can this occur without movement on your part?'[45] Some degree of ontological likeness is thus required not only for representation, but for causation as well.

> How can there be effort directed against anything, or motion set up in it, unless there is mutual contact between what moves and what is moved? And how can there be contact without a body when, as is transparently clear by the natural light, 'naught apart from body, can touch or yet be touched'?[46]

It is hard to see, Gassendi continues, how on Descartes' principles there can even be a union between mind and body in a human being. As we have seen, Descartes had suggested that

the mind is 'intermingled' with the body. Gassendi does not
understand how this is possible.

> You will have to explain how that 'joining and, as it were,
> intermingling' or 'confusion' can apply to you if you are
> incorporeal, unextended and indivisible . . . for there can
> be no intermingling between things unless the parts of
> each of them can be intermingled . . . Must not every union
> occur by means of close contact? And, as I asked before,
> how can contact occur without a body? How can some-
> thing corporeal take hold of something incorporeal so as
> to keep it joined to itself? And how can the incorporeal
> grasp the corporeal to keep it reciprocally bound to itself,
> if it has nothing at all to enable it to grasp or be grasped?[47]

These are the earliest statements of the so-called mind–body
problem facing Cartesian dualism, a problem that Descartes'
seventeenth-century followers tried to address in various ways, and
that would haunt the philosophy of mind down to the twenty-first
century.[48] Descartes himself was not very troubled by it, at least at
first. He never really responded to this particular objection in his
initial replies to Gassendi. Later he did write to his good friend
and eventual literary executor Claude Clerselier (1614–1684)
to say only that 'the whole problem contained in such questions
arises simply from a supposition that is false and cannot in any
way be proved, namely, that if the soul and the body are two
substances whose nature is different, this prevents them from
being able to act on each other.'[49]
    Gassendi's objections were the longest of all, and they clearly
rubbed Descartes the wrong way. Things did not get off to a good
start, with Gassendi sarcastically addressing Descartes as 'O Mind',
and Descartes returning the favour by calling Gassendi, whom
he took to be a materialist, 'O Flesh'. The tone of the debate only

degenerates from there, with Descartes complaining about Gassendi's 'tedious and repetitious assertions' and accusing him of 'using the imagination to examine matters that are not within its proper province'. Any careful reader will see, Descartes concludes, 'that he should not judge how many arguments you [Gassendi] have from the number of words you produce'.[50]

Interestingly, Descartes was much less dismissive of the challenge of accounting for mind–body union and causal interaction when the problem was raised for him a few years later. The change in his demeanour might have been partly due to the fact that his correspondent this time was a princess.

IF, DURING HIS EARLIER travels in Germany and his time with the Catholic army of the Duke of Bavaria, Descartes was present at (and even participated in) the Battle of White Mountain in 1620, he unwittingly observed (and perhaps helped facilitate) the downfall of the father of someone who would become a close friend and confidant.

Frederick V was the Elector of the Palatinate – one of the principalities charged with selecting the emperor of the Holy Roman Empire – and the leader of the Protestant Union. In 1618, with sectarian conflicts roiling the region, the Protestant states of Bohemia rebelled against the sitting emperor, Matthias, and their king-elect and Matthias's designated successor, Ferdinand II, both Catholics from the House of Habsburg. (Among the Bohemians' first steps was to throw two of Ferdinand's representatives out of a third-storey window, in the famous 'Defenestration of Prague'.) The Bohemian crown was then offered to Frederick, who accepted it in the summer of 1619. Matthias had died that March, and so, just a few days after Frederick's coronation, Ferdinand was elected Holy Roman Emperor. Among the new emperor's first acts was to send his army and the forces of the Catholic League into

Bohemia to restore his rule there. Frederick soon lost the support of many of his Protestant allies, and his remaining forces were soundly defeated at White Mountain, near Prague. Frederick and his wife Elizabeth Stuart, daughter of James I of England, fled their German lands. By 1621 they were settled in the Dutch Republic, where they were offered refuge in The Hague by the stadholder, Prince Maurits of Nassau. It was a family affair, as Maurits was Frederick's maternal uncle (Frederick's mother was Louise Juliana of Nassau, a daughter of Willem the Silent and thus Maurits's sister).

Among the many children of Frederick and Elizabeth – now nicknamed the 'Winter King and Queen' because of the brevity of their Bohemian reign – was a brilliant and learned daughter, Elisabeth (1618–1680), erstwhile princess of Bohemia and the Palatinate.[51] In the late 1620s, after a few years under the protection of her sister Charlotte, who was married to the Elector of Brandenburg, Elisabeth joined her parents in The Hague. It was from their Dutch court that, in the spring of 1643 and with the help of Descartes' friend Pollot, Elisabeth, who knew Latin, initiated a long-term correspondence with the author of the *Meditations*.

In her first letter to Descartes, in May 1643, Elisabeth gets right to the point. She immediately raises the problem of mind– body relations.

> I ask you please to tell me how the soul of a human being (it being only a thinking substance) can determine the bodily spirits, in order to bring about voluntary actions. For it seems that all determination of movement happens through the impulsion of the thing moved, by the manner in which it is pushed by that which moves it, or else by the particular qualities and shape of the surface of the latter. Physical contact is required for the first two

conditions, extension for the third. You entirely exclude the one [extension] from the notion you have of the soul, and the other [physical contact] appears to me incompatible with an immaterial thing.[52]

Descartes, writing from Egmond aan den Hoef, responds to Elisabeth's query with much more patience than he showed in his non-response to the same question from Gassendi. 'I can say with truth that the question your Highness proposes seems to me that which, in view of my published writings, one can most

Gerard van Honthorst, *Elisabeth of Bohemia*, 1636, oil on canvas.

rightly ask me.'[53] He explains that in the *Meditations* he was more concerned with proving the distinction of mind and body and with how the mind thinks than with their union and how the mind can act on and be acted upon by the body. But now he is happy to help her understand this latter set of issues.

There are, he says, three 'primitive notions' on which all our knowledge of mind and body is formed. The first is the notion of extension, through which we can understand all the properties and powers of bodies and which serves as the basis for inquiries in physics. The second is the notion of thought, which regards the soul alone, its perceptions and volitions. Neither of these primitive notions can help us understand the relationship between mind and body. For example, we should not try to understand mind–body interaction on the model of body–body interaction. For that, rather, we call upon a third primitive notion, which concerns the union of mind and body and 'on which depends that [notion] of the power the soul has to move the body and the body to act on the soul, in causing its sensations and passions'.[54] It is this conception, Descartes says, that philosophers have used, falsely, to explain how gravity works. The real quality of 'heaviness' that the Scholastics attributed to bodies was supposed to be an immaterial cause united with the body that, by some means other than physical contact, made it fall to the earth. He suggests that Elisabeth think of the mind–body union and interaction in precisely the same way.

The princess does not find any of this very illuminating. Indeed, she says, it simply begs the question. She cannot conceive of any mode of causal interaction other than the mechanistic one, which requires bodily contact. Moreover, she rightly observes that the exact same difficulty of understanding how an immaterial thing can act on a material thing applies to the case of Scholastic gravitation by way of a 'real quality' as to the case of Cartesian mind–body union. 'I admit', she says, 'that it is easier for me to concede matter and extension to the soul than to concede the capacity to move a body and to be moved by it to an immaterial thing.'[55]

Descartes explains in a subsequent letter that the first two primitive notions belong to 'the pure understanding' alone. We know what extension and thought are through the intellect working on those concepts. The mind–body relation, however, is 'known very clearly by the senses'. Thus one should not try to understand how mind can act on body and vice versa by way of intellectual inquiry. Rather, 'it is in using only life and ordinary conversations and in abstaining from meditating and studying those things which exercise the imagination that we learn to conceive the union of the soul and the body.'[56] In other words, if one wants to know about the union and interaction between mind and body, it is better simply to pay attention, through introspection, to what is going on within oneself.

But, Elisabeth protests, all that such sensory and volitional experience can tell her is that the mind and the body *do* interact, and this is something of which she was already perfectly aware. What she wants to know is *how* this is possible if the mind is an immaterial substance. 'I find that the senses show me that the soul moves the body, but they teach me nothing (no more than the understanding and the imagination) of the way in which it does so.'[57] Perhaps, she suggests, there is more to the soul than Descartes is willing to allow, something like extension that, while not necessary for thinking itself, allows the soul to move and respond to the body.

Descartes and Elisabeth would engage in a philosophically rich correspondence – with occasional meetings in person – for the next six years, until Descartes left the United Provinces for Sweden. In nearly sixty letters – a volume exceeded only by Descartes' correspondences with Mersenne and Huygens – they covered a large range of topics. The metaphysical question of mind–body relations never really arose again, although they often discussed how one's mental state (especially beliefs) can affect one's physical health, and vice versa. Descartes, avoiding the hard problem of interaction, simply explains that 'the construction of our body is such that certain movements follow in it naturally from certain thoughts.'[58] They also reviewed various mathematical and scientific matters, including rather specific explanations of phenomena in mechanistic physics and chemistry. In a letter of August 1644 Descartes told Elisabeth that

> even if we were to admit that particles of water and those of quicksilver [mercury] were of the same size and shape and that their movements were similar, to explain how quicksilver ought to be much heavier than water, it suffices to suppose only that each particle of water is like a little cord which is very soft and very loose and that those of quicksilver, having fewer pores, are like other little cords which are much harder and tighter.[59]

Much of their correspondence, though, is devoted to the emotions and mental and physical health. Descartes sympathetically informs Elisabeth that 'the most common cause of a low-grade fever', from which she seems to have been suffering, 'is sadness.' He cites how

> the stubbornness of fortune in persecuting your house continually gives you matters for annoyance which are so public and so terrible that it is necessary neither to conjecture very much nor to be particularly experienced in social matters to judge that the principal cause of your indisposition consists in these.[60]

Elisabeth, in turn, thanks Descartes for the comfort he provides in the midst of her family's travails. 'Your letters, when they do not teach me, always serve as the antidote to melancholy, turning my mind from the disagreeable objects that come to it every day to the happiness that I possess in the friendship of a person of your merit, to whose counsel I can commit the conduct of my life.'⁶¹

This discussion of well-being led, naturally, to ethics and the pursuit of happiness. They compare notes on Aristotle, Seneca and Epictetus, and it is in Descartes' letters to Elisabeth – as well as in his late treatise *The Passions of the Soul*, which he wrote at her prompting – that we find his views on moral philosophy. 'True happiness', he tells her, 'consists . . . in a perfect contentment of mind and an internal satisfaction that those who are the most favoured by fortune ordinarily do not have and that the sages acquire without fortune's favour.' The means to achieving this contentment requires a person merely to follow three fairly simple rules:

> The first is that he always try to make use of his mind as well as he can, in order to know what must be done, or not done, in all the events of life. The second is that he have a firm and constant resolution to execute all that reason advises him to do, without having the passions or appetites turn him away from it. It is the firmness of this resolution that I believe ought to be taken to be virtue . . . The third is that, while he so conducts himself as much as he can in accordance with reason, he keep in mind that all the goods he does not possess are, each and every one of them, entirely outside of his power.⁶²

Descartes has clearly profited from his reading of Seneca and Epictetus. His definition of virtue as firmness in the resolution to abide by the dictates of reason and pursue only those goods to which that faculty directs us; his reminder that most of the goods of this world are subject to fortune and thus beyond our control; and his recommendation that we should therefore focus more on our judgements and attitudes towards things, which *are* in our control, and accept calmly whatever God brings our way – all of this clearly recalls the ethical doctrines of the ancient Stoics, which were enjoying a revival in the seventeenth century.[63]

God does indeed bring *all* things our way, Descartes reminds Elisabeth, including the things that depend on our wills and, apparently, even the volitions themselves. This led her to inquire, in a series of letters in the autumn of 1645, how such universal providence might be reconciled with any kind of meaningful freedom in human beings. 'Since we feel ourselves to have [free will], it seems that it is repugnant to common sense to think it dependent on God in its operations as well as in its being.' Her assumption is that for the will to be free, it must be undetermined by causes, especially an omnipotent divine cause. 'I confess to you as well that even though I do not understand how the independence of our will is no less contrary to the idea we have of God than its dependence is to its freedom, it is impossible for me to square them.'[64]

Descartes is not very troubled by the conundrum. 'The independence that we experience and feel within us and that suffices for rendering our actions praiseworthy or blameworthy is not incompatible with a dependence that is of another nature, according to which all things are subject to God.' He helps himself, though, by changing the terms of the problem somewhat and referring not so much to God's omnipotence or causal power as to God's omniscience. A king who knows that two of his subjects who are mortal enemies will inevitably fight if he orders them both to a place where he also knows they will necessarily encounter each other does not take away their freedom and responsibility for the duel that follows; the king's foreknowledge of what will happen and his actions in arranging the circumstances so that it does happen does not *compel* the two men to do what they do.

'His knowledge, and even his will to determine them there in this manner, do not alter the fact that they fight one another just as voluntarily and just as freely as they would have done if he had known nothing of it.' Similarly, God's foreknowledge of how human beings will choose to act in certain circumstances, and even God's having originally put those inclinations in them and so disposing conditions around them such that they do act on those inclinations, does not constrain or compel them to so act, and thus does not detract from the freedom of their choice.[65] Still, Descartes admits elsewhere, an understanding of how divine providence leaves the human will free is beyond our finite intellects. 'We can easily get ourselves into great difficulties if we attempt to reconcile . . . divine preordination with the freedom of the will, or attempt to grasp both of these things at once . . . We cannot get a sufficient grasp of [God's infinite power] to see how it leaves the free actions of men undetermined.'[66]

In the dedicatory letter to the *Principles of Philosophy* (*Principia philosophiae*) of 1644, Descartes says to Elisabeth that

> the outstanding and incomparable sharpness of your intelligence is obvious from the penetrating examination you have made of all the secrets of these sciences, and from the fact that you have acquired an exact knowledge of them in so short a time. I have even greater evidence of your powers – and this is special to myself – in the fact that you are the only person I have so far found who has completely understood all my previously published works. . . . Your intellect is, to my knowledge, unique in finding everything equally clear; and this is why my use of the term 'incomparable' is quite deserved.

Even making allowance for the exaggerated encomiums characteristic of early modern book dedications, it is clear that Descartes'

respect for Elisabeth as a fellow intellectual is sincere. Were the
two *more* than just colleagues in the Republic of Letters? More
than just good friends? Elisabeth never married; an arrangement
with Ladislav IV, king of Poland, fell apart when Elisabeth refused
to convert to Catholicism. The difference in social rank between
her and Descartes – she was royalty, after all – makes a romantic
relationship unlikely.[67]

IN NOVEMBER 1641, shortly after the appearance of the *Meditations*
in Paris, Descartes wrote to Mersenne to inform him that the
work was now also being printed in Amsterdam. The problem
was that the exclusive permission (*privilège*) granted to Michel
Soly was enforceable only within France. This left the door open
for publishers elsewhere to come out with their own pirated
editions. To forestall this, and also to be able to make corrections
to the work, Descartes commissioned a Dutch publisher to
produce a second edition.

> One of my friends had told me that several houses [in
> the United Provinces] wanted to publish [my *Meditations*],
> and that I could not stop it, since the licence to publish
> owned by Soli is valid only for France, and they are so free
> here that even a licence for the States would not hold
> them back. So I preferred there to be one publisher who
> would undertake it with my approval and my correc-
> tions, and who by advertising the project would stop the
> plans of others; this seemed better than letting an edition
> come out without my knowledge, which would be found
> to be full of mistakes.

Descartes gave the exclusive permission to the firm run by
Louis Elzevir in Amsterdam, 'on condition that he does not send

any copies to France so as not to do any wrong to Soli [*sic*]'. Not
that Descartes was very happy with his collaboration with Soly.
'I have no cause to be very satisfied with Soli: it is now three
months since the book was published and he has still not sent
me any copies.'[68]

The second edition came out later than expected, in the spring
of 1642, due to 'the negligence of the publisher'.[69] The volume
contained not only corrections to the first edition, but a new
subtitle; instead of 'In which the existence of God and the immortality of the soul are demonstrated', it read 'In which the existence
of God and the distinction of the human soul from the body are
demonstrated'. Descartes apparently came to realize that he does
not, in fact, demonstrate the soul's immortality in the work,
although he does lay the metaphysical groundwork for it. Descartes
now also included something that he had kept out of the first
edition: his engagement with Arnauld's questions about transubstantiation. His speculations on a topic so sensitive among Catholics
would be less risky in a book published in a Protestant land.[70]

The second edition had an additional, seventh set of objections
as well, from the Jesuit Pierre Bourdin (1595–1653), a professor
of mathematics at Clermont College in Paris. These came to
Descartes unsolicited; he says, 'I certainly do not remember ever
having asked the writer for his opinion.' At first, they were not
entirely unwelcome. Descartes thought that engaging Bourdin
might help in his campaign to gain an endorsement of the work
from the Jesuit camp and increase the chances of his writings
being added to the curriculum in their schools – ideally, to replace
the Scholastic textbooks then in use. Once he started reading
Bourdin's objections, however, he quickly realized that this was
not going to be a productive discussion.

The exchange with Bourdin is almost as long as the one with
Gassendi. And to Descartes, it was just as annoying, perhaps
even more so. Bourdin says he is addressing Descartes' 'method

for investigating truth', but most of his comments are on the
procedure of doubt of the First Meditation and the start of the
reconstruction of knowledge in the Second Meditation. Some
of Bourdin's complaints, while not tactfully put, are not entirely
unreasonable, and were taken up by later critics. This includes
his protest that in the First Meditation Descartes has played
the sceptic all too well and taken doubt to such an extreme that
he actually leaves himself with no means to climb back out of
the hole he has dug and establish a solid body of knowledge.
'The method goes astray by failing to reach its goal, for it does
not attain any certainty. Indeed, it cannot do so, since it has itself
blocked off all the roads to the truth . . . your method cuts its
own throat or cuts off all hope of attaining the light of truth.' By
the end of the First Meditation, in other words, Descartes seems
to have fatally undermined the ability of reason to resolve the
epistemological crisis into which he has drawn himself. As Bourdin
puts it, 'everything is doubtful . . . and hence we have nothing
left which will be the slightest use for investigating truth.'[71]

Descartes was not impressed. He sees the long attack on what
is really just a propaedeutic exercise in the *Meditations* as a hack job.
Bourdin is mocking, derisive, condescending and dismissive.
Referring to one of the 'rules' of Descartes' method of doubt,
whereby anything even remotely dubitable should in fact be
doubted, he proclaims that 'if anyone were to understand the rule
in the sense just described and wanted to use it in order to discover
what is true and certain, he would be wasting his time and effort by
working without any reward, since he would no more achieve his
goal than its opposite.'[72] Turning, then, to Descartes' discovery of
his first absolutely indubitable truth, 'I am, I exist,' Bourdin remarks
sarcastically 'This is excellent, my distinguished friend! You have
found your "Archimedean point", and without doubt you can now
move the world if you so wish. Look: the whole earth is already
shaking.' As for Descartes' general strategy, Bourdin says: 'Permit

me here to admire your skill once again. In order to discover what is certain, you make use of what is doubtful. To bring us out into the light, you order us down into the darkness.'[73]

Needless to say, Descartes did not see Bourdin's objections as worthy of a respectable member of the Society of Jesus, one whom he had hoped would give his treatise an honest and constructive examination. Descartes finds his rambling commentary to be thoroughly disingenuous. The French Jesuit misrepresents his arguments and does not take his epistemological project seriously. Descartes had a hint that this would be the case well beforehand.

> When, some eighteen months ago, I saw a preliminary attack of his against me which, in my judgement, did not attempt to discover the truth but foisted on me views which I had never written or thought, I did not hide the fact that I would in future regard anything which he as an individual produced as unworthy of a reply.[74]

Initially under the impression that Bourdin's objections were composed 'at the instigation of the Society as a whole', he now sees that it would be 'a sin to suspect that this work was produced by men of such sanctity'. It is too full of quibbles, sophisms, abuse and 'empty verbiage'. Nonetheless, Descartes felt that since Bourdin was a representative of the Jesuits – 'a society which', he adds 'is very famous for its learning and piety' – he should take the trouble to read the objections and do his best to reply to his cavils.

Descartes decided to write, as well, to Bourdin's superior, Father Jacques Dinet (1584–1653), the head of the Jesuits in France. Dinet had been prefect of studies at La Flèche when Descartes was a student there. Part of the purpose of the letter was to complain about Bourdin. 'I thought that what I had before me was not just one man's essay but the balanced and careful assessment that your entire Society had formed of my views. When I read the essay, however, I was astounded to realize that I would have to revise my view completely.' Anyone reading Bourdin's piece, he says, would have to 'regard this essay as having been written with such bitterness as would be unseemly for a layman, let alone one whose vows require him to be more virtuous than ordinary men'.[75] While the Seventh Replies are a harsh retort to Bourdin, Descartes reassures Dinet that they should certainly not be taken as directed at the Jesuits themselves.

> The essay which the Reverend Father [Bourdin] has produced makes it quite clear that he does not enjoy the health and good sense which are to be found elsewhere in your Society. We do not think less of the head, or the whole person, just because there may be malign humours infecting his foot or finger, against his will and through no fault of his own.[76]

More important, though, was Descartes' wish to inform Dinet of 'something of the philosophy which I am writing at the moment' – namely, the *Principles of Philosophy*, a work in which he will 'submit to the public the sum total of my few reflections on philosophy' – and to defend himself against some very public criticisms he was lately receiving. He wants to assure this Jesuit leader that 'there is no need to fear my opinions will disturb the peace of the Schools' and that, 'since one truth can never be in conflict with another', his philosophical views pose no threat to theological orthodoxy. Despite several times referring to his philosophy in the letter as 'the new philosophy', he does not want his theories to be regarded as novelties. Fully aware of the paradox, he proclaims that 'everything in peripatetic [Aristotelian-Scholastic] philosophy . . . is quite new, whereas everything in my philosophy is old.' Whatever Aristotle himself may have said, his views were and continue to be controversial. Moreover, his philosophy seems to change depending on 'the fashion in the Schools, and hence it is exceedingly new, since it is still being revised every day'.[77]

Descartes anticipated that his letter to someone so high up among the Jesuits might make possible the inroads with that order that clearly were not going to come through Bourdin. Towards the end of the letter he expresses to Dinet his desire that 'you will take my views under your protection . . . Since you are in charge of that section of the Society which can read my work with particular ease since a substantial proportion of it is written in French, I am convinced that you are particularly well placed to help in this matter.'[78] Either way, Descartes says in closing, he would be grateful if the good Father would let him know 'the verdict that you and your members reach'.

It is unclear how successful Dinet was in gaining a positive hearing for Descartes among the Jesuits, either for the *Meditations* or, later, for the *Principles of Philosophy*. He would, however, organize a meeting in Paris between Descartes and Bourdin in the autumn of 1644, during one of Descartes' periodic visits to France. It was a cordial encounter, and the two men were able to reconcile somewhat and put the bad feelings behind them. Descartes even sent Bourdin a dozen copies of the just-published *Principles* so he could distribute them among other members of his order.[79] At the same time, Descartes made the rounds of Paris and did his own lobbying work among Jesuit acquaintances, hoping to rely on his credentials as a Jesuit-educated scholar. He even wrote to one of his former teachers at La Flèche, Father Etienne Charlet, to let him know of his dream that one day 'they [the Jesuits] will find in it [his philosophy] so many things that will appear true to them, and that can easily be substituted for the common opinions [that is, Aristotelian philosophy], and serve advantageously in explaining the truths of the faith'.[80]

THE LICENCE to print a book, or *privilège*, was one thing. It was essentially a copyright within a particular domain conferred by the secular authorities – in France, the king. Securing an *approbation* from a theology faculty was an entirely different thing, but, in some respects, no less important. Where a *privilège* provides one with financial protection and intellectual property rights, an *approbation* provides one with ecclesiastic protection. It essentially proclaims that there is nothing theologically objectionable about this work.

Did Descartes receive for the *Meditations* the *approbation* from the Sorbonne that he so desperately desired and for which he seems to have lobbied vigorously? Scholarly opinion is divided on this. On the one hand, the title page of the Paris edition does declare that it is published *Cum Privilegio et Approbatione Doctorum*, 'With privilege and the approval of the learned doctors [of the Sorbonne]'. (Such a royal privilege and Sorbonne approval would be meaningless for the Amsterdam edition, published in a Protestant republic, which is why it is not indicated on the title page of that edition.) The Paris edition also, as we have seen, contains a laudatory dedicatory preface to doctors of the Sorbonne.

Now a manuscript copy of the *Meditations* was presented to the theological faculty in the summer of 1641, and a review of its contents was commissioned. Because there was no subsequent condemnation, it has been claimed that the examiners did indeed approve the work, albeit one month after it was actually published. Moreover, the argument goes, no reputable printer would have dared put out a book whose title page proclaimed 'cum approbatione' if approval had not in fact been obtained.[81] Nonetheless, some scholars continue to insist that the effort to gain Sorbonne approval failed.[82]

By 1644, however, any trouble that might come Descartes' way from French Catholic theologians was of less concern than more immediate and dangerous threats that he was facing from within Reformed circles in the United Provinces.

SEVEN

The Cartesian Textbook

etween April 1641 and May 1643, Descartes was living in the castle of Endegeest, just outside of the university town of Leiden. The French physician and scholar Samuel Sorbière (1615–1670), writing in 1642 after a visit to Descartes, notes that the philosopher 'lives near Leiden in a comfortable retreat, like another Democritus. He is taken up with his speculations and he communicates his thoughts and experiences to no mortal, except to Picot and to a chemist from Leiden, Hogeland. He will publish his Physics in two years time.'[1] Around the same time, Descartes himself told Huygens that 'I am philosophizing here [in Endegeest] very peaceably and in my usual way, that is, without rushing.'[2]

What neither Sorbière nor Descartes mentions is that the peace and quiet of Descartes' country retreat was now being disrupted in a most unpleasant way. He was in the early stages of a series of quarrels that would make things very difficult for him for the next several years and would lead him to think seriously of leaving the Dutch Republic altogether.

IF THE *DISCOURSE ON METHOD* and its accompanying essays had introduced Descartes to the European intelligentsia as a major, albeit not uncontroversial, thinker, the *Meditations* only increased his fame (or, to some, his infamy). He was now gaining

Jan Lievens, *René Descartes*, 1644–9, chalk on paper.

adherents, most notably in Dutch university arts and medical faculties. Cartesian metaphysical and physical principles were on their way to becoming the century's scientific paradigm, at least among progressive and independent minds. Later natural philosophers, such as Leibniz and Newton, would be able to offer their theories only against the background of, and in explicit opposition to, Cartesian science. This growing influence of Descartes' ideas was a matter of great concern to many academic and ecclesiastic authorities.

As we have seen, Descartes believed, with unreasonable optimism, that his philosophy had a chance of being adopted in schools and universities to replace that of Aristotle. This explains why, even before finishing the *Meditations*, he started work on a broad presentation of his entire system, from metaphysics to physics, including detailed causal explanations of a variety of celestial and terrestrial wonders, 'in an order which makes it easy to teach'. The 'Physics' to which Sorbière refers is Descartes' *Principles of Philosophy* (which Descartes himself, throughout his writings, refers to as 'ma physique'). Descartes was nearing completion of this textbook that, he hoped, would finally satisfy all those who clamoured to know how everything fitted together, and especially how his mechanistic accounts of light, gravity, magnetism, combustion, tides and other phenomena could be 'deduced' from the most general principles of nature, which in turn are secured by indubitable metaphysical starting points. The *Principles* – which Descartes finished after moving 'near Alkmaar op de hoef [that is, Egmond aan den Hoef], where I have rented a house'[3] – includes a good deal of material that he had hoped to publish in *The World* (in French) a decade earlier, before the condemnation of Galileo. In fact, he describes his work on the *Principles* as a matter of 'teaching [*The World*] to speak Latin'.[4]

Descartes knew the Scholastic textbook tradition well. He had studied from these *compendia* and *summae philosophiae* when he was at La Flèche. In the winter of 1640–41, in order to prepare himself for the objections to his *Meditations* that he expected to receive from theologians and despite his general disinclination to read the books of others, he took some time to reacquaint himself with a number of 'the most commonly used' of such works, particularly by Jesuit authors.[5] The typical Aristotelian textbook, used for teaching in the liberal arts curriculum in preparatory colleges and university faculties – for example, the *Summa philosophiae quadripartita* by the French theologian Eustachio a Sancto Paulo (a member of the Feuillants, a Cistercian order), which Descartes was busy reading that winter and even referred to as 'the best book of its kind ever made'[6] – was divided by broad philosophical topics. Thus the four parts of Eustachio's *Summa* were Logic, Ethics, Physics and Metaphysics. Descartes' own four-part *summa philosophiae* follows this model, sort of. He reversed the order of metaphysics and physics. Moreover, while there are some propositions of a moral or ethical nature in the work, he replaced logic with a preliminary discussion of the method and theory of knowledge – essentially, a detailed review of his epistemological progress in the *Meditations* towards clear and distinct ideas and the proper use of the will, only now presented more in the style of a systematic treatise than as a series of first-person, meditative reflections.[7]

Because Descartes' primary aim in the *Principles* is to present in full the metaphysical principles that he had long held back, along with the physics for which they provide the justificatory foundations, he is concerned in Part One ('The Principles of Human Knowledge') and the early articles of Part Two ('The Principles of Material Things') to elaborate on the conceptions of mind and body that he introduced in the *Discourse* and the *Meditations*. He is especially careful now to explain the basic ontology that underwrites the mind–body dualism.

Mind and body are, he insists once again, two distinct kinds of substance, where 'substance' is now defined – following a tradition going back to Aristotle – as 'nothing other than a thing which exists in such a way as to depend on no other thing for its existence'.[8] A substance is an ontologically independent, individual thing, something that exists by itself and can be conceived by itself. Strictly speaking, only God, the infinite being, is a substance, since God does not depend on anything else for his existence. However, Descartes grants that the term 'substance' is not univocal, and there are also finite substances – things that depend only on God for their existence and are independent from each other.

Each substance has its own 'principal attribute' or essential nature, which makes it the kind of stuff it is. For the mind, that principal attribute is thought, which Descartes now identifies in terms of consciousness: 'By "thought" I understand everything which we are aware of as happening within us, in so far as we have awareness of it.'[9] Body, however, is, as he discovered in the *Meditations*, nothing but extension; to be a body is simply to be spatially dimensional.[10] It follows that the properties that belong to thought and the properties that belong to extension are radically dissimilar and mutually exclusive: 'There are various modes of thought such as understanding, imagination, memory, volition, and so on; and there are various modes of extension, or modes which belong to extension, such as all shapes, the positions of parts, and the motions of the parts.'[11] Sensations (such as colour, warmth and pain), just like emotions and appetites, belong to thought; they are not 'real things existing outside the mind'.[12] Sense perception, Descartes warns once again, 'does not show us what really exists in things, but merely shows us what is beneficial or harmful to man's composite nature'.[13] The only properties really existing in bodies are shape, size, position and motion or rest. Bodies, in other words, are merely geometrical entities, with actually existing bodies also endowed with impenetrability.

If body is nothing but extension, Descartes continues, then, as he had suggested in *The World* and now explicitly argues, there is neither truly empty space nor atoms, 'pieces of matter that are by their very nature indivisible'. Any three-dimensional space – any extension – is a body, and any corpuscle of matter, no matter how small, just because it is extended in three dimensions, can be further divided.[14]

What does in fact break the material plenum up into parts, and thereby introduce physical diversity into the universe, is motion. This is where the great number and variety of individual bodies comes from. 'All the variety in matter, all the diversity of its forms, depends on motion.'[15] Different bodies are simply different ways in which matter is in motion and rest. And any particular body is the body it is because it is a collection of material parts that are at rest, or at least a consistently stable position, relative to each other but in motion relative to surrounding bodies. By 'motion', Descartes means only the transference of a body from the vicinity of one set of bodies that are in immediate contact with it to the immediate vicinity of another set of bodies; in other words, nothing other than the change of position of a parcel of matter relative to other parcels of matter.

Much of this would have been familiar to readers of *The World* (had there been any at the time – not even Mersenne saw a copy), the *Discourse* and the *Meditations*, only now presented and argued for in greater detail. But in the metaphysical parts of the *Principles* Descartes also lays out in programmatic form some of the basic theoretical parameters that are to guide scientific inquiry. Perhaps the most important of these is the elimination of teleology, or 'final causes', from explanations in natural philosophy. A final cause is the end towards which some thing or process is purposively moving or at which some action aims. An Aristotelian botanist would say that the final cause of an acorn's development is the full-grown oak tree, and the final cause of an athlete's training is victory in competition. For certain medieval and early modern theologians, the final cause of God's creation of the cosmos is his own glory. According to Descartes, however, appeals to God's purposes or to any kind of goal-orientated behaviour within nature – like Aristotelian bodies 'seeking' their natural resting place, or things behaving or having the properties they do for the sake of achieving some end – have no place in physics. Explanations are to be framed solely in terms of what we have seen the Aristotelians call 'efficient causation', whereby an effect follows simply and necessarily from the nature, power and activity of a causal agent.

> It is not the final but efficient causes of created things that we must inquire into. When dealing with natural things we will never derive any explanations from the purposes which God or nature may have had in view when creating them . . . For we should not be so arrogant as to suppose that we can share in God's plans.[16]

This is an important methodological principle of the new mechanistic philosophy. With the reduction of matter to extension and the identification of motion as the sole agent of change in nature, Descartes has now sanctioned the only legitimate terms of scientific explanation. When inquiring into why certain natural phenomena come about, one may not appeal to divine providence or purposiveness within nature. Descartes, good Catholic that he is, certainly is not claiming that there is no providence in the cosmos. The correlations of the mind–body arrangement, for one – feeling pain when one puts one's hand into fire – are testimony to God's goodness, as they are established by God for our own well-being. Indeed, the whole course of nature is the effect of divine providence. Later, in the *Passions of the Soul*, Descartes is careful note that 'nothing can possibly happen other than as Providence has determined from all eternity.'[17] But within the domain of scientific inquiry, nothing is to be explained because God wished it so or because it exists 'for the sake of' anything else. Nor, as Descartes has been saying all along, is it acceptable to introduce any kind of spiritual or vital elements in bodies. Rather, the explanation of any phenomenon should be framed solely in terms of the way in which material particles, moving according to the laws of nature, arrange by impact and adhesion to produce an organism of a certain complex structure and function and bring about certain effects.

With the metaphysics in place – the 'roots' of the tree of knowledge – Descartes is prepared to turn to the most general physical principles of the cosmos (the 'trunk'), including the mechanics of hard and fluid bodies. His first move is to inquire into the laws of nature of a world created by a God whose essence is simple, whose activity is immutable, and who is the first and sustaining cause of motions among bodies. In this transition from metaphysics to physics in Part Two of the *Principles*, Descartes satisfies a promissory note from years before and carries out an argument only sketchily presented in earlier writings. In the *Discourse*, he recalls that

> I showed [in *The World*] what the laws of nature were, and without basing my arguments on any principle other than the infinite perfections of God, I tried to demonstrate all those laws about which we could have any doubt, and to show that they are such that, even if God created many worlds, there could not be any in which they failed to be observed.[18]

Descartes now, in the *Principles*, provides a more explicit deduction and demonstrates, a priori and with absolute certainty, what the most general laws of nature are (and must be) from his understanding of the divine attributes alone (although, in keeping with the stricture against teleology, treating God only as an efficient cause, without any appeal to divine purposes). For the discovery of these laws, no controlled experimentation or even basic observation of the world is necessary. He does not need to witness apples falling from trees, examine the motions of the planets or do any mathematical calculations. He does offer some empirical examples to illustrate the laws – such as the centrifugal force exerted by a stone being swung around in a sling as a case of the tendency to rectilinear motion – and make their content familiar to his readers. But all he really needs to know to carry out his deduction of these most universal physical principles is that the cosmos was created by a God having certain attributes. This theological information, supplemented by already demonstrated metaphysical claims about matter and motion, is sufficient to ground a logical derivation of the laws. (Unlike Newton, Descartes is not really interested in formulating the precise mathematics of force and motion, but only in specifying in broad quantitative terms very general kinematic rules that cover the basic movement and interaction of ideal geometric bodies.)

Descartes begins his deduction of the laws of nature with the claim that 'God is the primary cause of motion' in the universe who 'in His omnipotence created matter along with its motion and rest'. When God created the world out of nothing, he introduced a certain amount of motion into the matter composing it. With this premise in hand, Descartes believes he can immediately demonstrate that the most universal law of nature governs the conservation of motion. This law states that the total quantity of motion in the universe (measured in any body as the product of its mass and its speed) is constant and will never change. Any gain or loss of motion in one part of the cosmos must be compensated for by an equivalent loss or gain of motion in some other part. This law follows immediately from the immutability of God:

God's perfection involves not only his being immutable in Himself, but also his operating in a manner that is always utterly constant and immutable. Now there are some changes whose occurrence is guaranteed either by our own plain experience or by divine revelation, and either our perception or our faith shows us that these take place without any change in the creator; but apart from these we should not suppose that any other changes occur in God's works, in case this suggests some inconstancy in God.

There are continual changes in the motions of individual bodies everywhere; some bodies speed up, others slow down and even come to rest, owing to their collisions. But there can be no change in the overall quantity of motion in Creation, for this would imply a change in the immutable creator who first implanted and now conserves motion in it, which would be absurd. God does not change his mind or his activity.

God imparted various motions to the parts of matter when He first created them, and He now preserves all this matter in the same way, and by the same process by which he originally created it; and it follows from what we have said that this fact alone makes it most reasonable to think that God likewise always preserves the same quantity of motion in matter.[19]

This same divine immutability, in tandem with the conservation law, provides Descartes with justification for his first subordinate law of nature, essentially a law of inertia: 'Each and every thing, in so far as it can, always continues in the same state; and thus what is once in motion always continues to move.' There is no change unless there is a cause or reason for the change, and thus no body changes its state of motion or state of rest unless such change is brought about by an external cause.

Descartes' argument for this first law, in both the *Principles* and *The World*, is rather opaque, and amounts only to the claim that because God is immutable, 'always acting in the same way, He always produces the same effect.'[20] But the underlying reasoning seems to be that if there were a spontaneous gain or loss of motion in a body – a gain or loss not brought about by some causal interaction with another body – there would be no compensating loss or gain of motion elsewhere. This self-generated change in motion would therefore be something that appears out of nowhere, and thus would amount to an increase or decrease in the total quantity of motion in the universe, which would be a violation of the conservation law.[21]

The second subsidiary law of nature is that 'all motion is in itself rectilinear.' All bodies in motion have a natural tendency to move in a straight line, and they will do so unless their path is impeded by some other body. Any body that is moving in a circle (such as a stone in a sling) still has a centrifugal tendency to move in a straight line away from the centre of the circle it is describing. (These first two laws of nature formulated by Descartes appear in Newton's physics as a single law of inertia.) Descartes says that 'the reason for this second rule is the same as the reason for the first rule, namely the immutability and simplicity of the operation by which God preserves motion in matter.'[22]

The argument here relies on a principle that was a commonplace among medieval and early modern theologians and philosophers – and Descartes was no exception – namely, that God, after initially creating the world, must continuously conserve it from moment to moment to keep it in existence. God, in other words, is not only a 'cause of becoming' (of coming into being; in Latin, *causa secundum fieri*) but a sustaining cause, a 'cause of being' (*causa secundum esse*). Were God to cease the creative action by which He brought the world into being, the world would cease to be, much as the light and heat of the sun would disappear were the sun to stop actively causing it. In this respect, God's causal action is fundamentally different from that of a housebuilder who, having once built a house, no longer needs to act for the house to persist in existence. This is true not only of the world at large but of each and every existing thing within it. God's activity is required to conserve in being each and every body and soul he has created. Now when God conserves an individual body, he takes into account only the motion that is occurring in that body at a single instant, 'at the very moment when He preserves it, without taking any account of the motion which was occurring a little while earlier'. Therefore, Descartes argues, the tendency or determination of motion of a body at any given moment can be only along a straight line, since curvilinear motion requires reference to at least two moments of motion and the relation between them.

The third law of nature states that 'if a body collides with another body that is stronger than itself, it loses none of its motion; but if it collides with a weaker body, it loses a quantity of motion equal to that which it imparts to the other body.'[23] Both parts of this law are simply the application of the universal conservation of motion principle to collisions between perfectly hard bodies; the law ensures that in these interactions no overall gain or loss of motion occurs in the physical world. In order for the collisions and resulting transfers of motions among bodies to preserve the total quantity of motion in the universe, any loss or gain of motion in one part must be compensated for by a reciprocal gain or loss of motion in another part. If a body collides with another body that is so much stronger than itself that it cannot move that second body, then while there is a reason why the first body's *direction* of moving should change, there is no reason why it should lose any of its motion. And if a body impacts upon a body that it *can*

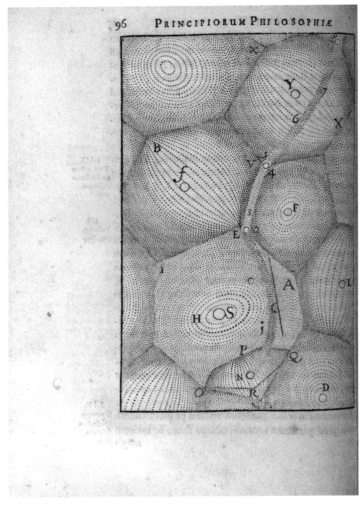

move, then its own loss of motion will be equivalent to any gain of motion by the body being moved.

Still operating in a purely deductive manner, Descartes proceeds to derive from these three general laws of nature a number

The cosmos and its vortices, from *Principia philosophiae* (1644).

of particular 'rules' governing the impact of solid bodies and the transference of motions that result from their collisions. For example, the first rule says that if two perfectly hard bodies of equal size and equal speed are moving towards each other in a straight line and collide, each will rebound in the direction from which it came without any loss of its speed. The second rule states that if one body is even slightly larger than the other (both still moving at the same speed) and thus has a greater overall quantity of motion (mass × speed), then only the second body will bounce back and both bodies will move together in the first body's line of direction at that body's original speed.[24]

All of these laws, which came in for rough treatment later in the century by Christiaan Huygens, Leibniz and others, state only abstract tendencies under ideal conditions, in an environment devoid of friction or elasticity. In reality, however – at least according to Descartes – there are no truly empty spaces. Therefore all bodies move in, with and through a plenum of matter. The material cosmos, in other words, functions essentially like a fluid. There are vortices everywhere, such as those described in *The World*, with all matter moving only relative to, and displacing, other matter. This means that there is no body that does not face some resistance to its motion, and so no actual observations can possibly confirm the laws. But for Descartes this is irrelevant. He has demonstrated the laws with deductive rigour from first principles about God, the creator of nature. That, he insists, is all he needs to give his natural science absolutely certain foundations.

THE METAPHYSICS OF GOD, mind and matter and the laws of nature presented in Parts One and Two of the *Principles* are discovered solely by 'the light of reason'. On this background, Descartes can proceed to consider 'the observable effects and parts of natural bodies and track down the imperceptible causes and particles which produce them'.[25] In the remainder of the treatise, Descartes frames mechanistic explanations behind nature's diverse phenomena. These explanations are no longer based on stipulated, freestanding 'assumptions', as they were in *The World*, but 'deduced' – in Descartes' broad sense of the term, to include experimental testing – in an unbroken chain of reasoning from those higher principles. The explanations also agree with the observed phenomena. Thus, he claims, they are as 'true and certain' as can be.

> If a cause allows all the phenomena to be clearly deduced from it, then it is virtually impossible that it should not be true. Suppose, then, that we use only principles which we see to be utterly evident, and that all our subsequent deductions proceed by mathematical reasoning; if it turns out that the results of such deductions agree accurately with all natural phenomena, we would seem to be doing God an injustice if we suspected that the causal explanations discovered in this way were false. For this would imply that God had endowed us with such an imperfect nature that even the proper use of our powers of reasoning allowed us to go wrong.[26]

Of course, as Descartes had noted in the *Discourse*, there are many ways in which the particular features of the universe might plausibly be deduced (explained) from the most general principles. Any one of different possible mechanisms, each consistent with the metaphysical and physical foundations and with the observations, could be at work both in the formation of the cosmos and underlying any present phenomenon. Descartes says it would be 'arrogant for us to assert that we have discovered the exact truth where others have failed'. Thus, until a sufficient number of crucial experiments can be carried out that will eliminate competing explanations, the specific causes he provides for the arrangement of the heavens and the facts on earth should be regarded as only 'hypothetical'.[27]

There is more than just epistemic humility at work here. Descartes needs to be careful, and he knows it – especially as he considers how the cosmos in its general structure came to be as it is. As he turns in Part Three to 'the visible universe', he thus gives due recognition in the opening articles to 'the infinite power and goodness of God' and the 'beauty and perfection of his works'. He notes that

> there is no doubt that the world was created right from the start with all the perfection it now has. The sun and earth and moon and stars thus existed in the beginning, and, what is more, the earth contained not just the seeds of plants but the plants themselves; and Adam and Eve were not born as babies but were created a fully grown people. This is the doctrine of the Christian faith, and our natural reason convinces us that it was so.[28]

The reader is further warned that because God's providential wisdom exceeds our understanding, we cannot grasp 'the ends which God set before himself in creating the universe'. Thus what he claims to offer is but a hermeneutical cosmogeny that, though strictly speaking 'false', provides a deeper understanding of things than the biblical account of creation. 'If we want to understand the nature of plants or of men, it is much better to consider how they can gradually grow from seeds than to consider how they were created by God at the very beginning of the world ... although we know for sure that [things] never did arise in this way.'[29]

Behind Descartes' strategy to present what is now a metaphysically grounded account of the origin of things – with matter, once put into motion by God, forming structures according to the laws of nature rather than God's will – still as merely hypothetical is prudence. He is hedging his bets. 'Our hypothesis', he concedes, may not be 'the exact truth', but it does have 'practical benefit for our lives . . . because we shall be able to use it just as effectively to manipulate natural causes so as to produce the effects we desire'.[30] Such cautious instrumentalism is no doubt a remnant from his experience with *The World* and the Galileo affair.

With the theological caveats in place – and their sincerity is questionable – Descartes proceeds to explain the formation and evolution of the cosmos and major celestial phenomena involving the sun, the moon, the stars, comets and planets (both the 'higher planets' – Mercury, Venus, Mars, Jupiter and Saturn – and the 'lesser planets', that is, the moons orbiting the planets). Among the topics covered are the placement of the different planets relative to the sun, the spinning of the earth on its axis (which is caused by the rotational motion of the material vortex in which the planet is embedded), the motion of comets through the celestial vortices, and 'why the moons of Jupiter move so fast while those around Saturn move so slowly or not at all'. There is a discussion of why stars seem to appear and disappear, why comets have tails but planets do not, and an extended account of sunspots, which he says are nothing other than the conglomeration of tiny particles of matter on the surface of the sun into large masses.

Retreating somewhat from his earlier reluctance to promote a heliocentric cosmos, Descartes now argues explicitly that 'Ptolemy's hypothesis does not account for the appearances.' He still cloaks his version of the Copernican theory as a 'hypothesis (or supposition that may be false) and not as the real truth.'[31] Nonetheless, he insists that it 'seems to be the simplest of all both for understanding the appearances and for investigating their natural causes'. He remains circumspect, however, and relies on a mere technicality to protect himself from theological censors.

Strictly speaking, Descartes says, the earth does *not* move. This is because it is always in the same position relative to the parts of the material vortex (or 'heaven') that surround it and that, through their own motion, cause its rotation. Given Descartes' definition of motion as translation of a body from the vicinity of immediately surrounding bodies, the earth is immobile with respect to the minute bodies of its vortex with which it is contiguous, and thus it is stationary.

> In the strict sense, there is no motion occurring in the case of the earth or even the other planets, since they are not transferred from the vicinity of those parts of the heaven with which they are in immediate contact, in so far as these parts are considered as being at rest.[32]

Nonetheless, the rotational motion of the larger vortex within which the earth's own rotating vortex is embedded carries the earth in revolutions around the sun. A similar mechanism is at work for the other planets. There is no mistaking Descartes' preferred cosmology: 'All the planets', he notes, 'are carried around the sun by the heaven.'[33]

Finally, in Part Four of the *Principles*, titled 'The Earth', Descartes considers such terrestrial phenomena as gravity, magnetism, the nature of water and the ebb and flow of the tides, fire and lightning, the formation of mountains, plains and seas, and the process of sensation in animals and human beings. Everything, of course – even the so-called occult qualities – takes place according to the principles of the mechanical philosophy. Thus gravity or heaviness is not some mysterious power acting at a distance. Rather, as explained in *The World*, it is an effect of larger parts of matter being forced downwards, towards the earth, by the vigorous motion of smaller and lighter particles centrifugally moving upwards through the motion of the vortex. In the article of the *Principles*

realis ejuſdem magnetis, verſus Auſtralem Terræ dirigi-
tur, ac neuter altero magis deprimitur, quia particulæ
ſtriatæ cum æquali vi ab utraque parte ad illos accedunt.
Sed in polo Terræ Boreali, polus *a* magnetis N omnino
deprimitur, & *b* ad perpendiculum erigitur. In locis autem

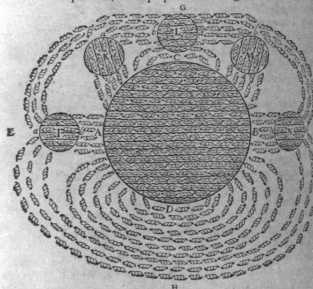

intermediis, magnes M polum ſuum *b* magis aut minùs
erigit, & polum *a* magis aut minùs deprimit, prout magis aut minùs vicinus eſt polo Terræ B. Quorum cauſſa
eſt quòd Auſtrales particulæ ſtriatæ, magnetem N ingreſ-
ſuræ,

Magnetism, from *Principia philosophiae* (1644).

titled 'How all the parts of the earth are driven downwards by the celestial matter, and so become heavy', Descartes explains that

> the power which the individual particles of celestial matter have to move away from the centre of the earth cannot achieve its effect unless, in moving upwards, the particles displace various terrestrial particles, thus pushing them and driving them downwards. Now all the space around the earth is occupied either by particles of terrestrial bodies or by celestial matter. All the globules of the celestial matter have an equal tendency to move away from the earth and thus no individual one has the force to displace any other. But the particles of terrestrial bodies do not have this tendency to so great an extent. So whenever any celestial globules have any terrestrial particles above them they must exert all their force to displace them.[34]

It is noteworthy that for Descartes gravity remains a force operative only on terrestrial bodies. He did not yet realize, as Newton would later, that gravity operates on *all* bodies in the cosmos – that it is the force, for example, that keeps the planets in their orbits.

Similarly, magnetism is not a mystical power of attraction acting between bodies across empty space and drawing them together. Rather, it is explained by minute, grooved particles of matter circulating throughout nature. The differently orientated grooves on these particles determine the direction of their passage through the poles of the earth – either south to north or north to south. As the particles come around the material ether surrounding the planet to head back into the pole from which they started, they enter the tiny pores found in iron but not other bodies.

The magnet attracts iron, or rather, a magnet and a piece of iron approach each other. For in fact there is no attraction there. Rather, as soon as the iron is within the sphere of activity of the magnet, it borrows force from the magnet, and the grooved particles that emerge from both the magnet and the piece of iron expel the air between the two bodies. As a result, the two approach each other in the same way as two magnets do.[35]

Matter, motion and impact: for Descartes, and for later partisans of the mechanistic world picture – whether or not they agree with Descartes on the constitution of body or the details of particular explanations – all natural phenomena can be explained in these simple terms. As he proclaims, 'I have described this earth and indeed the whole visible universe as if it were a machine.'[36]

There remains, however, a particular item in the world that escapes explanation by mechanistic principles. The human mind or soul, being an immaterial substance, is a domain unto itself and not subject to the deterministic laws that govern the behaviour of material things. The faculties of intellect and will operate according to their own principles. At the same time, the human soul is intimately connected with the human body, and many (but not all) mental events are, by divine institution, correlated in law-like ways with physical events in that body.

A sword strikes our body and cuts it; but the ensuing pain is completely different from the local motion of the sword or of the body that is cut – as different as colour or sound or smell or taste. We clearly see, then, that the sensation of pain is excited in [the mind] merely by the local motion of some parts of our body in contact with another body.[37]

Descartes' account of human sensory experience in the *Principles* finally brings to the public some of his physiological views from the *Treatise on Man*. Motions are communicated from the body's extremities to the brain via the nerves, 'which stretch like threads from the brain to all the limbs' and whose channels are inflated with 'animal spirits'.[38] When these fluid-like spirits carry the motions to the centre of the brain, they cause a movement there of the pineal gland, which Descartes now calls 'the seat of the soul'. The different ways in which this gland is moved is naturally coordinated with various sensations, emotions and appetites in the mind. When the gland is moved one way, there occurs in the mind a feeling of pain referred to some body part; when it is moved another way, a feeling of warmth, and so on.

The brief discussion of sensation – what Descartes calls 'a few observations' – appears towards the end of Part Four. He tells the reader that his original plan for the *Principles* was to include two additional parts, one devoted to biological phenomena (animals and plants) and one devoted to the human being. The latter would presumably have been a fuller presentation of material from the *Treatise on Man*. It might also have included a more extensive discussion of the soul alone, including its passions and actions. However, none of this material on vegetation, animal or human physiology, or human psychology ever made it into the *Principles*. Descartes confesses, towards the end of the work, that, even at this late point, 'I am not yet completely clear about all the matters which I would like to deal with there, and I do not know whether I shall ever have enough free time to complete these sections.'[39]

THE PRINCIPLES is just as ambitious a treatise as Descartes envisioned *The World* to be, perhaps even more so. With extraordinary confidence – or what his critics considered impertinent boldness – Descartes intended his textbook to provide the metaphysical and physical tools for a thorough understanding of the celestial and terrestrial realms. In the letter to Abbé Picot that serves as the preface to the 1647 French translation of the work, he insists that 'in order to arrive at the highest knowledge of which the human mind is capable there is no need to look for any principles other than those I have provided.'[40] Nothing lies outside the scope of Descartes' project. Having established the principles of 'immaterial or metaphysical things', and then 'deducing' from these an account of the most general features of the cosmos and concrete theories to explain a wide range of particular topics, he boasts that 'there is no phenomenon of nature which has been overlooked in this treatise.'[41] All of those phenomena – except for those that take place within the human mind – are explained solely according to the clear and distinct notions that inform his philosophy of nature.

> This is much better than explaining matters by inventing all sorts of strange objects which have no resemblance to what is perceived by the senses (such as 'prime matter', 'substantial forms', and the whole range of qualities that people habitually introduce, all of which are harder to understand than the things they are supposed to explain).[42]

At the same time, and in a rhetorical gesture intended to forestall his potential critics, he insists that 'this philosophy is nothing new but is extremely old and very common . . . in attempting to explain the general nature of material things I have not employed any principle which was not accepted by Aristotle and all other philosophers of every age.'[43] True enough, perhaps; but what Descartes does not say is that he has also *not* employed many elements essential to the Aristotelian picture.

Descartes believed that his philosophy would open up the world to view and make its operations transparent to human reason. His explanations cover some of the most puzzling and opaque processes of nature, and even show why the laws of nature themselves are what they are. His boldness goes well beyond that of Galileo just a decade earlier. While the Florentine scientist played an important role in the mathematization of the study of nature and was, as we have seen, likewise committed to a corpuscularian account of phenomena, he was not interested in an investigation into the metaphysical foundations of physics. And though Galileo was occupied, like Descartes, with explaining such things as sunspots, the earth's tides and the solidity of bodies, he did not aspire to provide an exhaustive and systematic account of the world's phenomena.

Descartes' ambitions went too far even for the great scientist at the other end of the century. Isaac Newton was, compared with Descartes, a rather reserved natural philosopher. In his own *Principia* – the *Philosophiae naturalis principia mathematica* (Mathematical Principles of Natural Philosophy) – he focused primarily on the mathematical laws of bodily forces. In several writings he vigorously remonstrated against making metaphysical or even phyiscal assumptions and engaging in speculation about the ultimate and hidden causes of these forces. He was no less committed than Galileo and Descartes to the corpuscular philosophy of nature, and was on occasion willing to consider various material mechanisms behind gravitational attraction. (When pressed, he suggested at one point that it was the result of a material *aether* operating on bodies.) But Newton generally resisted such conjectures that go so far beyond what is empirically verifiable and mathematically demonstrable. 'Hypotheses non fingo' – 'I frame no hypotheses' – he famously says in the General Scholium that appears in the second edition (1713) of his *Principia* when discussing the ultimate causes of nature's forces.

Hitherto I have not been able to discover the cause of those properties of gravity from phenomena, and I frame no hypotheses; for whatever is not deduced from the phenomenon is to be called an hypothesis; and hypotheses, whether metaphysical or physical, whether of occult qualities or mechanical, have no place in experimental philosophy.[44]

It is clear that with this remark Newton had Descartes' physics in mind. Its various hypotheses about mechanical causes, such as the subtle matter that is supposed to explain gravity by pushing bodies downwards, are, to Newton's mind, no more justified than the occult qualities and other metaphysical hypotheses of the Aristotelians.

By the end of the *Principles*, and despite finally showing how 'the whole of my physics' rests on metaphysical foundations, Descartes' own confidence in the status of his theories appears to waver. He seems torn between standing by his original ambition for absolute certainty and settling for something less exalted and more realistic, a kind of pragmatic certainty. He says that 'my explanations appear to be at least morally certain . . . that is, as having sufficient certainty for application to ordinary life, even though they may be uncertain in relation to the absolute power of God.'[45] But such a concession may be more a formal expression of piety than a serious epistemological doubt about what he has accomplished. For Descartes immediately goes on to say that 'my explanations possess more than moral certainty.' Absolute certainty, he notes, 'arises when we believe that it is wholly impossible that something should be otherwise than we judge it to be'. Perhaps, in light of God's omnipotence, it is possible, in principle, that things might be different from what the light of nature has compelled him to believe. However, since that intellectual faculty has been provided by a benevolent and non-deceiving God, '[it] cannot lead us into error, so long as we are using it properly and are thereby perceiving something distinctly.' Because Descartes has 'deduced these results of mine in an unbroken chain from the first and simplest principles of human knowledge', any other explanation of the world is, for all intents and purposes, unintelligible.[46]

Still, Descartes closes the *Principles* with the requisite disclaimer. 'I submit all my views to the authority of the Church.'

WHEN DESCARTES LEFT FRANCE for good in 1628, interruptions from family, friends and even total strangers were not the only things he was fleeing. In the Dutch Republic, he was able to put some distance between himself and the less tolerant intellectual milieu under Louis XIII and his prime minister, Cardinal Richelieu. He knew the power wielded by the Church in his Catholic homeland. French theologians who were troubled by his philosophy and would regard his ideas as inconsistent with religious dogma could easily – and with royal authority behind them – make life difficult for him.

By contrast, Frederik Hendrik, the stadholder of Holland at the time, was the most tolerant and enlightened person to hold that position in the first half of the century. While the prince was occasionally at odds with the liberal regents who governed the towns of this most liberal of the provinces, and while he was not above colluding with the more conservative Calvinists when it suited his political purposes, he refused to be beholden to Reformed ecclesiastics. In the late spring of 1637, Descartes told Huygens, Frederik Hendrik's secretary, that 'I would never have decided to retire to these provinces and to prefer them to many other places . . . had I not been persuaded by my great respect for his Highness [Frederik Hendrik] to entrust myself entirely to his protection and government.'[47]

Descartes believed early on that, despite straying from Aristotelian orthodoxy, and thus at risk of being seen as promoting novelties in philosophy, he was less likely to be persecuted for this in Holland. Many years later, he was still certain that, on the whole, he had made the right choice. Near the end of his time in the United Provinces, Descartes expressed his overall satisfaction with the life he had been allowed to lead there. It could be a relatively peaceful place, especially for a resident foreigner who was smart enough not to get involved in Dutch political and religious affairs. In a letter to Brasset in April 1649, Descartes says that

> it was not considered strange if Ulysses left the enchanted islands of Calypso and Circe, where he could enjoy all imaginable pleasures, and that he so scorned the song of the Sirens, in order to go live in a rocky and infertile country, insofar as this was the place of his birth. But I [speak as] a man who was born in the gardens of Touraine, and who is now in a land where, if there is not as much honey as there was in the land that was promised by God to the Israelites, there is undoubtedly more milk.[48]

The Dutch Republic was certainly no paradise. But the freedoms it offered and the relative laissez-faire attitude in intellectual matters – especially in the province of Holland – suited Descartes' purposes well.

Still, even in this tolerant land, where neither Rome nor the bishops of Paris had any influence, one had to be careful in navigating a complicated and often treacherous theological-political landscape. The Remonstrant controversy especially, in both its religious and political dimensions, while somewhat quiescent in the 1630s and early 1640s, still smouldered. Descartes, unfortunately, was not always careful to keep a low profile, and much of his time during his final decade in the Netherlands was taken up by some very nasty disputes.

Soon after the publication of the *Discourse* in 1637, Descartes acquired several admirers in Dutch universities. Among these was Henricus Regius (Hendrik de Roy, 1598–1679), a professor in the faculty of medicine at the University of Utrecht. Regius had obtained permission to teach physics as well, and he used this opportunity to introduce Cartesian scientific principles in his lectures. Descartes' philosophy had already begun appearing in some of the university's courses and disputations, but Regius was bolder than most and quite popular among students. He also went beyond anything that Descartes himself would have sanctioned.

While Regius' regular teaching in opposition to 'the traditional philosophy' raised some hackles, the problems in Utrecht really began with a series of disputations held under his direction. These were devoted to very Cartesian theses about body and the material world and the elimination of all spiritual items from nature other than the human soul. Especially problematic was a defence of the claim that the union of soul and body in a human being was only 'accidental' rather than 'substantial'.

Descartes' dualism of mind and body had to be handled carefully, lest one either anchor the soul too much in the body and thereby undermine its independence and immortality or, at the other extreme, exaggerate its independence from the body to the detriment of what theologians traditionally considered the unity of human nature. At one point, Descartes would caution Regius that what he is saying about the mutual independence of mind and body made the union of these two substances in a human being too much of a merely accidental conjunction rather than a real union. True, Descartes told Regius, the soul can exist without the body; indeed, it does so, in its immortal condition after the death of the body. But in this lifetime, the soul can properly be described as being – and here Descartes diplomatically recommends Aristotelian-Scholastic terminology – the 'substantial form' of the body, intimately united with it and dependent on it for many of its mental states (sensations and passions) and functions. In late 1641, while examining a draft of a disputation sponsored by Regius, Descartes wrote to his disciple to point out those things that are likely 'to give offence to theologians'. Most important, he warns Regius, is that 'in your theses you say that a human being is an *ens per accidens* [an entity by accident, rather than an *ens per se*, or an entity by itself]. You could scarcely have said anything more objectionable and provocative.'[49] If the body is not truly an *essential* part of a human being, then the doctrine of the resurrection of the body, an important element in orthodox Reformed dogma – and something about which Remonstrants had reservations – would be undermined.

Among those provoked by Regius' theses – which he took to be Descartes' theses as well – was Gisbertus Voetius (Gijsbert Voet), an influential Reformed minister in Utrecht and, in 1641, the rector of the university. Voetius was a conservative firebrand, a raving Counter-Remonstrant, anti-Catholic and, not least, an antisemite. He was deeply troubled by Regius' abandonment of Aristotelian natural philosophy. In his own series of disputations, endorsed by the Faculty of Theology, he soundly attacked his Utrecht colleague for introducing the 'new philosophy' into the studies which he supervised. Suggesting that 'there is so much that we do not know', and that therefore one should be content with the learning handed down by the Schools, Voetius angrily accused the Cartesian philosophers in his university of arrogance and even delusions of divine grandeur in making bold claims to knowledge about the cosmos.[50]

Descartes in turn advised Regius on how to deal with his superior. He suggested that Regius take a respectful, even obsequious approach – 'Remember that there is nothing more praiseworthy in a philosopher than a candid acknowledgement of his errors'

– and directed him to make some harmless concessions in matters of language: 'Why did you need to reject openly substantial forms and real qualities?'[51]

Despite recommending that Regius put aside his ego and take a more conciliatory tack, Descartes was himself growing annoyed with Voetius. In a subsequent letter to Regius, he offers a harsh assessment of the rector's character and the unreasonable degree of control he exercised in Utrecht. 'I did not know that he reigned over your city, and I believed it to be more free . . . I pity that city that it is so willing to serve so vile a pedagogue and so miserable a tyrant.'[52] It was now Descartes' battle as much as Regius', since it was ultimately his own philosophy (albeit poorly represented by Regius) that was being maligned. Descartes was not one to back down, but then neither was Voetius.

Much to Descartes' vexation, Regius continued to make things worse. He rejected the cautionary advice of Descartes and of

Anna Maria van Schurman, *Gisbertus Voetius*, 1647, engraving.

sympathetic but more moderate university colleagues. In February 1642 he made a very public reply to Voetius in the form of a pamphlet aggressively defending his philosophical principles. In this *Responsio*, Regius went on the counterattack and accused the Aristotelians of atheism and of implying that the human soul, as the substantial form of the body, is itself material.[53]

Voetius was apoplectic to be so publicly rebuffed, and by one of his own professors. This had gone too far. He convened the university senate and directed it to ask the city council to order the seizure of all copies of Regius' pamphlet and to censure the theories it defended. The Utrecht councillors followed suit, and in April 1642 they issued a condemnation of the 'new philosophy'. Meanwhile, the university stripped Regius of his right to give lectures on physics and restricted his teaching to medicine. It also forbade the further teaching of Descartes' ideas.[54] The members of the university's senate declared that they

> reject this new philosophy, first, because it is contrary to the ancient philosophy which, up to now and for good reason, has been taught in all the Academies of the world, and subverts its foundations; and second, because it turns the youth from the old and good philosophy and keeps them from achieving the peak of erudition . . . Therefore it is established that everyone teaching philosophy in this Academy must henceforth abstain from such [philosophy].[55]

Descartes had managed, for the most part, to stay personally out of the dispute. His role to this point, aside from being the author of the offending philosophical system, was limited to counselling Regius on how to handle things. Still, he was starting to feel the heat. In March 1642 he wrote to Mersenne to tell him about 'the impudence of Voetius'.

His great animosity against me comes from the fact
that there is a professor at Utrecht [Regius] who teaches
my philosophy, and his students, having had a taste of
my manner of reasoning, despise the common philosophy so much that they openly mock it. This has excited
an extreme jealousy against him [Regius] by all the other
professors, whose head is Voetius; and every day they
plead with the magistrates to get them to prohibit this
kind of teaching.[56]

If Descartes truly wanted to remain outside the fray, he made
a serious tactical misstep when, with the second edition of the
Meditations, he published his letter to Father Dinet. Aside from the
complaint about Bourdin, Descartes in this letter recounts at
length his unjust treatment in Utrecht, in the hope of receiving
more considerate treatment by the Jesuits. He defends himself
against the charges of atheism and corrupting the youth 'with
the principles of this presumed philosophy',[57] as well as the accu-
sation that his philosophy is opposed to the philosophy of the
ancients. Descartes also presents Voetius, referring to him not by
name but as 'the Rector', in highly unflattering terms. He suggests
that the theologian never actually read the books he cites in his
attack on Cartesian philosophy, only the tables of contents. He
also calls him 'malicious' and 'grumpy [*mordaces*]', and says that now
that, in 1642, Voetius is no longer rector, Utrecht need not deal
with the shame, ignominy and dishonour that he brought to the
university.

Descartes' letter to Dinet was easily accessible to Dutch
readers, especially after the more provocative parts were translated that same year. This very public indictment of Voetius
and of the University of Utrecht, which Descartes accuses of
preferring a slavish devotion to tradition over the pursuit of
truth, was not a wise step for someone who wanted only to be

left alone to continue his work and who wished to avoid distract-
ing quarrels. If Descartes thought his missive would put an end
to the matter, he was sorely mistaken. Indeed, the Dinet letter
only exacerbated things.

Voetius commissioned one of his minions, an Aristotelian
professor of logic and physics at Groningen named Martin
Schoock, to compose a response to Descartes' 'venomous letter' and the 'injuries, sarcasms and lies by which he [Descartes]
tried in vain to taint and tarnish the irreproachable reputation of
Doctor Voetius'.⁵⁸ Schoock opened a full offensive on Descartes'
philosophy, as well as on his character. With respect to mechanistic physics, for example, he argues that there is a radical
difference between the ways in which artificial machines and
natural organisms work, such that the former cannot be used as
a model to understand the latter.

> While we cannot deny that, with respect to certain works
> of nature, created *ex nihilo* by God – the omnipotent and
> wise architect of everything that exists – one can, in a
> certain measure, discover the same structure as that
> which is visible in certain machines produced according
> to the laws of mechanics, this should not be taken in such
> a way as to become the norm and the rule of all the works
> of nature, nor lead one to insist that, if one knows per-
> fectly the interior of machines, one is thereby immediately
> competent with respect to the works of nature.⁵⁹

Moreover, Schoock claims, not only does Descartes' master
argument against scepticism fail, but Descartes himself must *be*
a sceptic and an atheist. 'While giving the appearance of being
very worried about atheism, he does everything he can to teach
it and disseminate it.'⁶⁰ Descartes' demonstrations of God's existence are so 'weak and deceitful' that they were clearly designed

intentionally to lead people to conclude that God does not in fact exist. Descartes is thus, like the infamous atheist Lucilio Vanini (1585–1619), a man who 'presents himself as fighting atheism through Achillean arguments but who, subtly and secretly, injects the poison of Atheism in those who, because of their weakness of intellect, cannot discover the snake in the grass'.[61] For good measure, Schoock insinuates that Descartes has something to hide in his personal life. 'It is difficult to understand anything about his conduct in practical affairs. Who can explain all his hiding places and his changes of residence?' Descartes obviously has a guilty conscience, most likely because of his sexual licentiousness. '[Descartes] finds his pleasures among the madames whom he does not hesitate, it seems, to embrace passionately.'[62]

Descartes was not going to take this lying down. In the spring of 1643 he countered, perhaps imprudently, with a long (book-length) and accusatory open 'letter' to Voetius (*Epistola ad Voetium*), whom he understood to be behind, and perhaps the true author of, Schoock's offensive. Descartes insists that the vigour of the attacks against him are due to the fact that his opponents know that his philosophy is the true one. He denies once again that he is an atheist, although he also takes the opportunity to add some clarifications to his demonstrations of God's existence. Indeed, he claims, it is Voetius who is securing the spread of atheism through his intemperate condemnations. 'No one will ever again write against Atheists,' Descartes says, for fear of receiving like treatment from the irascible theologian.[63] In Part Seven of the letter, 'On the Merits of Gisbert Voetius', Descartes shows that he can give as good as he gets when it comes to character assassination. While he claims to be 'known to be a lover of peace and quiet above all other things', Voetius, he says, is 'exceedingly contentious, bitter and inappropriate'.[64] The theologian also lacks the one character trait that he appears to value, 'the most basic and fundamental of all virtues': charity. Voetius is nothing but an 'arrogant and obstinate [preacher who] does things that disturb the peace and harmony of the Republic'.[65]

The affair in Utrecht led to years of trouble for Descartes. A committee from the city council, to whom Descartes had sent copies of the *Epistola*, found it to be libellous. The council summoned him to come to Utrecht and respond to the charge by providing 'such verifications of his intentions that he judges to be useful'.[66] Although Descartes, living in Holland, was technically outside the jurisdiction of the Utrecht magistrates, there were extradition agreements between the two provinces. Descartes was sufficiently worried that he asked Henri Brasset to have his superior, the French ambassador, intervene with the stadholder and have the summons set aside. By 1645 the Utrecht city councillors were so tired of the whole affair and the trouble it was causing that they issued a decree forbidding the printing or dissemination of books *for or against* Descartes. The proscription was not consistently enforced, however, and the wrangling continued, with the fallout consuming a good deal of Descartes' time and energy well into the late 1640s.

As for Regius, whose lectures started the whole affair, it seems that when it came to philosophy he just could not get it right, or at least to Descartes' satisfaction. Having argued in 1641 for a merely 'accidental' union of mind and body, he later went to the other extreme and in his *Fundamentals of Physics* (*Fundamenta physices*, 1646) and *Explication of the Human Mind* (*Explicatio mentis humanae*, 1647) so deeply embedded the activities of the mind in the body that it was unclear in what sense it was an independent, and immortal, substance. There was, he maintained, no natural cause for the separation of soul from body, not even the death of the body; we can be certain of the soul's immortality only by faith and Scripture.

Descartes was not pleased. He accused Regius of both plagiarism (stealing parts of the unpublished *Treatise on Man*) and distorting his views. 'It appears that everything he wrote was taken from my writings,' Descartes charges in the Preface to the 1647 French translation of his *Principles*. 'But because he copied down the material inaccurately and changed the order and denied certain truths of metaphysics on which the whole of physics must be based, I am obliged to disavow his work entirely.'[67] Writing to Mersenne in October 1646, he angrily complains that

> A few days ago I saw a book which will make me hence-
> forth much less free in communicating my thoughts than
> I have been hitherto; it is a book by a professor at Utrecht,
> Regius, entitled *Foundations of Physics*. In it he repeats most
> of the things I put in my *Principles of Philosophy*, my *Optics*
> and my *Meteorology*, and piles up whatever he has had from
> me in private, and even things he could only have had by
> indirect routes and which I did not want him to be told.
> Moreover, he retails all this in such a confused manner,
> and provides so few arguments, that his book can only
> make my opinions look ridiculous, and give a handle to
> my critics in two ways. Those who know that he hitherto
> made great profession of friendship with me, and fol-
> lowed blindly all my opinions, will blame all his faults on
> me. And if I ever decide to publish the views I have not
> yet published, it will be said that I have borrowed them
> from him, since they will have some resemblance to what
> he has written.[68]

More than disavowing Regius' book, Descartes would go on to publish a booklet in which he harshly criticizes his ex-friend's writings. In the *Comments on a Certain Broadsheet* (*Notae in programma quoddam*, 1648), he expresses his puzzlement over just what Regius' inconsistent account of the mind–body union is. He also defends and explains his own account of innate ideas, which Regius had rejected in favour of an empiricism. Descartes never meant to say that there are fully formed ideas actually in the mind; rather, what is innate or in the mind by its very nature is a propensity to think certain thoughts and call up specific ideas (such as the idea of God).[69]

Any intellectual relationship, much less friendship, between Descartes and his troublesome disciple was over. 'I am forced to admit that I blush with shame to think that in the past I have praised this author as a man of the most penetrating intelligence, and have written somewhere or other that "I do not think he teaches any doctrines which I would be unwilling to acknowledge as my own."'[70]

Meanwhile, no sooner did Descartes feel that he had things in Utrecht under control – although Voetius continued with his attacks – than a similar battle over Cartesian philosophy was brewing in Leiden. This could be more problematic for Descartes from a legal perspective. Leiden was in the province of Holland, and so any formal measures taken by that city against Descartes personally – such as a summons to answer a charge of libel, should one be issued – would be enforceable.

The trouble in Leiden began, as in Utrecht, when a number of faculty at the university there started promoting Cartesian ideas. Adriaan Heereboord (1614–1661), a professor of logic, argued in a 1644 disputation that only Descartes' philosophy offered the possibility of true knowledge of nature. He said that the Aristotelians were interested in nothing more than slavishly following their ancient master and in conflating his philosophy with theology. 'A monstrous and monastic kind of philosophy was born which, with its boring and futile sophistries, corrupted everything.'[71] Heereboord and others defended Cartesian method in philosophical inquiry – beginning with doubt and proceeding only by assenting to what is known clearly and distinctly – and the tenets of Cartesian metaphysics and physics.

The attack on Aristotle in Leiden was received just as it had been in Utrecht. Conservative academics, led by the Counter-Remonstrant theologian (and sometime poet) Jacobus Revius (1586–1658), described the new philosophy as 'dangerous' to faith and morals and accused Descartes' local partisans of encouraging scepticism and freethinking. In 1646 the University of Leiden senate proclaimed that only Aristotelian philosophy could be taught and discussed. Descartes' philosophy was now officially banned – at least in public lessons – at two Dutch universities.

Descartes subsequently wrote to the curators at Leiden to protest some of the personal attacks that had been made against him by individual professors – he had been called, among other things, 'a blasphemer' – as they battled their Cartesian colleagues. In an attempt to calm things down, the university curators in May 1647 ordered professors in the faculties of theology and philosophy to cease any and all discussion of Descartes' philosophy, pro or con. Furthermore, they wrote to Descartes himself and requested that he stop causing trouble with his new and controversial opinions. In a letter to Elisabeth, Descartes complained that in Leiden 'they are turning a minor disagreement into a major dispute' and that the theologians 'want to subject me to an inquisition more severe than the Spanish one, and turn me into an opponent of their religion'.[72]

The controversy over Descartes' philosophy continued to spread, and by the end of the decade rancorous debates erupted in other universities throughout the Republic – Groningen, for example. The tranquil life of the mind that Descartes had sought in his rural Dutch retreat was becoming harder to sustain. It was enough to make him think twice about remaining in what was once 'this peaceful land' and consider a return to France. Writing from Egmond Binnen in May 1647, he tells Elisabeth:

> As for the peace I had previously sought here, I foresee
> that henceforth I may not get as much of that as I would
> like. For I have not yet received all the satisfaction that is
> due to me for the insults I suffered at Utrecht, and I see
> that further insults are on the way. A troop of theologians
> [at Leiden], followers of scholastic philosophy, seem to
> have formed a league in an attempt to crush me by their
> slanders.

He tells the princess that 'in the event I cannot obtain justice
(and I foresee that it will be very difficult to obtain), I think I
am obliged to leave these provinces altogether.'[73]

In fact, within the month Descartes was off to Paris and
Brittany, but only for a visit. He went primarily to deal with
some family and financial affairs and to see old friends, although
he also took advantage of the opportunity to oversee work on
the French translation of the *Principles*. While in Paris, he paid
a call on the mathematician and religious thinker – and one of
Arnauld's fellow Jansenists – Blaise Pascal (1623–1662). Pascal
showed Descartes the calculating machine he had designed, and
they discussed potential experimental testing of the possibility
of a vacuum. The trip undoubtedly provided a welcome respite
from the unpleasant tangles with Dutch theologians.

Still, despite all the trouble in Utrecht and Leiden – just the
kind of attacks on his philosophy from theologians that he had
hoped to avoid when he left France for the United Provinces
– Descartes very soon missed Holland. It was now his home, and
he had long come to appreciate, even to depend upon, its advantages and pleasures. He kept the trip to France short, and by early
autumn he was back in 'the happiness of a tranquil and retired
life' in Egmond-Binnen.

EIGHT

'A land of bears, rocks and ice'

y the mid-1640s an exhausted and decimated Europe was ready to put an end to decades of war that had cost nearly 8 million lives. After several years of negotiations on multiple fronts, delegations from France, Sweden, the Holy Roman Empire, the Papal States and the Dutch Republic, along with their allies in smaller principalities and federations, finally met in the Westphalian towns of Münster and Osnabrück in 1648 to ratify a series of peace agreements.

What had been a mere thirty years of war for most of those states was, for the Dutch and the Spanish, eighty years of conflict. When representatives from the two sides signed their names to the Treaty of Münster in May 1648, the outcome was not just peace but the formal recognition of the United Provinces as a sovereign and independent nation.

Not all of the Dutch provinces had been in favour of coming to terms with their former overlord. Holland – and Amsterdam in particular – led the pro-peace camp, but there was opposition in Utrecht, Zeeland and other quarters on political, military and economic grounds. They feared, especially, that their commercial interests would suffer with the reopening of ports in the southern Low Countries, still loyal to Spain, and a revival of the Flemish city of Antwerp. In the end, as usual, Holland and its allies in the peace party prevailed in the States General.

The preamble to the agreement signed by the Dutch and Spanish is an impressive document, even given the pro forma literary ornamentation that diplomacy demands.

> In the name of God and in his honor. Let all persons know that, after a long succession of bloody wars which for many years have oppressed the peoples, subjects, kingdoms and lands which are under the obedience of the Lords, King of Spain, and States General of the United Netherlands, these Lords, the king and the States, moved by Christian pity, desire to end the general misery and prevent the dreadful consequences, calamity, harm and danger that the further continuation of these wars in the Low Countries would bring in their train . . . and to put in the place of such baleful effects on both sides a pleasing, good, and sincere peace.

The first article of the treaty announces that 'this Lord King [Philip IV of Spain] declares and recognizes that the Lords States General of the United Netherlands and the respective provinces thereof . . . are free and sovereign states, provinces and lands upon which . . . he, the Lord King, does not now make any claim.' Subsequent articles detail the terms of the peace, including such contentious matters as trade in the East and West Indies, tariffs and taxation. Spain lifted the embargoes against Dutch ships, the Dutch agreed to allow Catholics in their lands to worship freely, and the two sides settled territorial claims in Flanders and Brabant, with Spain – despite pressure from some Dutch quarters for a reunification of the northern and southern provinces – keeping whatever was now in its possession. The treaty also stipulated that Spanish Catholics who travelled to the Dutch Republic and Dutch Protestants who travelled to Spain would each be 'required to conduct themselves in the matter of public exercise of religion with all piety, giving no scandal by word or deed and speaking no slander'.[1]

Throughout the Republic, news of independence was received with jubilation. Celebratory observances were held in The Hague, Amsterdam and other towns as people gathered to hear public readings of the treaty. Unfortunately, Frederik Hendrik, who as stadholder was the supreme commander of Dutch armed forces during the final two decades of the conflict, could not be present at any of the festivities. He did not live to see the peace for which he had so ardently lobbied among the combative Dutch constituencies. In March 1647 the 63-year-old Prince of Orange, under whose political and military leadership there was remarkable flourishing of Dutch art and culture in the first half of the century, died. The stadholdership of the major provinces of Holland, Utrecht, Zeeland, Gelderland and Overijssel passed to his son, the 21-year-old Willem II, Prince of Orange (and grandson of Willem the Silent).

The new stadholder had been no fan of peace with Spain, and accepted it only grudgingly. He would rather have continued the war, in league with France, not least to regain the Dutch-speaking lands of the southern Low Countries. His mother, Frederik Hendrik's wife Amalia van Solms, however, wished to see an end to the hostilities through which her husband had so brilliantly guided the Republic. This split within the family was but a microcosm of a greater and more dangerous division in Dutch society. The Peace of Münster did not really bring much peace, at least within the Republic. It was approved by the States General by only a narrow majority.

Willem II lacked his parents' sophistication and taste for high culture. He was also a bully. Where Frederik Hendrik generally preferred a conciliatory approach to domestic affairs, his son had a more aggressive style. Willem's main adversaries were Holland's regents. Amsterdam and Haarlem, especially, were centres of opposition to Willem's belligerent policies. Among the more contentious issues was the size of the army. Willem was at constant loggerheads with the liberal camp, whose leaders wanted to see a decrease in troops and in military expenditure now that the long war was over. A large standing army in peacetime was a drain on the economy, which had only recently begun to recover from a recession in the 1630s. The stadholder and his Orangist allies, however, insisted that Dutch homeland security was at stake. The Republic would not be safe from its enemies without strongly fortified garrisons along its borders. The robust debate – carried out in speeches, pamphlets, periodicals and proclamations – was often framed in terms of patriotism, with each side accusing the other of betraying the Republic and working on behalf of its adversaries.

Equally critical was the question of religious toleration. Willem was not an especially pious man, but he was not above catering to the more conservative elements of the Dutch Reformed Church when it was to his political advantage. He thus sought greater confessional uniformity in the Republic, partly for the sake of centralizing and consolidating his power. Despite the terms agreed to in the Peace of Münster, he instituted a clampdown on Catholicism. Priests were expelled, Catholic chapels and other institutions confiscated and 'cleansed', and worship forced to go underground, into *schuilkerken* (hidden churches – some of which, in fact, were well above ground, in attics).

What was really at stake in these final years of the 1640s was the political nature of the Dutch Republic itself. What kind of nation was it going to be: a decentralized federation, with power primarily in the provincial executive bodies (the States) and a relatively weak national government, or a unified realm under a monarch-like ruler? Would true sovereignty lie in the provinces, where the regent class held sway, or in the generality, dominated by the stadholder?

In the summer of 1650, his patience with Holland and the States party at an end, Willem went on the offensive. The stadholder laid siege to Amsterdam with a force of 10,000 soldiers. The city councils there and elsewhere were once again purged of anti-Orangist agitators and Remonstrant sympathizers, and leading regents were arrested and thrown into prison.

The Orangist triumph was short-lived, however. By November Willem II was dead, a victim of smallpox. His son Willem III – born just after the death of his father – would be in his minority for quite some time. Not for another 22 years would there be a stadholder installed in the major provinces. The political pendulum that had swung one way in 1618, under Maurits, now swung back to the other side. Power devolved to the regents and the provincial assemblies. For the next two decades the Republic would enjoy the period of 'True Freedom', a stadholderless era (for most of the provinces) under the national leadership of the grand pensionary of the States of Holland, Johan de Witt, and his partisans.[2]

The brief but repressive regime of Willem II, and especially his campaign against Catholics in the United Provinces, had to be of some concern to Descartes. It was one thing to take on fuming theologians in the schools. Descartes could hold his own in intellectual debate. He could even deal with university senates and city councils that, while formally banning discussion of the new philosophy, typically dragged their feet when it came to enforcement. But a broad retreat from the relatively tolerant policies of Frederik Hendrik could spell trouble for an independent-minded French philosopher who claimed to be willing to 'bear public witness to the fact that I am a Roman Catholic'.[3] It must have been especially worrisome to some close friends with whom Descartes was passing the time during the long, cold Dutch winters.

IN THE MIDST OF THE TURMOIL in Utrecht, Leiden and Groningen, Descartes was able still to take advantage of the relative peace and quiet in Egmond-Binnen to pursue his philosophical investigations and manage his growing correspondence. Among other things, he was engaged in revising the *Treatise on Man*, expanding it into the 'description of the functions of animals and men' that would turn up in the posthumous inventory of his papers as a manuscript titled *The Description of the Human Body* (*La Description du corps humain*).[4] Like the earlier treatise, this was an account of the formation and operations of the body without any participation of a soul.

With each passing year in his isolated quarters, though, the wintry weather during Europe's 'Little Ice Age' was wearing him down. Already in March 1641, while still living in Leiden, he had written to Mersenne that 'I have plenty of time and paper, but I do not have any material, if only because winter has begun once again in this country, and it snowed so much last night that one can now travel in the street by sled.'[5] Now that Descartes was living in the countryside of North Holland, procuring the amenities of daily life was even more difficult. He was often forced to put off a journey because of a particularly cold stretch.[6] In March 1646, he wrote to Chanut, in Stockholm, that

> the extraordinary rigour of this winter has obliged me to make frequent wishes for your good health and that of your family; for it is said around here that there has not been so severe [a winter] since 1608. If it is the same in Sweden, you will have seen there all the glaciers that Septentrion [the northern regions] can produce.[7]

The tedium of the cold months and the solitary philosophical pursuits in Egmond in the early 1640s were at least relieved somewhat by visits with friends. Back when Descartes was living 'near Alkmaar', in the mid-1630s, he got to know two Catholic priests in nearby Haarlem: Johan Albert Ban (1597–1644) and Augustijn Bloemaert (1584–1659). Their company was now a source of great pleasure to him, and offered some distraction from the Voetius affair.

It was Huygens who first introduced Descartes to Ban. The stadholder's secretary had a manuscript copy of Descartes' unpublished *Compendium musicae* and shared it with the musically inclined priest. Ban, an accomplished composer and harpsichordist, was suitably impressed, and sought out the philosopher in his rural retreat. Descartes told Huygens a few years later that

> if you had never said anything good about me, I would perhaps never have become familiar with any priest in these parts; for I have got to know only two, one of whom is Monsieur Ban, whose acquaintance I have acquired through the esteem that he heard you express over the little treatise on music that at an earlier time escaped from my hands.[8]

Ban, for his part, wrote to William Boswell, secretary to the English ambassador to the United Provinces, that 'I had an excellent opportunity to confer with Descartes, a man, as you know, of great skill and second to none in natural and mathematical subjects. I received him in my home with a ten-part piece of music, with voices and instruments . . . He admired it and praised it.'[9] Descartes and Ban enjoyed discussing various musical topics, including intervals and the division of octaves, and they compared notes over Mersenne's new system of tuning instruments in his book *Harmonie universelle* (1636).

Descartes admired Ban's personal qualities – 'so virtuous', he called him – and appreciated his skills on the keyboard. The two were soon joined by Bloemaert, Ban's 'intimate friend', and the trio formed a regular little floating party. They met frequently in Haarlem to listen to music and converse over philosophical, artistic and perhaps religious matters. As Baillet describes it, 'Descartes left the solitude of Egmond from time to time to go see [Ban and Bloemaert]; and because they were hardly greater drinkers or gamblers than he was, the debauchery in which they ordinarily engaged in together was some musical concert with which Monsieur Ban was accustomed to regale them.'[10] Ban and Bloemaert, in turn, visited Descartes in Egmond, sometimes bringing him his mail, since Descartes had instructed Mersenne and Huygens to address their letters to him by way of Bloemaert.

Reporting on his friendship with these two Dutch Catholics, Descartes tells Huygens in 1639 that 'I find them to be such fine gentlemen . . . so exempt from those qualities which have led me ordinarily to avoid the society of those of their robe in this country, that I count their acquaintance among the debts that I owe you.' The Dutch need not be troubled simply because they are priests doing mission work on behalf of the pope, he said. 'If anyone should be excused [for this crime], I am certain that there is no one who deserves it more than these two.' As for those critics in France who fault Descartes for spending his life in a Protestant nation that officially forbids Catholic worship, and that under Willem II was actively persecuting Catholics, Descartes replied that the time he spends with these two priests eases his religious conscience.[11]

Sadly, Ban died in the summer of 1644. Descartes was in France at the time, and was told of his friend's passing by Bloemaert upon his return to Holland. Even without the diversion of Ban's music, Descartes and Bloemaert continued to spend time together. There seems to have been a particular warmth in their fellowship, and the Haarlem priest remained a valued companion in Descartes' final years in the country.

IT WAS DURING THOSE final years that Descartes set to work on a treatise inspired by his correspondence with Elisabeth. The princess had pressed Descartes to explain the human emotions according to the principles of his philosophy. Her interest was not purely intellectual. She suffered from a variety of physical ailments, including gastrointestinal issues and abscesses on her hands. But what she found especially distressing were the emotional ups and downs in her life, due in no small part to her family. She attended to her younger sister, Henriette, during a life-threatening illness. Even more bothersome was the humiliating behaviour of her brother, Edward.

> His folly has troubled the health of my body and the tranquillity of my soul more than all the misfortunes that have already come my way. If you take the trouble to read the newspaper, you could not fail to know that he has fallen into the hands of a certain group of people who have more hatred for our house than affection for their religion, and he has let himself be taken in by their traps to such a degree as to change his religion and make himself a Roman Catholic . . . I must see someone whom I loved with as much tenderness as I know how to have, abandoned to the scorn of the world and the loss of his soul (according to my belief).[12]

She asked Descartes, who in effect served as her spiritual counsellor, to help her towards a better understanding of 'the perturbations of the mind', in the hope that she might thereby find some relief. 'I would also like to see you define the passions, in order to know them better.'[13] In his letters to her, Descartes explained how all those involuntary states of mind caused by external objects acting on the body and its animal spirits are 'passions' in the broad sense of being passive rather than active mental events; thus all our sensory perceptions are passions. But passions in the stricter sense – emotions such as joy and sadness, and whatever may be troubling Elisabeth – are the result of particularly strong agitations of the spirits.[14] He also clarified that he was not in favour of eliminating the passions altogether, as some ancient Stoics had advocated. Rather, the key to finding happiness is to moderate or 'tame' the passions, to draw them away from excess and 'render them subject to reason'.[15]

By early 1646 Descartes composed something for Elisabeth's benefit, 'a little treatise' that, he hoped, would arm her against a sea of troubles.[16] This was most likely the first two parts of what would eventually be his last publication, *The Passions of the Soul* (*Les Passions de l'âme*). The work presents Descartes' most sustained discussion of the relationship between mind and body, and it is appropriate that he composed it for the person who, more than anyone else, challenged him to explain their interaction.

In Part One, subtitled 'the whole nature of man', Descartes reviews some of the physiological material on the human body presented in the *Treatise on Man* and the *Principles*. This includes the variety of ways in which external objects can affect the motions of the animal spirits and the different kinds of 'thoughts' in the soul that such motions, once they reach the pineal gland, can stimulate. (Descartes is quite explicit here that 'the seat of the passions' is the brain, not the heart.[17]) Those thoughts that are generated not by the soul itself, through the will, but by the body are all passive perceptions. These include ordinary perceptual sensations and the ideas of the imagination. But among those passive thoughts in the soul are a subset that Descartes calls *émotions*; 'because of all the kinds of thought which the soul may have, there are none that agitate and disturb it so strongly.'[18]

The key to controlling the emotional passions – as much as this is possible – is not through will-power alone, at least not directly. One cannot moderate these passions simply by wanting them to be less disturbing. Rather, one must think about things that are connected, psychologically, with emotions that one desires and avoid thinking about things that bring about emotions one wants to avoid.

> Our passions cannot be directly aroused or suppressed by the action of our will, but only indirectly through the representation of things which are usually joined with the passion we wish to have and opposed to the passion we wish to reject. For example, in order to arouse boldness and suppress fear in ourselves, it is not sufficient to have the volition to do so. We must apply ourselves to consider the reasons, objects or precedents which persuade us that the danger is not great; that there is always more security in defence than in flight; that we shall gain glory and joy if we conquer, whereas we can expect nothing but regret and shame if we flee.[19]

The right (voluntary) thoughts will generate the right motions of the pineal gland and thus of the spirits, which in turn will cause the desired (passive) thoughts in the soul. We can even, in this way, modify the natural connections between bodily motions and mental states. An item of food that once caused disgust can, through training and habituation, become associated with delight.

The strength of the soul to resist the undesirable passions, rather than being carried away by them, and enjoy the useful ones lies in 'knowledge of the truth' – in particular, a knowledge of what is good and what is bad, accompanied by firm judgements on this basis 'for the guidance of conduct'. We can thereby come to associate pleasant feelings with things that are good, and unpleasant feelings with things that are bad. Armed with rational knowledge and a resolute will, aided by the imagination, Descartes

concludes, 'there is no soul so weak that it cannot, if well-directed, acquire an absolute power over its passions.'[20]

Parts Two and Three of the treatise are devoted to a catalogue of the passions, all of which are variations on six 'primitive' or basic passions: wonder, love, hatred, desire, joy and sadness. Thus esteem and contempt are species of wonder; we esteem or have

Jan Baptist Weenix, *René Descartes*, c. 1647–9, oil on canvas.

contempt for something when we wonder at its greatness or insignificance. Scorn, however, is a form of hatred; shame is an expression of sadness; and jealousy is 'a kind of anxiety' arising from the desire to preserve the possession of some good.

The Passions of the Soul is essentially Descartes' moral treatise. Repeating what he had told Elisabeth in their correspondence, he declares virtue to be the power to abide by the better judgements of reason and the general capacity to have desirable, rational thoughts on the appropriate occasions. The individual virtues, in turn, are just those specific 'habits in the soul' to have the particular right thoughts and, when called for, to bring them into action. Generosity, for example, is the 'firm and constant resolution' to use one's freedom well and to 'undertake and carry out whatever [one] judges to be best'.[21] Courage is the ability to avoid fear in the face of danger by turning one's mind away from the reasons for flight and towards the thought of the security and honour in resistance.

Moral philosophy in the early modern period, as it was among the ancients, is concerned not so much with right action and duties towards others, as it would be for Kant and later thinkers, as with achieving eudaimonia, one's own well-being or flourishing. For Descartes, what is essential for achieving this supreme condition is that mastery of the passions. 'It is on the passions alone that all the good and evil of this life depends.' Of course, the passions do not always turn out to be beneficial.

> The persons whom the passions can move most deeply are capable of enjoying the sweetest pleasures of this life. It is true that they may also experience the most bitterness when they do not know how to put these passions to good use and when fortune works against them. But the chief use of wisdom lies in its teaching us to be masters of our passions and to control them with such skill that

the evils which they cause are quite bearable, and even become a source of joy.²²

The passions are all, by their own nature, good, he insists. 'We have nothing to avoid but their misuse or their excess.'²³

IN EARLY 1649 *The Passions of the Soul* was on its way to being published in Amsterdam and Paris. In the meantime, Descartes' views on the emotions, which circulated in manuscript and by word of mouth, had attracted some notice in high places.

The learned daughter of Gustavus Adolphus II of Sweden and Maria Eleonora of Brandenburg, Christina (1626–1689), was now the queen of Sweden.²⁴ Her exposure to Descartes' philosophy seems to date only to early 1647. The occasion was a report by her French physician, François du Ryer, after he had paid a visit to Chanut, Descartes' diplomat friend in Stockholm who would soon be named French ambassador. Ryer had obtained a copy of something that Descartes wrote in February of that year in reply to a letter from Chanut. Chanut had asked for Descartes' views on love, both the love of other human beings and the love of God. In Descartes' long response – Baillet calls it 'a lovely dissertation on love' – he distinguishes between a 'purely intellectual or rational love' and love as a passion. The former is the soul's clear and distinct perception of some good, whether present or absent, with which it desires to unite itself, as two parts of a whole; this kind of love can be in the soul whether or not it is joined to a body. Love as a passion is a 'sensual or sensitive' state of mind that arises because the soul is joined to a body. Whereas intellectual love is accompanied by knowledge of the value of its object, love as a passion involves only a 'confused idea'. In the ordinary course of things, however, these two kinds of love often accompany each other. 'When the soul judges that an

object is worthy of it, this immoderately disposes the heart to
motions that excite the passion of love.'[25] Given the topic at hand,
Descartes also felt the need to provide in his letter to Chanut a
summary of his not-yet-published account of the passions. Ryer
showed his copy of the letter to his philosophically inclined queen,
and it piqued her interest.

Christina, who would later abdicate the Swedish throne,
convert to Catholicism and move to Rome, also took an interest
in Descartes' account of the extent of the cosmos: was it finite
or infinite. She was concerned that the hypothesis of an infinite
universe, which she took to be Descartes' view, was contrary to the
Christian religion. In a letter to Chanut intended to address her
qualms, Descartes explains that the attribute 'infinite' should be
reserved only for a being that could be demonstrated positively
to be infinite, that is, God. But neither is the universe finite.
Because matter is just extension, beyond any alleged limit or
boundary to the universe there will be more space, and thus more
extension – that is, more matter.

> We cannot say that something is infinite without a reason
> to prove this such as we can give only in the case of God;
> but we can say that a thing is indefinite simply if we have
> no reason which proves that it has bounds. Now it seems
> to me that it is impossible to prove or even to conceive
> that there are bounds in the matter of which the world
> is composed.[26]

A few months later, in September, Christina sought Descartes'
opinion on 'the supreme good'. Descartes told Chanut that it
was his general policy 'to refuse to write down my thoughts concerning morality', for two reasons. 'One is that there is no other
subject in which malicious people can so readily find pretexts for
vilifying me; and the other is that I believe that only sovereigns, or

those authorized by them, have the right to concern themselves with regulating the morals of other people.'[27] However, since the request came from a queen, Descartes felt he had sufficient authorization to put his views down on paper, on the condition that only Christina and Chanut would see them.

Writing to Christina in November, Descartes explains that, of course, absolutely speaking, God is the supreme good. But then there are things that are supreme goods in a relative way – relative to us, that is, in the sense that 'our having [them] is a perfection.' Moreover, what qualifies as such a relatively supreme good must be something that we either actually possess or have the power to possess through our own resources, independently of good or bad luck. Since goods of the body are all subject to fortune, the supreme good must be a good of the soul. Now knowledge is certainly a worthy good of the soul, but whether or not one has knowledge is often beyond one's control. Therefore the supreme good for a human being must be a condition of the will: its unswerving obedience to reason (rather than to the passions), 'which is absolutely within our disposal'. Just as Descartes had explained earlier to Elisabeth, so he now tells Christina that the supreme good

> consists only in a firm will to do well and the contentment which this produces. My reason for saying this is that I can discover no other good which seems so great or so entirely within each man's power. . . . I do not see that it is possible to dispose it [the will] better than by a firm and constant resolution to carry out to the letter all the things which one judges to be best, and to employ all the powers of one's mind in finding out what these are.[28]

What is noteworthy about Descartes' account is that, once again – and contrary to ancient eudaimonist theories of ethics, such as

Aristotle's — happiness or contentment is not itself the *summum bonum*, but only its consequence.

Baillet reports that Christina said she could not properly assess Descartes' account of passionate love, 'because, she said, having never felt this passion, she could not judge a painting without knowing the original'.[29] Still, the queen was very impressed.

David Beck, *Queen Christina of Sweden*, 1647–51, oil on canvas.

According to Chanut, who was with the queen when she was perusing the *Principles of Philosophy* and who was charged with helping her understand the finer points of the work, 'this princess, who esteems nothing in the world more than truth and virtue, judges you greatly for the love of the one and the other.'[30] Christina wanted to know more about the philosopher, 'all the particulars of his person and his life'.[31] Chanut told her what he could. It was enough to make her want Descartes to become a part of her circle of intellectuals in Stockholm. Thus, just as *The Passions of the Soul* was ready to go to press – both Christina and Elisabeth had been provided with manuscript copies – it looked as if Descartes' quiet life by the North Sea dunes might be coming to an end.

DESCARTES HAD TOLD CHANUT in late 1646 that he was not particularly interested in royal patronage. When he learned that his friend was planning to present Christina with a copy of the French translation of the *Meditations*, he made it clear that 'I have never been so ambitious as to desire that persons of that rank should know my name.' Nonetheless, he thought that some royal backing would not be a bad thing to have, given his recent troubles in Utrecht and elsewhere. With the attacks by 'countless Schoolmen, who look askance at my writings and try from every angle to find in them the means of harming me, I have good reason to wish to be known by persons of greater distinction'.[32]

What Descartes did not expect was an invitation to join a monarch's entourage, much less end up in the northern climes of Scandinavia. In fact, he remarked to Chanut in 1646 that, with him in Holland and Chanut in Sweden, there seemed to be little chance that the two of them would have the opportunity to 'converse privately' in the near future. 'I would count myself extremely fortunate, I assure you, if I could do this with you; but I do not

Frans Hals, *René Descartes*, 1649, oil on panel.

think I shall ever go to the places where you are, or that you will retire to this place.'[33] And yet, within three years, Descartes was packing up most (but not all) of his belongings. In February 1649 Chanut was asked by the queen to issue a formal invitation to Descartes to come to Sweden, for just a while, until the long Swedish winter settled in. She wanted him to be her tutor in philosophy, and especially to provide lessons in Cartesian science.

Descartes was, at least on this occasion, a reluctant traveller. He told Chanut that he was afraid that on the voyage to Sweden 'I shall simply find myself waylaid by highwaymen who will rob me or involved in a shipwreck which will cost me my life.'[34] He certainly did not want to give up the comfortable routine that had allowed him to carry out his researches without interruption, something that would be hard to maintain while catering to the wishes of a queen and dealing with the protocols of a royal court in a foreign and unfamiliar land. While flattered by the honour, he much preferred to stay in Egmond, where he could see the *Passions* through to publication and work on the planned additional parts of the *Principles*. He wavered over whether or not to accept the invitation. In the spring of 1649 he wrote to Brasset to express his difficulty in deciding to leave 'this land in order to live in a land of bears, rocks and ice'.[35]

In the end, after months of dithering, and a conversation with Chanut when the ambassador was passing through the United Provinces in May 1649, Descartes determined that it was hard to refuse the offer to be Christina's philosopher-in-residence and that, despite his misgivings, he should undertake the journey. He told Elisabeth a month later that 'I still intend to go there [Sweden] provided the queen indicates that she still wishes me to. A week ago Monsieur Chanut, our resident in that country, passed through here on his way to France. He spoke so glowingly of this marvellous queen that the voyage no longer seems so long and arduous as it did previously.'[36] Descartes procrastinated further, however, and did not actually embark until the end of September, just as summer was coming to an end.

Many of Descartes' Dutch acquaintances were saddened by his impending departure and apprehensive about how he would fare in new and strange surroundings. Baillet says that 'several of his friends in Holland who wanted to come to Amsterdam [from where Descartes would sail to Sweden] to say goodbye could not leave him without expressing their affliction that [Descartes'] pre-monitions about his destiny gave them.' He adds that 'among those who were most touched . . . was the pious Monsieur Bloemaert, whom [Descartes] saw in Haarlem on frequent and extended visits during his time in Egmond.'[37] The Catholic priest counted on Descartes for company and for intellectual stimulation. Perhaps they still talked about their late friend Ban's music and reminisced about his concerts.

Bloemaert decided that he wanted a memento before Descartes set sail. 'Monsieur Bloemaert could not let Descartes leave without taking the liberty of having him captured by a painter, in order that he might at least find some light consolation in the copy of an original that he risked losing.'[38] The priest was quite familiar with Haarlem's art world, as he had an extensive collection of paintings by local masters. He went with the best portraitist that the city had to offer. Frans Hals's oil sketch on wood panel, almost certainly done from life (and reproduced on the cover of this book), remains our standard image of the philosopher and served as a model for numerous copies, including the one by an anonymous artist now in the Louvre.[39]

IT WAS SUPPOSED TO BE only a temporary sojourn. Writing to Elisabeth in March 1649, before his departure, Descartes tells her that 'I am counting on passing the winter in that country and returning only next year.'[40]

Soon after his arrival in Stockholm, at the beginning of October, he seems unsure what the arrangement is with Christina. He informs Elisabeth soon after settling in that 'I have so far had the honour of seeing the queen only once or twice.'[41] He was apparently at her beck and call, and the summons were unpredictable. '[I am] going to the castle only at the times when it pleases her to give me the honour of speaking with her.' Unfortunately, those times did not suit well Descartes' usual habits. This man who was reportedly accustomed to lying in bed until late in the morning was, according to Baillet, expected to attend to the queen in her library at 5 a.m.[42] Still, at this point at least, before the dark Swedish winter had set in, he did not regard this as a major inconvenience. 'It will not be hard for me to perform my courtly duties, and that suits my temperament very well.'[43] He seems, moreover, suitably impressed by Christina's personality and intellect. He praises her 'generosity and majesty' and notes that 'she is strongly drawn to scholarly pursuits', although he is unsure how he can be of help to her. 'Because I do not know that she has ever read any philosophy, I cannot judge her tastes in this subject, or whether she will have time for it.'

In fact, Christina seems to have had very little time for philosophy. She was quite busy with celebrations surrounding the recently completed Peace of Münster, following the wars in which Sweden played a major role. Baillet says that she did call upon her new resident philosopher to compose verses to accompany a ballet, titled *La Naissance de la paix* (The Birth of Peace), during those festivities, although, Baillet reports, she was unable to persuade him also to participate in the dance.[44] Even by mid-January 1650 Descartes complains to his friend Nicolas de Flécelles de Brégy, the French ambassador to Poland whom he had met while De Brégy was on a diplomatic mission in Stockholm, that since early December he has seen the queen 'only four or five times'. She had just returned from several weeks away in Uppsala, and he has

Louis-Michel Dumesnil, *Queen Christina of Sweden and Her Court* (detail showing
Christina listening to Descartes), before 1739, oil on canvas.

not seen her since her arrival, so there has been no opportunity for philosophical lessons – indeed, for any kind of intellectual engagement. 'This makes me think that during the winter here men's thoughts are frozen, like the water.'[45]

As if the idleness and the inconvenient hour at which his presence in the queen's library was required did not make life at court unpleasant enough, it seems that other members of the queen's cohort of *savants* were growing resentful of the famous Frenchman in their midst. What may have made them especially jealous was that Christina assigned Descartes a lead role in the planning of a scholarly institute devoted to 'the search for truth', a kind of Swedish Academy of Sciences, and even had him draw up the statutes. Baillet reports that one of the 'regulations' of this academy, of which Christina would be the head, was that membership was reserved for 'only natural born subjects of this realm', presumably leaving Descartes out of luck.[46]

Writing to Elisabeth in October 1649, after only a couple of weeks in Sweden, he tells her that 'I do not think that anything is capable of keeping me in this country longer than next summer.'[47] One can only imagine his state of mind by the middle of a frigid January.

Unfortunately, he would never leave Sweden to return to his beloved *hermitage* in Egmond. In mid-January 1650 Chanut became sick with a pulmonary infection after an outdoor stroll with Descartes. The philosopher attended to his friend during his illness, which lasted for several weeks. No sooner had Chanut begun to get better than Descartes himself started suffering from the same symptoms, inflammation of the lungs and a fever. Unlike the diplomat, he never recovered. Descartes died in Stockholm on 11 February 1650.

There were rumours that the cause of Descartes' death was poisoning, perhaps by his rivals at court for Christina's favours.[48] Baillet dismisses this as being 'unworthy of the memory of the scholars who attended the queen, and who were men without malice, for the most part, and who discharged their envy not upon his [Descartes'] person but upon his philosophy'. Rather, Baillet insists, Descartes was just worn down by his duties. 'The true and sole cause of the illness of Monsieur Descartes was the apportioning of his care between the queen and the sick ambassador, in the middle of a season hostile to his temperament.'[49]

THE SEVENTEENTH CENTURY belonged to Descartes. His philosophy dominated the intellectual life of Europe for fifty years after his death. From the salons and academies of France, to the Royal Society and philosophical clubs of England, to Dutch and German universities, Cartesian metaphysical, epistemological and scientific ideas were the inescapable topic of conversation. They inspired research by partisans and attacks by opponents.

There were Cartesians, orthodox and otherwise, who saw their mission as defending Descartes' principles, even if this meant introducing clarifications, modifications, even corrections and major expansions into topics where Descartes himself had feared to tread. Their goal was to render the system more internally coherent and more plausible. This meant not only eliminating apparent inconsistencies but taking account of recent developments in physics, biology, physiology and other sciences.[50] Addressing the challenges posed by Gassendi and Elisabeth, they devoted their efforts to formulating a workable account of mind–body relations; in some cases this meant a retreat to a *deus ex machina* and appealing to God as the true and ubiquitous efficient cause of their mutually corresponding states. At the same time, second-generation Cartesians found body–body causation just as problematic to understand as mind–body causation. After all, if, as Descartes had insisted, bodies are nothing but pure, passive extension, then they must be devoid of any dynamic features. Active causal powers

– just the powers that Scholastics accounted for by introducing into bodies soul-like substantial forms and real qualities – cannot be properties of mere extension. Coming up with an explanation of force was a serious challenge for Cartesian physics.[51] Meanwhile, some of Descartes' more courageous (or perhaps foolhardy) followers waded into fraught theological territory by addressing the difficulties around Eucharistic transubstantiation and the problem of the status of the eternal truths relative to God's will.[52]

Among the Cartesian philosophy's more prominent contemporary critics were the Dutch Jewish thinker Bento (Baruch) de Spinoza (1632–1677) and the German polymath Gottfried Wilhelm Leibniz (1646–1716). Spinoza started out as an expositor of Descartes' philosophy but eventually formulated his own highly original philosophical system, one that scandalized Europe. He departed in a radical way from the Cartesian notion of substance: only God is a true substance, he argued, and as such God is identical to Nature. Everything else – including human beings – is a 'mode' of God or Nature. Leibniz, who also seems to have gone through a Cartesian period, for his part rejected Descartes' theory of body on both metaphysical and physical grounds; bodies must be more than mere passive extension if the phenomena of nature are to be what they are. He also corrected Descartes' account of the most basic laws of nature. He showed, for example, that what is conserved in the universe is not the total quantity of motion (mass × speed) but the total quantity of force or kinetic energy (which he measured as mass × velocity^2).

The nail in the coffin for Cartesianism, however, came from an Englishman. Isaac Newton, as we have seen, eschewed (for the most part) the kind of speculating ('hypothesizing', he called it) about the metaphysical foundations of the laws of nature and physical phenomena that was so central to Descartes' philosophy. He also introduced attractive and repulsive forces 'acting at a distance' between bodies, and substituted absolute motion

for Descartes' relative motion. By replacing the kinetics of the Cartesian cosmos with the dynamics of classical mechanics, Newton raised the mechanical philosophy to a much more mathematically sophisticated level.[53] As Voltaire would write in the 1730s,

A Frenchman arriving in London finds quite a change, in philosophy as in all else. Behind him he left the world

Laurent Guyot, 'Jardin Elysée, Vue du Tombeau de Descartes', engraving from Alexandre Lenoir, *Musée des monuments français*, vol. v (1806).

full; here he finds it empty. In Paris one sees the universe composed of vortices of subtle matter; in London one sees nothing of the sort . . . According to your Cartesians, everything is done by means of an impulse that is practically incomprehensible; according to Mr Newton it is by a kind of attraction, the reason for which is no better known.[54]

Despite Cartesian science being eclipsed by Newtonian mechanics – and later, of course, by Einsteinian relativity theory and quantum physics – Descartes was of indisputable influence in the modern development of both philosophy and science. The philosophy of mind, for example, has long wrestled with the mind–body problem bequeathed by Cartesian dualism. Most philosophers of mind now tend to be materialists rather than dualists about the mind. They reject the notion of the soul as a separate, non-physical kind of stuff (the so-called 'ghost in the machine', to use the dismissive phrase of the British philosopher Gilbert Ryle). Rather, they identify mental states with neurological and physiological states of the brain. However, the problem of consciousness – what is it? 'Where' is it? How does it arise? – is part of Descartes' legacy, and remains intractable. As for science, to the extent that contemporary physics is still wedded to the idea that there are fundamental items in nature – atoms, subatomic particles, 'strings' – whose behaviour is governed by laws, it really is a continuation of the project of the rational, experimental mechanical science of the seventeenth century to which Descartes contributed so much.

Was Descartes 'the father of modern philosophy'? It depends, of course, on what is meant by 'modern'. There were certainly more radical and original thinkers who might have an equally plausible claim to the title: Spinoza in the seventeenth century, Hume in the eighteenth. But there can be no question that

Descartes played a crucial role in the renewal of philosophy (including the philosophy of nature or 'science') in the seventeenth century and did much to put it on more rational foundations. In very important ways, he helped set the agenda for a good deal of future philosophizing. But he was one of many, and a more complete picture would situate him among a coterie of major figures in that period – Hobbes, Spinoza, Boyle, Locke, Leibniz, Newton – who also made important contributions to that renewal. So, maybe not *the* father of modern philosophy, but certainly one of its parents.

CHRONOLOGY

Historical events are indicated by *italics*.

Amsterdam, Leiden, Deventer and the coastal villages of
Egmond), with occasional trips back to France

1632–3   *Galileo publishes 'Dialogue Concerning the Two Chief World Systems';*
         he is condemned by Catholic Church and sentenced to house arrest

1630–33 Works on *The World* (*Treatise on Light* and *Treatise on Man*), which
         is abandoned after news of Galileo's condemnation in Rome

1634–5   Meets Helena Jansdr van der Stroom; their daughter
         Fransintge (Francine) is born

1637   Publishes *Discourse on Method* and essays *Geometry*, *Dioptrics* and
         Meteors

1640   Fransintge dies of scarlet fever

1641   Publishes *Meditations on First Philosophy* in Paris, along with six
         sets of objections and replies. Beginning of controversy at
         the University of Utrecht, with opposition led by the rector
         Gisbertus Voetius

1642   Second edition of *Meditations* published in Amsterdam, with
         the seventh set of objections and the letter to Father Dinet.
         Cartesian philosophy condemned by the city council of
         Utrecht

1643   Publishes *Letter to Voetius*. Begins correspondence with
         Elisabeth of Bohemia

1644   Publishes *Principles of Philosophy*. New controversy over
         Descartes' philosophy brewing at the University of Leiden

1647   Travels to Paris; meets with Blaise Pascal. University of
         Leiden curators forbid discussion of Cartesian philosophy.
         Queen Christina of Sweden begins studying Descartes'
         works

1647   *Frederik Hendrik dies; succeeded by his son Willem II*

1648   Publishes *Comments on a Certain Broadsheet*, in critical response
         to his Utrecht disciple Henricus Regius

1648   *Treaty of Münster, end of war between Dutch Republic and Spain; the*
         United Provinces become a sovereign nation

1649   *Willem II dies; beginning of stadholderless period under the leadership*
         of Johan de Witt, Grand Pensionary of Holland

1649   Queen Christina invites him to Stockholm to tutor her in
         philosophy. Travels to Sweden in October. Publishes *Passions*
         of the Soul

1650   Dies in Stockholm on 11 February

REFERENCES

Abbreviations

AT   *Oeuvres de Descartes*, ed. Charles Adam and Paul Tannery, 11 vols (Paris, 1974–83)

CSM   *The Philosophical Writings of Descartes*, ed. and trans. John Cottingham, Robert Stoothoff and Dugald Murdoch, 2 vols (Cambridge, 1984)

CSMK   *The Philosophical Writings of Descartes*, vol. III: *The Correspondence*, ed. and trans. John Cottingham, Robert Stoothoff, Dugald Murdoch and Anthony Kenny (Cambridge, 1991)

G   *Descartes: The World and Other Writings*, ed. and trans. Stephen Gaukroger (Cambridge, 1998)

M   *René Descartes: Principles of Philosophy*, ed. and trans. Valentine Rodger Miller and Reese P. Miller (Dordrecht and Boston, MA, 1983)

S   *The Correspondence Between Princess Elisabeth of Bohemia and René Descartes*, ed. and trans. Lisa Shapiro (Chicago, IL, 2007)

Introduction

1   The label, meant initially as a pejorative, was provided by their critics, who opposed their innovations in philosophy (and, by implication, in theology). On the *novatores*, see Daniel Garber, 'Novatores', in *The Cambridge History of Philosophy of the Scientific Revolution*, ed. David Marshall Miller and Dana Jalobeanu (Cambridge, 2022), pp. 35–57; and on Descartes' relationship to them, see Garber, 'Descartes Among the *Novatores*', *Res Philosophica*, 92 (2015), pp. 1–19.

2   Letter/Preface to the French translation of *Principles of Philosophy*, AT IX–B.15/CSM 1.187.

1 Man of Touraine

1 Descartes to Brasset, 23 April 1649, AT V.349/CSMK 375.
2 On the fate of Descartes' body, see Russell Shorto, *Descartes' Bones: A Skeletal History of the Conflict Between Faith and Reason* (New York, 2008).
3 Catherine Descartes, 'Relation de la mort de M. Descartes', in *Bibliothèque Politique* (Paris, 1745), vol. III, pp. 238–50 (p. 239).
4 Richard A. Watson, *Cogito Ergo Sum: The Life of René Descartes* (Boston, MA, 2007), p. 51.
5 Isaac Beeckman, *Journal tenu par Isaac Beeckman de 1604 à 1634*, vol. I: *1604–1619*, ed. Cornelis de Waard (The Hague, 1939), pp. 237, 244, 257.
6 Descartes to Elisabeth, AT IV.220–21/CSMK 250–51.
7 See the account of his earliest years in Desmond Clarke, *Descartes: A Biography* (Cambridge, 2006), pp. 12–14.
8 On these family professional connections, see Watson, *Cogito Ergo Sum*, pp. 43–6.
9 Allan P. Farrell, *The Jesuit Ratio studiorum of 1599* (Washington, DC, 1970), p. 62. This is a complete translation of the text of the *Ratio studiorum*.
10 Ibid., p. 43.
11 Ibid., p. 40.
12 There is some debate as to when exactly Descartes began at La Flèche. Most likely it was 1607; this is the date defended in Geneviève Rodis-Lewis, *Descartes: Biographie* (Paris, 1995); and Clarke, *Descartes*. Descartes' early biographer Baillet puts it, implausibly, in 1604 (Adrien Baillet, *La vie de Monsieur Desartes*, 2 vols (Paris, 1691)), while Stephen Gaukroger (*Descartes: An Intellectual Biography* (Oxford, 1995) and Watson (*Cogito Ergo Sum*) claim 1606.
13 *Discourse on Method*, AT VI.5–6/CSM I.113.
14 Descartes [to Debeaune], 12 September 1638, AT II.378/CSMK 124.
15 *Discourse on Method*, AT VI.5–6/CSM I.113.
16 *Discourse on Method*, AT VI.17/CSM I.119.
17 *Discourse on Method*, AT VI.16/CSM I.119.
18 Farrell, *The Jesuit Studio ratiorum*, p. 40.
19 The placard of Descartes' theses was not discovered until 1981, attached with other papers to the back of an engraving as support. See the annotated transcription and translation in Jean-Robert Armogathe, Vincent Carraud and Robert Feenstra, 'La licence en droit de Descartes', *Nouvelles de la République des lettres*, 8 (1988), pp. 123–45.

20 *Discourse on Method*, AT VI.4/CSM I.112–13.
21 *Discourse on Method*, AT VI.9/CSM I.115.
22 Descartes [to Debeaune], 12 September 1638, AT II.378/CSMK 123–4.

2 'The great book of the world'

 1 On this, see Leszek Kolakowski, *Chrétiens sans Église: La Conscience religieuse et le lien confessionnel au XVIIe siècle* (Paris, 1969), chap. 2; and Jonathan Israel, *The Dutch Republic: Its Rise, Greatness and Fall, 1477–1806* (Oxford, 1995), pp. 421–75.
 2 Adrien Baillet, *La vie de Monsieur Descartes*, 2 vols (Paris, 1691), vol. 1, p. 43. According to J. A. van Ruler, who finds Baillet's source in the earlier biographical text by Daniel Lipstorp (1653), the details of Baillet's narrative may be fictitious, but Descartes and Beeckman did in fact meet that same day; see 'Philosopher Defying the Philosophers: Descartes's Life and Works', in *The Oxford Handbook to Descartes and Cartesianism*, ed. Steven Nadler, Tad Schmaltz and Delphine Antoine-Mahut (Oxford and New York, 2019), pp. 3–24 (p. 11).
 3 AT X.58–61.
 4 See Descartes to Beeckman, 26 March 1619, AT X.155/CSMK 2. Beeckman comments on Descartes' approach to this problem in his journal entry of 11 November 1619 (Isaac Beeckman, *Journal tenu par Isaac Beeckman de 1604 à 1634*, vol. 1: *1604–1619*, ed. Cornelis de Waard (The Hague, 1939), p. 237).
 5 Descartes to Beeckman, 24 January 1619, AT X.152/CSMK 1.
 6 Descartes to Beeckman, 24 January 1619, AT X.153/CSMK 1. Beeckman claims that Descartes wrote the treatise 'on my account [*mea causa*]'; see Beeckman, *Journal*, p. 257. The treatise was not published in Descartes' lifetime.
 7 *Compendium Musicae*, AT X.89.
 8 Descartes to Beeckman, 26 March 1619, AT X.156–7/CSMK 2.
 9 Descartes to Beeckman, 26 March 1619, AT X.156–7/CSMK 2–3.
10 *Rules for the Direction of the Mind*, Rule 4, AT X.378/CSM I.19.
11 Descartes to Beeckman, 24 January 1619, AT X.151/CSMK 1.
12 Descartes to Beeckman, 24 January 1619, AT X.153/CSMK 1.
13 Descartes to Beeckman, 23 April 1619, AT X.163/CSMK 4.
14 Descartes to Mersenne, 18 December 1629, AT I.94/CSMK 17.
15 *Discourse on Method*, AT VI.11/ CSM I.116. He is referring to the Thirty Years War, which generally (but not exclusively) pitted Catholic armies against Protestant forces.

16 The letter is no longer extant, but see Baillet, *La vie de Monsieur Descartes* (vol. I, p. 118), who claims to be quoting from it.

17 *Discourse on Method*, AT VI.28/CSM I.125.

18 According to research by Erik-Jan Bos, 'Descartes en Italie: pour vendre des mulets', *Bulletin Cartésien*, 51 (2020), pp. 164–70.

19 Baillet, *La vie de Monsieur Descartes*, vol. I, p. 118.

20 *Olympica*, AT X.218/CSM I.5.

21 Descartes to Mersenne, 11 October 1638, AT II.380. In this letter, Descartes says, referring to Galileo, 'je ne l'ay jamais vu, ny n'ay eu aucune communication avec luy' (388).

22 Descartes to Balzac, 5 May 1631, AT I.204/CSMK 32.

23 Descartes to Mersenne, 13 November 1639, AT II.623.

24 Baillet, *La vie de Monsieur Descartes*, vol. I, pp. 117–22.

25 *Meteors*, AT VI.316.

26 Desmond Clarke, *Descartes: A Biography* (Cambridge, 2006), p. 71.

27 *Discourse on Method*, AT VI.11/CSM I.116.

28 AT X.216/CSM I.4.

29 The account of the dreams and of Descartes' interpretation of them is in Baillet, *La vie de Monsieur Descartes*, vol. I, pp. 81–6. This section of the notebook is titled *Olympica*. Richard Watson believes that Baillet is making up most of the material on the dreams (*Cogito Ergo Sum: The Life of René Descartes* (Boston, MA, 2007), pp. 109–14).

30 AT X.216/CSM I.3.

31 Baillet, *La vie de Monsieur Descartes*, vol. I, p. 81.

32 *Discourse on Method*, AT VI.10/CSM I.116.

33 *Discourse on Method*, AT VI.16/CSM I.119.

34 *Discourse on Method*, AT VI.3/CSM I.112.

35 The ever-sceptical Watson thinks that Baillet just makes up a lot of this story (*Cogito Ergo Sum*, pp. 142–9).

36 Baillet, *La vie de Monsieur Descartes*, vol. I, pp. 160–63.

37 *Rules for the Direction of the Mind*, Rule 1, AT X.359/CSM I.9.

38 *Rules for the Direction of the Mind*, Rule 3, AT X.368/CSM I.14.

39 *Rules for the Direction of the Mind*, Rule 3, AT X.369–370/CSM I.15.

40 *Rules for the Direction of the Mind*, Rule 7, AT X.388/CSM I.25.

41 *Rules for the Direction of the Mind*, Rule 2, AT X.364-5/CSM I.12.

42 The *mathesis universalis* appears in Rule 4. However, it may be a late addition to the text. It does not appear in the contemporary manuscript recently discovered by Richard Serjeantson (the 'Cambridge manuscript'), which many believe is an early version of the work. Scholars are divided on whether *mathesis universalis* is

the method itself or a substantive body of science, a set of true propositions discovered through the method. On this, compare Jon Schuster, *Descartes Agonistes: Physico-Mathematics, Method and Mechanism, 1618–1633* (Dordrecht, 2013) against Daniel Garber, *Descartes Embodied: Reading Cartesian Philosophy through Cartesian Science* (Cambridge, 2001), p. 38 n. 8, and Daniel Garber, 'Review of Jon Schuster, *Descartes Agonistes: Physico-Mathematics, Method and Mechanism, 1618–1633*', *Les Archives du Séminaire Descartes*, 23 May 2015.

43 *Rules for the Direction of the Mind*, Rule 4, AT X.374/CSM I.17.
44 *Discourse on Method*, AT VI.19–20/CSM I.120.
45 *Rules for the Direction of the Mind*, Rule 4, AT X.371–372/CSM I.16.
46 It is now known as 'Snell's Law', after the Dutch astronomer Willebrord Snell (1580–1626), who also discovered the mathematical formula but never published it in his lifetime.
47 A nice account of Descartes' 'method' as applied to the problem of the anaclastic is in Daniel Garber, 'Descartes and Experiment in the *Discourse* and *Essays*', in Garber, *Descartes Embodied*, pp. 85–110 (pp. 87–9).
48 *Rules for the Direction of the Mind*, Rule 17, AT X.459/CSM I.70.
49 A few things have been clarified somewhat, but not completely, by the Cambridge manuscript.
50 Garber, in *Descartes Embodied*, argues that the method of the *Rules* does inform Descartes' later work, at least up to the *Discourse on Method* of 1637.

3 A Fabulous New World

1 The Stockholm inventory is in AT X.1–12.
2 It is possible that item X in the inventory, 'Soixante & neuf feuillets, dont la suite est interrompue en plusier endroits, contenans la doctrine de ses principes en françois & non entierement conformes à l'imprimé latin' (AT X.12), refers to *Le Monde*. However, when the inventory was made, in the early 1650s, there was as yet no published Latin edition ('l'imprimé latin') of the work. Sophie Roux suggests, nonetheless, that *Le Monde* may have been one of the manuscripts that Pierre d'Alibert brought back from Stockholm around 1666; see Sophie Roux, 'Une enquête sur Jacques du Roure', *Bulletin cartésien*, 50 (2021), pp. 20–30. Moreover, in correspondence with me, she makes the compelling point that the 'printed Latin' work being

referred to here is the *Principles of Philosophy*, many of the doctrines of which were in the earlier text; and so the work in the inventory might very well be *Le Monde*.

3 *Discourse on Method* IV, AT VI.30/CSM I.126.
4 AT VIII-B.110–11.
5 *Discourse on Method* IV, AT VI.31/CSM I.126.
6 Descartes to Balzac, 5 May 1631, AT I.202-3/CSMK 31.
7 Descartes to Mersenne, 4 March 1630, AT I.125.
8 Descartes to Mersenne, 2 December 1630, AT I.191. The 'subterfuge' was to be the claim of ignorance. Descartes was, in fact, interested in going to England to meet with the Hartlib circle there, although he never made the trip.
9 In May 1616 Cardinal Bellarmine noted that the pope and the Sacred Congregation of the Index had warned Galileo only that 'the doctrine attributed to Copernicus (that the earth moves around the sun and the sun stands at the center of the world without moving from east to west) is contrary to Holy Scripture and therefore cannot be defended or held'; see the document in Maurice Finocchiaro, ed., *The Galileo Affair: A Documentary History* (Berkeley and Los Angeles, CA, 1989), p. 153. The nature of the warning that Galileo received in 1616 has been subject to different interpretations ever since Galileo himself claimed that he had not been forbidden to *discuss* the Copernican doctrine. On this, see Finocchiaro, *The Galileo Affair*, pp. 32–71.
10 For a good discussion of the philosophical and historical complexities, see the Introduction to Finocchiaro, *The Galileo Affair*. J. L. Heilbron, *Galileo* (Oxford, 2010), is the best recent biography of Galileo in English, which includes a good general account of the affair.
11 Galileo Galilei, *Discoveries and Opinions of Galileo*, ed. Stillman Drake (Garden City, NY, 1957), p. 45.
12 Ibid., p. 57.
13 Dedicatory Letter to Cosimo II de Medici, ibid., p. 24.
14 Ibid., pp. 102, 106.
15 Ibid., p. 144.
16 Ibid., p. 177.
17 The text of this assessment is in Finocchiaro, *The Galileo Affair*, p. 146.
18 Ibid., p. 148. Copernicus' treatise was put on the Index *donec corrigitur* ('until it is corrected'). Corrections were duly made, and it was removed from the Index in 1620.

19 The text of this 'special injunction' is ibid., p. 147.
20 Galileo's Second Deposition, ibid., p. 278.
21 The text of the Inquisition's sentence is ibid., pp. 287–91.
22 Descartes to Mersenne, 8 October 1629, AT I.23/CSMK 6.
23 Descartes to Mersenne, 25 November 1630, AT I.179/CSMK 28.
24 Descartes to Mersenne, 13 November 1629, AT I.70/CSMK 7.
25 Descartes to Mersenne, 13 November 1629, AT I.71/CSMK 8.
26 Descartes to Mersenne, January 1630, AT I.113/CSMK 18.
27 Descartes to Mersenne, 25 November 1630, AT I.178–9/
    CSMK 28.
28 *Discourse on Method*, AT VI.42/CSM I.132.
29 AT I.254/CSMK 39.
30 AT I.263/CSMK 40.
31 *Discourse on Method*, AT VI.56/CSM I.139.
32 *Discourse on Method*, AT VI.55/CSM I.139.
33 *Discourse on Method*, AT VI.57/CSM I.140.
34 *Discourse on Method*, AT VI.59/CSM I.141.
35 There is some difference of scholarly opinion over whether the
    title *Le Monde* applies to the whole composed of both treatises
    together, or only to the *Traité de la lumière*. The earliest editions
    of these works all use *Le Monde* only with respect to the *Traité de la
    lumière*. Florent Schuyl's 1662 Latin edition of the *Traité de l'homme*
    – *De homine* – and Clerselier's 1664 French edition of that work
    do not have *Le Monde* in the title. (There was a 1664 edition of *Le
    Monde de Mr. Descartes ou le Traité de la lumière* published by Jacques du
    Roure (according to Roux, 'Une enquête sur Jacques du Roure').)
    Moreover, Clerselier's 1677 edition containing both treatises has
    the following title: *L'Homme de René Descartes . . . a quoy l'on a ajouté
    Le Monde ou Traité de la lumière du mesme auteur.* In Clerselier's view,
    then, only the *Traité de la lumière* is *Le Monde*. The editors of CSM, the
    standard English edition of Descartes' writings, take his lead, and
    reserve *The World* only for the *Treatise on Light.* It seems clear from
    Descartes' correspondence, however, that the work he refers to
    as 'mon Monde' includes both parts. For example, he tells Mersenne
    that 'my discussion of man in *The World* will be a little fuller than
    I had intended, for I have undertaken to explain all the main
    functions in man' (AT I.263/CSMK 40) – which is precisely what
    he does in the *Traité de l'homme*. The editors of AT, still the standard
    critical edition of Descartes' writings, include both treatises under
    Le Monde, as have I.

36 See the summary in *Discourse on Method*, AT VI.40−44/CSM I.131−4.

37 In fact, it is a little more complex than this. The human body itself is a substance whose matter is informed by the substantial form that makes it a living human body; that human body substance then takes on the substantial form that is the human soul, which endows it with rationality and the other human psychic functions.

38 See, for example, Thomas Aquinas, *De ente et essentia*, sections 17−18.

39 See Duarte Madeira Arrais, *Novae philosophiae et medicinae de qualitatibus occultis, pars prima* (Lisbon, 1650), pp. 1−19.

40 Collegium Conimbricense, *In octo libros physicorum Aristotelis* (Coimbra, 1602), VIII.4.i.3.

41 *Principles of Philosophy*, Preface to the French translation, AT IX−B.8/CSM I.182−3.

42 Act 3, third interlude, ll. 58−66.

43 See Roger Ariew and Marjorie Grene, 'The Cartesian Destiny of Form and Matter', *Early Science and Medicine*, 2 (1997), pp. 300−325 (p. 313).

44 Descartes to Mersenne, 26 April 1643, AT III.648/CSMK 216.

45 *The World*, AT XI.25−6/CSM I.89.

46 *The World*, AT XI.27/CSM I.89.

47 *The World*, AT XI.20/CSM I.87.

48 *The World*, AT XI.34−35/CSM I.91.

49 Galileo, *Discoveries and Opinions*, pp. 274−7.

50 *Treatise on Man*, AT XI.120/G 99.

51 *Treatise on Man*, AT XI.130/ G 107.

52 *Treatise on Man*, AT XI.143/ G 119.

53 *Treatise on Man*, AT XI.145−6/ G 120.

54 *The World*, AT XI.3−4/CSM I.81.

55 There are, of course, important differences among these early modern scientists. Some of them (Boyle, Locke, Gassendi) are atomists and others (Descartes and most of his followers) are not. Leibniz insists on the need for a metaphysical ground of force within bodies (similar, he admits, to Aristotelian forms), while Descartes denies this. And Newton, in some contexts, seems to countenance action at a distance. Nonetheless, in the domain of physics proper, for all of these thinkers the only relevant considerations are matter and motion and the mathematical formulation of the laws governing these.

56 Descartes to Mersenne, 15 April 1630, AT I.145/CSMK 23.

57 Descartes to Mersenne, 6 May 1630, AT I.149/CSMK 24.

58   Descartes [to Mersenne?], 27 May 1630, AT I.151–2/CSMK 25.
     The editors of AT are uncertain whether this letter is indeed
     addressed to Mersenne.
59   Descartes to Mersenne, 19 April 1630, AT I.146/CSMK 23.
60   *Discourse on Method*, AT VI.59/CSM I.141.
61   Descartes to Mersenne, 25 November 1630, AT I.182/CSMK 29.

4 Rebuilding the House of Knowledge

1   Jonathan Israel, *The Dutch Republic: Its Rise, Greatness and Fall, 1477–1806*
     (Oxford, 1995), p. 559.
 2   Throughout this book, I use the standard abbreviations for Dutch
     patronyms. Thus 'Cornelisz' is short for 'Corneliszoon' (Cornelis's
     son), and 'Jansdr' is short for 'Jansdochter' (Jan's daughter).
 3   On the book trade in Amsterdam, see M. M. Kleerkooper and W. P.
     van Stockum, *De Boekhandel te Amsterdam voornamelijk in de 17e eeuw*, 2 vols
     (The Hague, 1914–16), as well as, more recently, Andrew Pettegree
     and Arthur der Weduwen, *The Bookshop of the World: Making and Trading
     Books in the Dutch Golden Age* (New Haven, CT, 2019).
 4   Descartes to Mersenne, 18 December 1629, AT I.85–6.
 5   *The World*, AT XI.64–9/G 41–5. The diagrams in the work make
     the heliocentrism perfectly clear.
 6   *The World*, AT XI.48/G 32.
 7   *The World*, AT XI.31–2/G 21.
 8   Descartes to Mersenne, November or December 1632, AT I.262/
     CSMK 39–40.
 9   Descartes to Mersenne, November 1633, AT I.271/CSMK 41.
10   Descartes to Mersenne, December 1640, AT III.258/CSMK 160.
11   Descartes to Mersenne, February 1634, AT I.281–2/CSMK 41–2.
     The work was not published until after Descartes' death, when
     it appeared as two separate treatises: *Le Monde ou Traité de la Lumière*
     (1664) and the *Traité de l'homme* (1664; a Latin translation was
     published first, in 1662).
12   *The World*, AT XI.31/G 21.
13   *Discourse on Method*, AT VI.75/CSM I.149.
14   Descartes to Mersenne, 27 May 1638, AT II.141–2/CSMK 103.
15   *Discourse on Method*, AT VI.76/CSM I.150.
16   *Dioptrics*, AT VI.87.
17   *Dioptrics*, AT VI.83.
18   *Meteors*, AT VI.233.

19 Descartes [to Vatier], 22 February 1638, AT I.563/CSMK 87.

20 *Meteors*, AT VI.240.

21 *Meteors*, AT VI.325.

22 *Meteors*, AT VI.333.

23 Descartes to Mersenne, March 1636, AT I.339/CSMK 51.

24 Descartes to Mersenne, 27 February 1637, AT I.349/CSMK 53.

25 *Discourse on Method*, AT VI.22–7/CSM I.122–4.

26 This is how I read this difficult passage from the *Discourse* in which
    Descartes describes the procedure of investigation in *The World*. In
    practice, things may have been a little more complicated than he says
    in his exposition, and are certainly more complicated (and opaque)
    in the later *Principles of Philosophy*, where it is even less clear at what
    point Descartes begins arguing hypothetically from phenomena to
    causes. My thanks to Daniel Garber for discussing this issue with me;
    see also Daniel Garber, 'Descartes and Experiment in the *Discourse*
    and *Essays*', in Daniel Garber, *Descartes Embodied: Reading Cartesian
    Philosophy through Cartesian Science* (Cambridge, 2001), pp. 85–110.
    Meanwhile, Stephen Gaukroger has told me that, as he reads *The
    World*, the heavens and so on are not actually discovered a priori.

27 *Discourse on Method*, AT VI.64–5/CSM I.144.

28 *Discourse on Method*, AT VI.56–7/CSM I.139–40.

29 *Discourse on Method*, AT VI.57–8/CSM I.140. See also Descartes to
    the Marquess of Newcastle, 23 November 1646, AT IV.569–76/
    CSMK 302–4. Descartes tells the Marquess that 'I cannot share the
    opinion of Montaigne and others who attribute understanding or
    thought to animals . . . the reason why animals do not speak as we do
    is not that they lack the organs but that they have no thoughts.' He
    also notes that 'none of our external actions can show anyone who
    examines them that our body is not just a self-moving machine, but
    contains a soul with thoughts, with the exception of spoken words.'

30 Descartes to Mersenne, March 1636, AT I.340/CSMK 51.

31 *Discourse on Method*, AT VI.77/CSM I.151.

32 Descartes [to ?] AT I.370/CSMK 58.

5 'I think, therefore I am'

1 Descartes to Mersenne, 27 May 1638, AT II.152–3.

2 According to a report by Baillet; see AT V.280.

3 According to Baillet; AT V.280.

4 Descartes to Plempius, 15 February 1638, AT I.526/CSMK 81.

5 Descartes to Mersenne, 2 November 1646, AT IV.555.
6 This is how he describes his life in Holland in a letter to Constantijn Huygens, 12 June 1637, AT I.638/CSMK 60.
7 *Discourse on Method*, AT VI.75/CSM I.149.
8 *Discourse on Method*, AT VI.46—55/CSM I.134—9.
9 This is Descartes' paraphrase of Froidmont's objection, AT I.414/CSM I.62.
10 Descartes to Plempius, 3 October 1637, AT I.410/CSMK 60.
11 Descartes to Plempius, 20 December 1637, AT I.475/CSMK 76.
12 Descartes to Plempius, 20 December 1637, AT I.475/CSMK 76.
13 Fermat to Mersenne, April or May 1637, AT I.357.
14 Fermat to Mersenne, April or May 1637, AT I.355.
15 Descartes to Mersenne, 5 October 1637, AT I.451/CSMK 74.
16 Descartes to Mersenne, January 1638, AT I.486.
17 See Roberval's text of April 1638, AT II.104—14.
18 Descartes to Mersenne, 27 July 1638, AT II.274—5.
19 Descartes to Mydorge, March 1638, AT II.13.
20 Descartes to Mersenne, 29 June 1638, AT II.193.
21 Descartes to Mersenne, 29 June 1638, AT II.175.
22 *Discourse on Method*, AT VI.68—9/CSM I.146.
23 Descartes to Mersenne, 5 October 1637, AT I.449.
24 Descartes to Vatier, 22 February 1638, AT I.560/CSMK 86.
25 Descartes to Vatier, 22 February 1638, AT I.561—3/CSMK 86—7.
26 Huygens to Descartes, 23 November 1637, AT I.462.
27 Huygens to Descartes, 15 May 1639, AT II.679.
28 See Descartes' paraphrases of Morin's objections in his letter to Morin of 13 July 1638, AT II.197—219/CSMK 106—11.
29 Morin to Descartes, 22 February 1638, AT I.537.
30 Descartes to Mersenne, 15 April 1630, AT I.144/CSMK 22.
31 Descartes to Huygens, 31 July 1640, AT III.751/CSMK 150.
32 Descartes to Mersenne, 11 November 1640, AT III.238—9/CSMK 158.
33 Descartes to Mersenne, 11 October 1638, AT II.380/CSMK 124.
34 Descartes to Mersenne, 28 January 1641, AT III.298/CSMK 173.
35 On the *Meditations* as an anti-sceptical project, see Edwin M. Curley, *Descartes Against the Skeptics* (Cambridge, MA, 1978).
36 The classic study is Richard H. Popkin, *The History of Skepticism from Erasmus to Spinoza* (Berkeley and Los Angeles, CA, 1979).
37 There are many fine and highly detailed scholarly studies of the *Meditations*, from very different perspectives. These include

Janet Broughton, *Descartes' Method of Doubt* (Princeton, NJ, 2001); John Carriero, *Between Two Worlds: A Reading of Descartes' Meditations* (Princeton, NJ, 2009); Martial Gueroult, *Descartes selon l'ordre des raisons*, 2 vols (Paris, 1953); Anthony Kenny, *Descartes: A Study of His Philosophy* (New York, 1968); Bernard Williams, *Descartes: The Project of Pure Enquiry* (Harmondsworth, 1978); and Margaret Wilson, *Descartes* (London, 1978).

38 Descartes to Mersenne, 11 November 1640, AT III.235/CSMK 157.

39 Preface to the French translation of *Principles of Philosophy*, AT IX.2.14/CSM I.186.

40 Ibid.

41 *Meditations*, Synopsis, AT IX.2/CSM II.9.

42 Seventh Set of Replies, AT VII.481/CSM II.324.

43 *Meditations*, First Meditation, AT VII.17/CSM II.12.

44 These are the two different ways of understanding the dream argument, suggested (respectively) by how Descartes describes it in the First Meditation (AT VII.19/CSM II.13) and in his recap in the Sixth Meditation (AT VII.77/CSM II.53). The difference is discussed by Wilson in her analysis of the argument (*Descartes*, pp. 13–31).

45 *Meditations*, First Meditation, AT VII.19–20/CSM II.13.

46 *Meditations*, Third Meditation, AT VII.36/CSM II.25. Scholars now call it 'hyperbolic' doubt; the phrase was introduced in Henri Gouhier, *Essais sur Descartes* (Paris, 1937).

47 *Meditations*, First Meditation, AT VII.21/CSM II.14.

48 Descartes was a fan of this sort of literature, and Cervantes's story may have played an influential role in the way in which Descartes conceived the doubts of the First Meditation; see Steven Nadler, 'Descartes' Demon and the Madness of Don Quixote', *Journal of the History of Ideas*, 58 (1997), pp. 41–55.

49 *Meditations*, Second Meditation, AT VII.25/CSM II.17.

50 *Meditations*, Second Meditation, AT VII.28/CSM II.19.

51 *Meditations*, Third Meditation, AT VII.41/CSM II.29.

52 *Meditations*, Fifth Meditation, AT VII.66/CSM II.46.

53 *Meditations*, Fourth Meditation, AT VII.53/CSM II.37.

54 AT VII.71/CSM II.49.

55 AT VII.62/CSM II.43.

56 Second Set of Replies, AT VII.141/CSM II.101.

57 *Meditations*, Sixth Meditation, AT VII.78/CSM II.54.

58 *Meditations*, Sixth Meditation, AT VII.79–80/CSM II.55.

59 For a provocative study of Descartes' account of embodied mind, and especially what he calls 'meum corpus', see Jean-Luc Marion, *Sur la pensée passive de Descartes* (Paris, 2013).

60 *Meditations*, Sixth Meditation, AT VII.80−81/CSM II.56.

61 In the second edition, published in 1642, this is changed to: 'in which are demonstrated the existence of God and the distinction between the human soul and the body.'

62 Descartes to Mersenne, 24 December 1640, AT III.266/CSMK 163.

63 Descartes [to Gibieuf], 11 November 1630, AT III.238/CSMK 158.

6 Loss and Conflict

1   Descartes to Mersenne, 24 December 1640, AT III.265/CSMK 163.

2   Descartes to Mersenne, 30 September 1640, AT III.183−4/CSMK 153.

3   Descartes to Mersenne, 28 January 1641, AT IIII.297/CSMK 172.

4   On Helena Jansdr van der Stroom, see Jeroen van de Ven, 'Quelques données nouvelles sur Helena Jans', *Bulletin Cartésien*, 32, *Archives de philosophie*, 67 (2004), pp. 163−6.

5   Desmond Clarke, *Descartes: A Biography* (Cambridge, 2006), p. 131.

6   Adrien Baillet, *La vie de Monsieur Descartes*, 2 vols (Paris, 1691), vol. II, p. 89.

7   Ibid., vol. I, p. ix.

8   For more on Helena's fate, see Clarke, *Descartes*, pp. 135−6; and Van de Ven, 'Quelques données nouvelles'. Van de Ven also discusses the dowry (p. 166), as does Richard A. Watson, *Cogito Ergo Sum: The Life of René Descartes* (Boston, MA, 2007), p. 188.

9   Descartes [to ?], 30 August 1637, AT I.393.

10 Baillet, *La vie de Monsieur Descartes*, vol. II, p. 90.

11 Ibid.

12 Descartes to Mersenne, 15 September 1640, AT III.175−81.

13 Helena, twice widowed, would die in 1683.

14 Descartes to Pollot, January 1641, AT III.278−9/CSMK 167.

15 First Set of Objections, AT VII.99/CSM II.72.

16 Second Set of Objections, AT VII.126/CSM II.90.

17 *Leviathan*, III.xxxiv.2.

18 *Leviathan*, I.i.1−2.

19 *Leviathan*, I.iii.12.

20 Descartes to Mersenne (for Hobbes), 21 January 1641, AT III.287/CSMK 170.

21 Descartes to Mersenne, 4 March 1641, AT III.320/CSMK 173.

22 Fourth Objections, AT VII.197–204/CSM II.139–44.

23 Fourth Objections, AT VII.207–14/CSM II.146–50.

24 Fourth Objections, AT VII.214/CSM II.150.

25 Council of Trent, Session 13, Chapter 4.

26 On this subject, see Jean-Robert Armogathe, *Theologia cartesiana: L'explication physique de l'Eucharistie chez Descartes et Dom Desgabet*, International Archives of the History of Ideas, 84 (The Hague, 1977).

27 Fourth Replies, AT VII.251/CSM II.175.

28 Descartes to Mesland, 9 February 1645, AT IV.163–9.

29 When Descartes' friend Claude Clerselier published his collection of Descartes' correspondence in 1657 he did not include this letter to Mesland, suspecting that its 'novelties' would be found 'suspect and dangerous' (Clerselier to Desgabets, 6 January 1672, AT IV.170).

30 Descartes to Arnauld, 4 June 1648, AT V.194/CSMK 355.

31 See Steven Nadler, 'Arnauld, Descartes and Transubstantiation: Reconciling Cartesian Metaphysics and Real Presence', *Journal of the History of Ideas*, 59 (1988), pp. 229–46.

32 Descartes to Mersenne, 28 January 1641, AT III.293/CSMK 171.

33 Descartes to Mersenne, 4 March 1641, AT III.330/CSMK 175.

34 Descartes to Mersenne, 18 March 1641, AT III.334/CSMK 175.

35 On Gassendi and early modern Epicureanism, see Catherine Wilson, *Epicureanism at the Origins of Modernity* (New York, 2008). On Gassendi's philosophy generally, see Antonia LoLordo, *Pierre Gassendi and the Birth of Early Modern Philosophy* (Cambridge, 2007).

36 On Gassendi's 'mitigated skepticism', see Richard H. Popkin, *The History of Skepticism from Erasmus to Spinoza* (Berkeley and Los Angeles, CA, 1979); and LoLordo, *Pierre Gassendi*, pp. 60–72.

37 Fifth Set of Objections, AT VII. 276–7/CSM II.192–3.

38 The phrase is from David Chalmers, 'Facing Up to the Problem of Consciousness', *Journal of Consciousness Studies*, 2 (1995), pp. 200–219.

39 Descartes does, it seems, miss Gassendi's point and accuse him of making a category mistake; Fifth Set of Replies, AT VII.359–60/CSM II.248–9.

40 Namely, in his *Syntagma philosophicum* of 1658.

41 Fifth Set of Objections, AT VII.260–62/CSM II.181–3.

42 On this, see John Yolton, *Thinking Matter: Materialism in Eighteenth-Century Britain* (Minneapolis, MN, 1984).

43 Fifth Set of Objections, AT VII.337/CSM II.234.

44 Fifth Set of Objections, AT VII.338/CSM II.234.

45 Fifth Set of Objections, AT VII.261/CSM II.182.

46 Fifth Set of Objections, AT VII.341/CSM II.237.

47 Fifth Set of Objecctions, AT VII.343–5/CSM II.238–9.

48 For studies of mind–body causal and epistemological relations
    in Descartes and later Cartesianism, see Richard A. Watson, *The
    Downfall of Cartesianism, 1673–1712: A Study of Epistemological Issues in Late
    Seventeenth-Century Cartesianism* (The Hague, 1966); Tad Schmaltz,
    Descartes on Causation (Oxford, 2007); Schmaltz, *Early Modern
    Cartesianisms: Dutch and French Constructions* (Oxford, 2017); Steven
    Nadler, *Occasionalism: Causation Among the Cartesians* (Oxford and New
    York, 2011); and Sandrine Roux, *L'Empreinte cartésienne: L'interaction
    psychophysique, débats classiques et contemporains* (Paris, 2018).

49 AT IX–A.213/CSM II.275.

50 Fifth Set of Replies, AT VII.390/CSM II.266–7.

51 For a biography of Elisabeth, see Renée Jeffery, *Princess Elisabeth of
    Bohemia: The Philosopher Princess* (Lanham, MD, 2018).

52 Elisabeth to Descartes, 6 May 1643, AT III.661/S 62.

53 Descartes to Elisabeth, 21 May 1643, AT III.664/S 63.

54 Descartes to Elisabeth, 21 May 1643, AT III.666/S 66.

55 Elisabeth to Descartes, 10 June 1643, AT III.685/S 68.

56 Descartes to Elisabeth, 28 June 1643, AT III.692/S 70.

57 Elisabeth to Descartes, 1 July 1643, AT IV.2/S 72.

58 Descartes to Elisabeth, 8 July 1644, AT IV.65/S 81.

59 Descartes to Elisabeth, August 1644, AT IV.137/S 85.

60 Descartes to Elisabeth, 18 May 1645, AT IV.201/S 86.

61 Elisabeth to Descartes, 22 June 1645, AT IV.233/S 93.

62 Descartes to Elisabeth, 4 August 1645, AT IV.264–5/S 97–8.

63 For example, through Justus Lipsius' *De constantia* (1583). On
    Descartes' moral philosophy, see John Marshall, *Descartes's Moral
    Theory* (Ithaca, NY, 1998); and Denis Kambouchner, *Descartes et la
    philosophie morale* (Paris, 2008).

64 Elisabeth to Descartes, 28 October 1645, AT IV.323/S 123, and
    30 November 1645, AT IV.336/S 127.

65 Descartes to Elisabeth, 3 November 1645, AT IV.333/S 126, and
    January 1646, AT IV.352–3/S 130. The analogy with the king is
    misleading, of course, since the king, unlike God, does not put those
    belligerent inclinations into his two subjects.

66 *Principles of Philosophy* I.40–41, AT VIIIA.20/CSM I.206. For Descartes'
    approaches to the problem of freedom, see C. P. Ragland, *The Will to
    Reason: Theodicy and Freedom in Descartes* (Oxford and New York, 2016).

67 Clarke suggests that Descartes' interest in her was grounded not in love but in her potential as a patron (*Descartes*, p. 274).

68 Descartes to Mersenne, 17 November 1641, AT III.448/CSMK 198–9.

69 Descartes to Mersenne, March 1641, AT III.543/CSMK 210.

70 This is the plausible explanation offered by Clarke, *Descartes*, p. 207.

71 Seventh Set of Objections, AT VII.529/CSM II.360.

72 Seventh Set of Objections, AT VII.463/CSM II.311.

73 Seventh Set of Objections, AT VII.479/CSM II.323.

74 Seventh Set of Replies, AT VII.452/CSM II.303.

75 Letter to Father Dinet, AT VII.564/CSM II.384–5.

76 Letter to Father Dinet, AT VII.565/CSM II.385.

77 Letter to Father Dinet, AT VII.580–581/CSM II.391–2.

78 Letter to Father Dinet, AT VII.602/CSM II.396.

79 See Descartes to Dinet and Descartes to Bourdin, both October 1644, AT IV.142–3.

80 Descartes to Charlet, 9 February 1645, AT IV.157.

81 Jean-Robert Armogathe, 'L'Approbation des *Meditationes* par la Faculté de théologie de Paris (1641)', *Bulletin Cartésien*, 21, *Archives de philosophie*, 57 (1994), pp. 1–3.

82 See, for example, Clarke, *Descartes*, pp. 206–7.

7 The Cartesian Textbook

1 Quoted in Desmond Clarke, *Descartes: A Biography* (Cambridge, 2006), p. 230. 'Hogeland' is Cornelis van Hogeland (1590–1662), a friend of Descartes' in Leiden.

2 Descartes to Huygens, 1 September 1642, AT III.792.

3 Descartes to Colvius, AT III.647.

4 Descartes to Huygens, 31 January 1642, AT III.523/CSMK 210.

5 Descartes to Mersenne, 30 September 1640, AT III.185/CSMK 153–4. Among the Jesuit authors he names are Francisco Toledo (1552–1596), Antonio Rubio (1548–1615) and the Coimbrian commentators on Aristotle.

6 Descartes to Mersenne, 11 November 1640, AT III.232/CSMK 156.

7 The *Principles* was originally conceived as a six-part work, including a Part Five on plants and animals and a Part Six devoted to the human being; it may be that ethics would have been consigned to this final part.

8 *Principles* I.51, AT VIII–A.24/CSM I.210.

9 *Principles* I.9, AT VIII–A.7/CSM I.195.

10 *Principles* II.4, AT VIII–A.42/CSM I.224.
11 *Principles* I.65, AT VIII–A.32/CSM I.216.
12 *Principles* I.68, AT VIII–A.33/CSM I.217.
13 *Principles* II.3, AT VIII–A.41/CSM I.224.
14 *Principles* II.11 and II.20, AT VIII–A.46/CSM II.227 and AT VIII–A.51/
     CSM I.231.
15 *Principles* II.23, AT VIII–A.52/CSM I.232.
16 *Principles* II.28, AT VIII–A.55/CSM I.234.
17 *Passions of the Soul,* II.145, AT XI.438/CSM I.380.
18 *Discourse on Method,* AT VI.43/CSM I.132. He is referring to what he
     does in *Le Monde,* chap. 7.
19 *Principles of Philosophy* II.36, AT VIII–A.61–2/CSM I.240.
20 *Le Monde,* AT XI.43/CSM I.96.
21 Garber argues that Descartes intends this law to apply only to
     inanimate bodies, so as to allow the human mind (which is not
     a subject of motion) to generate motion in its body; see Daniel
     Garber, 'Mind, Body and the Laws of Nature in Descartes and
     Leibniz', *Midwest Studies in Philosophy,* 8 (1983), pp. 105–33.
22 *Principles of Philosophy* II.39, AT VIII–A.63/CSM I.242.
23 *Principles of Philosophy* II.40, AT VIII–A.65/CSM I.242.
24 Some of the rules (presented in *Principles of Philosophy* II.46–52) are,
     as Huygens, Leibniz and even some later Cartesians discovered,
     incorrect.
25 *Principles of Philosophy* IV.203, AT VIII–A.326/CSM I.209.
26 *Principles of Philosophy* III.43, AT VIII–A.99/CSM I.255.
27 *Principles of Philosophy* III.44, AT VIII–A.99/CSM I.255.
28 *Principles of Philosophy* III.45, AT VIII–A.99–100/CSM I.256.
29 *Principles of Philosophy* III.45, AT VIII–A.100/CSM I.256.
30 *Principles of Philosophy* III.44, AT VIII–A.99/CSM I.255.
31 *Principles of Philosophy* III.19, AT VIII–A.86/CSM I.251. The bracketed
     words were added in the French edition published in 1647.
32 *Principles of Philosophy* III.28, AT VIII–A.90/CSM I.252.
33 *Principles of Philosophy* III.30, AT VIII–A.92/CSM I.253.
34 *Principles of Philosophy* IV.23, AT VIII–A.213/CSM I.269.
35 *Principles of Philosophy* IV.171, AT VIII–A.302/M 265.
36 *Principles of Philosophy* IV.197, AT VIII–A.321/CSM I.284.
37 *Principles of Philosophy* IV.197, AT VIII–A.321/CSM I.284.
38 *Principles of Philosophy* IV.189, AT VIII–A.315–16/CSM I.279–80.
39 *Principles of Philosophy* IV.188, AT VIII–A.315/CSM I.279.
40 AT IX–B.11/CSM I.184.

41 *Principles of Philosophy* IV.199, AT VIII−A.323/CSM I.285.
42 *Principles of Philosophy* IV.201, AT VIII−A.324−5/CSM I.287.
     The bracketed words were added in the French edition
     published in 1647.
43 *Principles of Philosophy* IV.200, AT VIII−A.323/CSM I.286.
44 Isaac Newton, *Mathematical Principles of Natural Philosophy and His System
     of the World*, trans. Florian Cajori, 2 vols (Berkeley and Los Angeles,
     CA, 1934), p. 547.
45 *Principles of Philosophy* IV.205, AT VIII−B.327/CSM I.289−90.
46 *Principles of Philosophy* IV.206, AT VIII−B.328−9/CSM I.290−91.
47 Descartes to Huygens, 12 June 1637, AT I.638.
48 Descartes [to Brasset], 23 April 1649, AT V.349.
49 Descartes to Regius, December 1641, AT III.460/CSMK 200.
50 Theo Verbeek, *Descartes and the Dutch: Early Reactions to Cartesian
     Philosophy, 1637−1650* (Carbondale and Edwardsville, IL, 1992),
     pp. 17−18.
51 Descartes to Regius, January 1642, AT III.492/CSMK 205.
52 Descartes to Regius, January 1642, AT III.510.
53 *Responsio, sive notae in appendicum ad Corollaria theologico-philosophica viri
     reverendi & celeberrimi D. Gisberti Voetii* (1642).
54 The text of the condemnation by the University of Utrecht is
     cited by Descartes in his letter to Dinet; see AT VII.590−93.
55 AT VII.592−3.
56 Descartes to Mersenne, March 1642, AT III.545−6.
57 It is interesting to note that these are precisely the charges that
     Socrates faced in Athens nearly two millennia earlier.
58 *Admiranda methodus novae philosophiae Cartesianae* (1643), Preface.
     A French translation of the work is in Theo Verbeek, *La Querelle
     d'Utrecht: René Descartes et Martin Schoock* (Paris, 1988), p. 161, along
     with other documents relative to the Descartes/Schoock stage
     of the Utrecht affair. For an account of Schoock's arguments,
     see Verbeek, *Descartes and the Dutch*, pp. 20−23. It has often been
     suggested that Voetius is actually the author of the work. But
     Verbeek, in his important study of the dispute, argues that
     'while the part that Voetius took in the composition of the
     Admiranda methodus is considerable, the book, such as it is, is,
     without any doubt, written by Schoock' (*La Querelle d'Utrecht*, p. 61).
59 *Admiranda methodus*, II.9; Verbeek, *La Querelle d'Utrecht*, p. 245.
60 *Admiranda methodus*, IV.3; Verbeek, *La Querelle d'Utrecht*, p. 315.
61 *Admiranda methodus*, Preface; Verbeek, *La Querelle d'Utrecht*, p. 160.

Descartes quotes this text from Schoock in his *Letter to Voetius* (*Epistola ad Voetium*), AT VIII–B.142.

62 *Admiranda methodus*, Preface; Verbeek, *La Querelle d'Utrecht*, p. 161.

63 *Letter to Voetius*, AT VIII–B.181–2.

64 *Letter to Voetius*, AT VIII–B.109–10.

65 *Letter to Voetius*, AT VIII–B.111, 116.

66 A French translation of the Dutch document can be found at AT IV.645–6.

67 AT IX–B.19/CSM I.189.

68 Descartes to Mersenne, 5 October 1646, AT IV.510/CSMK 295–6.

69 AT VIII–B.341–69/CSM I.294–311.

70 *Comments on a Certain Broadsheet*, AT VIII–B.364/CSM I.307.

71 Quoted in Verbeek, *Descartes and the Dutch*, p. 35.

72 Descartes to Elizabeth, 10 May 1647, AT V.18/CSMK 318–19.

73 Descartes to Elizabeth, 10 May 1647, AT V.15–16/CSMK 317.

8 'A land of bears, rocks and ice'

1 A translation of the text of the treaty is in Herbert H. Rowen, ed., *The Low Countries in Early Modern Times* (New York, 1972), pp. 179–87.

2 Willem Frederik of Nassau, a descendant of Willem the Great's brother Count Jan of Nassau, remained stadholder in Friesland, Groningen and Drenthe.

3 Descartes to Mersenne, March 1642, AT III.542–3/CSMK 210.

4 See Descartes to Elisabeth, 31 January 1648, AT V.112/S 168.

5 Descartes to Mersenne, 4 March 1641, AT III.332.

6 See the letter to Huygens of 11 March 1646, AT IV.786–7.

7 Descartes to Chanut, 6 March 1646, AT IV.376–7

8 Descartes to Huygens, October 1639, AT II.583–4.

9 AT II.153. The letter is from 15 January 1638.

10 Adrien Baillet, *La vie de Monsieur Descartes*, 2 vols (Paris, 1691), vol. II, p. 17.

11 Descartes to Huygens, October 1639, AT II.583–5.

12 Elisabeth to Descartes, 30 November 1645, AT IV.335–6/S 127.

13 Elisabeth to Descartes, 13 September 1645, AT IV.289/S 110.

14 Descartes to Elisabeth, 6 October 1645, AT IV.310/S 118.

15 Descartes to Elisabeth, 1 September 1645, AT IV.287/S 109.

16 Descartes to Elisabeth, May 1646, AT IV.407/S 134.

17 *Passions of the Soul*, I.33, AT XI.353/CSM I.340.

18 *Passions of the Soul*, I.28, AT XI.350/CSM I.339.
19 *Passions of the Soul*, I.45, AT XI.362–3/CSM I.345.
20 *Passions of the Soul*, I.50, AT XI.368/CSM I.348
21 *Passions of the Soul*, III.153, AT XI.445–6/CSM I.384. On Descartes'
    moral philosophy, see John Marshall, *Descartes's Moral Theory* (Ithaca,
    NY, 1998); and Denis Kambouchner, *Descartes et la philosophie morale*
    (Paris, 2008).
22 *Passions of the Soul*, III.212, AT XI.488/CSM I.404.
23 *Passions of the Soul*, III.211, AT XI.485–6/CSM I.403.
24 Her father had died in battle in 1632, and though her mother, the
    queen, was still alive, she had been declared unfit to serve as regent.
25 Descartes to Chanut, 1 February 1647, AT IV.603/CSMK 307.
26 Descartes to Chanut, 6 June 1647, AT VI.51–2/CSMK 320.
27 Descartes to Chanut, 20 November 1647, AT V.86–7/CSMK 326.
28 Descartes to Christina, 20 November 1647, AT V.82–3/CSMK 324–5.
29 Baillet, *La vie de Monsieur Descartes*, vol. II, p. 311.
30 Chanut to Descartes, 12 December 1648, AT V.254.
31 For Baillet's account of these events, see Baillet, *La vie de Monsieur
    Descartes*, vol. II, pp. 310–13.
32 Descartes to Chanut, 1 November 1646, AT IV.537/CSMK 299.
33 Descartes to Chanut, 1 November 1646, AT IV.537/CSMK 300.
34 Descartes to Chanut, 31 March 1649, AT V.329/CSMK 371. For
    a discussion of the invitation to Sweden, see Desmond Clarke,
    Descartes: A Biography (Cambridge, 2006), pp. 380–84 and
    chap. 14.
35 Descartes [to Brasset], 23 April 1649, AT V.349/CSMK 375.
36 Descartes to Elisabeth, June 1649, AT V.359-60/CSMK 378.
37 Baillet, *La vie de Monsieur Descartes*, vol. II, p. 387.
38 Ibid.
39 Hals's original is in the Statens Museum for Kunst, Copenhagen,
    Denmark.
40 Descartes to Elisabeth, 31 March 1649, AT V.330/S 179.
41 Descartes to Elisabeth, 9 October 1649, AT V.429/CSMK 382.
42 Baillet, *La vie de Monsieur Descartes*, vol. II, p. 411.
43 Descartes to Elisabeth, 9 October 1649, AT V.430/CSMK 383.
44 Baillet, *La vie de Monsieur Descartes*, vol. II, p. 395. Watson argues,
    however, that Descartes was not the author of the verses; see
    Richard A. Watson, *Descartes' Ballet: His Doctrine of the Will and His
    Political Philosophy* (South Bend, IN, 2007).
45 Descartes to De Brégy, 15 January 1650, AT V.466–7/CSMK 383.

46 For the statutes, see Baillet, *La vie de Monsieur Descartes*, vol. II,
    pp. 412–13.

47 Descartes to Elisabeth, 9 October 1649, AT v.431/CSMK 383.

48 The rumour circulated in the seventeenth century, but has also
    recently been argued for by Theodore Ebert, 'Did Descartes Die
    of Poisoning?', *Early Science and Medicine*, 24 (2019), pp. 142–85.

49 Baillet, *La vie de Monsieur Descartes*, vol. II, pp. 415–16.

50 On early modern developments in Cartesian physics, the classic
    study is Paul Mouy, *Le Développement de la physique Cartésienne, 1646–1712*
    (Paris, 1934).

51 On these issues, see Daniel Garber, *Descartes' Metaphysical Physics*
    (Chicago, IL, 1992); and Steven Nadler, *Occasionalism: Causation Among
    the Cartesians* (Oxford, 2011).

52 On these various developments in Cartesianism in the second half
    of the seventeenth century, see Sandrine Roux, *L'Empreinte cartésienne:
    L'interaction psychophysique, débats classiques et contemporains* (Paris, 2018);
    and Tad Schmaltz, *Descartes on Causation* (Oxford, 2002) and *Early
    Modern Cartesianisms: Dutch and French Constructions* (Oxford, 2017).

53 See, for example, Query 31 in the Latin edition of the *Opticks* (1706).

54 *Lettres philosophiques*, Lettre XIV, in Voltaire, *Philosophical Letters*, trans.
    Ernest Dilworth (Indianapolis, IN, 1961), p. 60.

BIBLIOGRAPHY

Ariew, Roger, *Descartes and the Last Scholastics* (Ithaca, NY, 1999)
—, *Descartes and the First Cartesians* (Oxford and New York, 2014)
—, and Marjorie Grene, eds, *Descartes and His Contemporaries: Meditations, Objections and Replies* (Chicago, IL, 1995)
—, and —, eds, 'The Cartesian Destiny of Form and Matter', *Early Science and Medicine*, 2 (1997), pp. 300–325
Armogathe, Jean-Robert, *Theologia Cartesiana: L'explication physique de l'Eucharistie chez Descartes et Dom Desgabet*, International Archives of the History of Ideas, 84 (The Hague, 1977)
—, 'L'Approbation des *Meditationes* par la Faculté de théologie de Paris (1641)', *Bulletin Cartésien*, 21, *Archives de philosophie*, 57 (1994), pp. 1–3
—, Vincent Carraud and Robert Feenstra, 'La licence en droit de Descartes', *Nouvelles de la République des lettres*, 8 (1988), pp. 123–45
Baillet, Adrien, *La Vie de Monsieur Descartes*, 2 vols (Paris, 1691)
Beeckman, Isaac, *Journal tenu par Isaac Beeckman de 1604 à 1634*, vol. 1: *1604–1619*, ed. Cornelis de Waard (The Hague, 1939)
Bos, Erik-Jan, 'Deux signatures de Descartes dan les registres de baptêmes; et la date de la mort de sa soeur Jeanne', *Bulletin Cartésien*, 47, *Archives de philosophie*, 81 (2018), pp. 171–4
—, 'Descartes en Italie: pour vendre des mulets', *Bulletin Cartésien*, 51, *Archives de philosophie*, 85 (2022), pp. 164–70.
Broughton, Janet, *Descartes's Method of Doubt* (Princeton, NJ, 2001)
Carriero, John, *Between Two Worlds: A Reading of Descartes's 'Meditations'* (Princeton, NJ, 2009)
Chalmers, David, 'Facing Up to the Problem of Consciousness', *Journal of Consciousness Studies*, 2 (1995), pp. 200–219
Clarke, Desmond, *Descartes: A Biography* (Cambridge, 2006)

Collegium Conimbricense, *In octo libros physicorum Aristotelis* (Coimbra, 1602)

Cook, Harold, *The Young Descartes: Nobility, Rumor, and War* (Chicago, IL, 2018)

Curley, Edwin, *Descartes Against the Skeptics* (Cambridge, MA, 1978)

Descartes, Catherine, 'Relation de la mort de M. Descartes', in *Bibliothèque Politique*, 3 (Paris, 1745), pp. 238–50

Ebert, Theodore, 'Did Descartes Die of Poisoning?', *Early Science and Medicine*, 24 (2019), pp. 142–85

Farrell, Allan P., *The Jesuit 'Ratio Studiorum' of 1599* (Washington, DC, 1970)

Finocchiaro, Maurice, ed., *The Galileo Affair: A Documentary History* (Berkeley and Los Angeles, CA, 1989)

Galileo Galilei, *Discoveries and Opinions of Galileo*, ed. Stillman Drake (Garden City, NY, 1957)

Garber, Daniel, 'Mind, Body and the Laws of Nature in Descartes and Leibniz', *Midwest Studies in Philosophy*, 8 (1983), pp. 105–33

—, *Descartes' Metaphysical Physics* (Chicago, IL, 1992)

—, 'Descartes and Experiment in the *Discourse* and *Essays*', in Daniel Garber, *Descartes Embodied: Reading Cartesian Philosophy through Cartesian Science* (Cambridge, 2001), pp. 85–110

—, *Descartes Embodied: Reading Cartesian Philosophy through Cartesian Science* (Cambridge, 2001)

—, 'Descartes Among the *Novatores*', *Res Philosophica*, 92 (2015), pp. 1–19

—, review of Jon Schuster, *Descartes Agonistes: Physico-Mathematics, Method and Mechanism, 1618–1633* (Dordrecht, 2013), *Les Archives du Séminaire Descartes*, 23 May 2015

—, 'Novatores', in *The Cambridge History of Philosophy of the Scientific Revolution*, ed. David Marshall Miller and Dana Jalobeanu (Cambridge, 2022), pp. 35–57

Gaukroger, Stephen, *Descartes: An Intellectual Biography* (Oxford, 1995)

—, *Descartes' System of Natural Philosophy* (Cambridge, 2002)

Gilson, Étienne, *Études sur le rôle de la pensée médiévale dans la formation du système cartésien* (Paris, 1984)

Gouhier, Henri, *Essais sur Descartes* (Paris, 1937)

Gueroult, Martial, *Descartes selon l'ordre des raisons*, 2 vols (Paris, 1953)

Heilbron, J. L., *Galileo* (Oxford, 2010)

Israel, Jonathan, *The Dutch Republic: Its Rise, Greatness and Fall, 1477–1806* (Oxford, 1995)

Jeffery, Renée, *Princess Elisabeth of Bohemia: The Philosopher Princesss* (Lanham, MD, 2018)

Kambouchner, Denis, *L'homme des passions. Commentaires sur Descartes*, vol. 1: *Analytique* (Paris, 1995)

—, *Les Méditations métaphysiques de Descartes* (Paris, 2005)

—, *Descartes et la philosophie morale* (Paris, 2008)

Kaplan, Benjamin, *Calvinists and Libertines: Confession and Community in Utrecht, 1578–1620* (Oxford, 1995)

Kenny, Anthony, *Descartes: A Study of His Philosophy* (New York, 1968)

Kleerkooper, M. M., and W. P. van Stockum, *De Boekhandel te Amsterdam voornamelijk in de 17e eeuw*, 2 vols (The Hague, 1914–16)

Kolakowski, Leszek, *Chrétiens sans Église: La Conscience religieuse et le lien confessionnel au XVIIe siècle* (Paris, 1969)

LoLordo, Antonia, *Pierre Gassendi and the Birth of Early Modern Philosophy* (Cambridge, 2007)

Marion, Jean-Luc, *Sur la pensée passive de Descartes* (Paris, 2013)

Marshall, John, *Descartes's Moral Theory* (Ithaca, NY, 1998)

Mouy, Paul, *Le Développement de la physique Cartésienne, 1646–1712* (Paris, 1934)

Nadler, Steven, 'Arnauld, Descartes and Transubstantiation: Reconciling Cartesian Metaphysics and Real Presence', *Journal of the History of Ideas*, 59 (1988), pp. 229–46

—, 'Descartes's Demon and the Madness of Don Quixote', *Journal of the History of Ideas*, 58 (1997), pp. 41–55

—, *Occasionalism: Causation Among the Cartesians* (Oxford and New York, 2011)

—, Tad M. Schmaltz and Delphine Antoine-Mahut, eds, *The Oxford Handbook to Descartes and Cartesianism* (Oxford and New York, 2019)

Newton, Isaac, *Mathematical Principles of Natural Philosophy and His System of the World*, trans. Florian Cajori, 2 vols (Berkeley and Los Angeles, CA, 1934)

Pettegree, Andrew, and Arthur der Weduwen, *The Bookshop of the World: Making and Trading Books in the Dutch Golden Age* (New Haven, CT, 2019)

Popkin, Richard H., *The History of Skepticism from Erasmus to Spinoza* (Berkeley and Los Angeles, CA, 1979)

Price, J. L., *Holland and the Dutch Republic in the Seventeenth Century* (Oxford, 1994)

Ragland, C. P., *The Will to Reason: Theodicy and Freedom in Descartes* (New York and Oxford, 2006)

Rodis-Lewis, Geneviève, *Descartes: Biographie* (Paris, 1995)

Roux, Sandrine, *L'Empreinte cartésienne: L'interaction psychophysique, débats classiques et contemporains* (Paris, 2018)

Roux, Sophie, 'Une enquête sur Jacques du Roure', *Bulletin cartésien*, 50, *Archives de philosophie*, 84 (2021), pp. 174–84

Rowen, Herbert H., ed., *The Low Countries in Early Modern Times* (New York, 1972)

Rozemond, Marleen, *Descartes's Dualism* (Cambridge, MA, 1998)

Schmaltz, Tad, *Radical Cartesianism: The French Reception of Descartes* (Cambridge, 2002)

—, *Descartes on Causation* (Oxford, 2007)

—, *Early Modern Cartesianisms: Dutch and French Constructions* (Oxford and New York, 2017)

Schuster, Jon, *Descartes Agonistes: Physico-Mathematics, Method and Mechanism, 1618–1633* (Dordrecht, 2013)

Shorto, Russell, *Descartes' Bones: A Skeletal History of the Conflict Between Faith and Reason* (New York, 2008)

Spaans, Joke, *Haarlem na de Reformatie: Stedelijk cultuur en kerkelijk leven, 1577–1620* (The Hague, 1989)

Van de Ven, Jeroen, 'Quelques données nouvelles sur Helena Jans', *Bulletin Cartésien*, 32, *Archives de philosophie*, 67 (2004), pp. 163–6

Van Ruler, J. A., 'Philosopher Defying the Philosophers: Descartes's Life and Works', in *The Oxford Handbook to Descartes and Cartesianism*, ed. Steven Nadler, Tad Schmaltz and Delphine Antoine-Mahut (Oxford and New York, 2019), pp. 3–24

Verbeek, Theo, *Descartes and the Dutch: Early Reactions to Cartesian Philosophy, 1637–1650* (Carbondale and Edwardsville, IL, 1992)

—, ed., *La Querelle d'Utrecht: René Descartes et Martin Schoock* (Paris, 1988)

Voltaire, *Philosophical Letters*, trans. Ernest Dilworth (Indianapolis, IN, 1961)

Watson, Richard A., *The Downfall of Cartesianism, 1673–1712: A Study of Epistemological Issues in Late Seventeenth-Century Cartesianism* (The Hague, 1966)

—, *Cogito Ergo Sum: The Life of René Descartes* (Boston, MA, 2007)

—, *Descartes's Ballet: His Doctrine of the Will and His Political Philosophy* (South Bend, IN, 2007)

Williams, Bernard, *Descartes: The Project of Pure Enquiry* (Harmondsworth, 1978)

Wilson, Catherine, *Epicureanism at the Origins of Modernity* (New York and Oxford, 2008)

Wilson, Margaret, *Descartes* (London, 1978)

Yolton, John, *Thinking Matter: Materialism in Eighteenth-Century Britain* (Minneapolis, MN, 1984)

ACKNOWLEDGEMENTS

I am deeply grateful to those friends and colleagues who helped me through-out this project, including answering queries, reading through a complete draft or individual chapters, and offering their comments, corrections and suggestions. Special thanks to Igor Agostini, Daniel Garber, Stephen Gaukroger, Denis Kambouchner, Denis Moreau, Sophie Roux, Han van Ruler (who, despite a bout of COVID, went through the entire manuscript), Erik-Jan Bos and Theo Verbeek. My thanks, as well, to Michael Leaman and Francis Quiviger for their comments on the manuscript, and especially for welcoming this volume into their wonderful series.

My work on this book was made possible by research support from the University of Wisconsin-Madison, including funding through the College of Letters and Science, the Evjue-Bascom Professorship and the Vilas Research Professorship (the William F. Vilas Trust).

PHOTO ACKNOWLEDGEMENTS

The author and publishers wish to express their thanks to the below sources of illustrative material and/or permission to reproduce it. Some locations of artworks are also given below, in the interest of brevity:

Bibliothèque nationale de France, Paris: p. 19; collection of Centraal Museum, Utrecht (purchase with support by the Vereniging Rembrandt, 1935), photo © Centraal Museum Utrecht: p. 234; Château de Versailles: p. 245; from René Descartes, *Discours de la methode . . .* (Leiden, 1637), photo Library of Congress, Lessing J. Rosenwald Collection, Washington, DC: p. 105; from René Descartes, *L'homme . . . et un traitté de la formation du foetus* (Paris, 1664), photos Bibliothèque nationale de France, Paris: pp. 84, 85; from René Descartes, *Principia philosophiae* (Amsterdam, 1644), photos Library of Congress, Lessing J. Rosenwald Collection, Washington, DC: pp. 196, 202; collection of Groninger Museum (loan from Municipality of Groningen, donation Hofstede de Groot), photo Marten de Leeuw: p. 184; Historisch Centrum Overijssel, Zwolle: p. 148; courtesy Koninklijke Verzamelingen (Royal Collection of the Netherlands), The Hague, photo © Niels den Haan: p. 170; from Alexandre Lenoir, *Musée des monuments français*, vol. V (Paris, 1806), photo Bibliothèque nationale de France, Paris: p. 249; Livrustkammaren (The Royal Armoury), Stockholm: p. 239; The Metropolitan Museum of Art, New York: p. 162; Musée d'art et d'histoire de Narbonne: p. 119; National Gallery of Art, Washington, DC: p. 6; National Portrait Gallery, London: p. 154; Rijksmuseum, Amsterdam: pp. 31, 38, 94, 95, 122, 213; Statens Museum for Kunst (SMK), Copenhagen: p. 241; © The Trustees of the British Museum, London: p. 156.

INDEX

Page numbers in *italics* refer to illustrations